The American History Series

SERIES EDITORS

John Hope Franklin, *Duke University*

Abraham S. Eisenstadt, *Brooklyn College*

Arthur S. Link
Princeton University
GENERAL EDITOR FOR HISTORY

James Kirby Martin
UNIVERSITY OF HOUSTON
Mark Edward Lender
KEAN COLLEGE OF NEW JERSEY

A Respectable Army

The Military Origins of the Republic, 1763–1789

HARLAN DAVIDSON, INC.
ARLINGTON HEIGHTS, ILLINOIS 60004

Library of Congress Cataloging in Publication Data

Martin, James Kirby, 1943–
    A respectable army.

    (The American history series)
    Bibliography: p.
    Includes index.
    1. United States—History—Revolution, 1775–1783—
Campaigns and battles. 2. United States. Continental
Army—History. I. Lender, Mark E., 1947–
II. Title. III. Series: American history series
(Harlan Davidson, Inc.)
E230.M34   973.3′3   81-17399
ISBN 0-88295-812-7   AACR2

Cover design: Roger Eggers

Cover illustration: "The March to Valley Forge, December 16 (sic),
1777" by William B. T. Trego, 1883. Courtesy of the Valley Forge
Historical Society.

Manufactured in the United States of America
93 92 91 90 89 7 8 9 10 BC

For
Frederick William Martin

Remember officers and Soldiers, that you are Freemen, fighting for the blessings of Liberty—that slavery will be your portion, and that of your posterity, if you do not acquit yourselves like men.
(George Washington, General Orders, New York, August 23, 1776)

In a Word, the next will be a trying Campaign and as All that is dear and valuable may depend upon the issue of it, I would advise that nothing should be omitted that shall seem necessary to our success. Let us have a respectable Army, and such as will be competent to every Exigency.
(George Washington, to the President of the Continental Congress, Headquarters at Keiths, Pennsylvania, December 16, 1776)

We therefore still kept upon the parade in groups, venting our spleen at our country and government, then at our officers, and then at ourselves for our imbecility in staying there and starving in detail for an ungrateful people who did not care what became of us, so they could enjoy themselves while we were keeping a cruel enemy from them.
(Private Joseph Plumb Martin of the Continental Army, reflecting back on 1780)

EDITORS' FOREWORD

Every generation writes its own history, for the reason that it sees the past in the foreshortened perspective of its own experience. This has certainly been true of the writing of American history. The practical aim of our historiography is to offer us a more certain sense of where we are going by helping us understand the road we took in getting where we are. If the substance and nature of our historical writing is changing, it is precisely because our own generation is redefining its direction, much as the generations that preceded us redefined theirs. We are seeking a newer direction, because we are facing new problems, changing our values and premises, and shaping new institutions to meet new needs. Thus, the vitality of the present inspires the vitality of our writing about our past. Today's scholars are hard at work reconsidering every major field of our history: its politics, diplomacy, economy, society, mores, values, sexuality, and status, ethnic, and race relations. No less significantly, our scholars are using newer modes of investigation to probe the ever-expanding domain of the American past.

Our aim, in this American History Series, is to offer the reader a survey of what scholars are saying about the central themes and issues of American history. To present these themes and issues, we have invited scholars who have made notable contributions to the respective fields in which they are writing. Each volume offers the reader a sufficient factual and narrative account for perceiving the larger dimensions of its particular subject. Addressing their respective themes, our authors have undertaken, moreover, to present the conclusions derived by the principal writers on these themes. Beyond that, the authors present their own conclusions about those aspects of their respective subjects that have been matters of difference and controversy. In effect, they have written not only about where the subject stands in today's historiography but also about where they stand on their subject. Each volume closes with an extensive critical essay on the writings of the major authorities on its particular theme.

The books in this series are designed for use in both basic and advanced courses in American history. Such a series has a particular utility in times such as these, when the traditional format of our American history courses is being altered to accommodate a greater diversity of texts and reading materials. The series offers a number of distinct advantages. It extends and deepens the dimensions of course work in American history. In proceeding beyond the confines of the traditional textbook, it makes clear that the study of our past is, more than the student might otherwise infer, at once complex, sophisticated, and profound. It presents American history as a subject of continuing vitality and fresh investigation. The work of experts in their respective fields, it opens up to the student the rich findings of historical inquiry. It invites the student to join, in major fields of research, the many groups of scholars who are pondering anew the central themes and problems of our past. It challenges the student to participate actively in exploring American history and to collaborate in the creative and rigorous adventure of seeking out its wider reaches.

John Hope Franklin

Abraham S. Eisenstadt

PREFACE

In the 1950s Walter Millis published an influential overview volume entitled *Arms and Men: A Study in American Military History*. He intended his book to be broad-ranging in scope and challenging in its assertions. Early on Millis dared to claim: "The United States was born in an act of violence. . . . In light of that beginning, it is strange how little attention later generations were to give to the military factor in the origins and development of our institutions." Millis sought to get beyond what some have called the narrow confines of traditional military history—the flow of guns, battles, and tactics that influence the immediate outcomes of martial conflicts. He also made it clear that the experience and impact of war on societies can have lasting reverberations and can influence the actual character of national ideals and values as they become institutionalized through time.

In recent years, a small band of scholars, the so-called new military historians, have carried forward in the spirit of Millis's dictim. We number ourselves among that company, and we have learned some key lessons along the way. To comprehend the impact of the War for Independence as it affected the experience of the Revolution and the creation of a republican polity in America, we have had to hurdle two major obstacles. First, we had to get beyond the deeply engrained national mythology about the essence of the war effort, so neatly personified by the imagery of the embattled freehold farmer as the quintessential warrior of the Revolution. Second, we had to integrate, not persist in keeping separate, the fascinating history of the real Continental army into the mainstream of writing about the nation-making experience of the United States.

Our conclusion is that the hard-core regulars of Washington's bedraggled and ill-treated army truly acted out the essence of republicanism and gave that concept concrete meaning in their era. What is so striking is that the army was able to contain its mounting bitterness toward the society that spawned and spurned it, permitting the soldiery to reach the highest of ideals. The army had to do so in the face of a population, ostensibly committed to Revolutionary idealism, that proved more adept at words than deeds, at talking more than doing. Washington's small standing army, so serious a potential threat to liberty in the ideological terms of the times, was ironically the lifeblood of freedom and republican virtue. Such irony helps to explain why the origins of America cannot be treated separately from military concerns.

In preparing this volume, we have sought to bring together the most striking findings of the new military history on Revolutionary America. We have also drawn upon our own research in an effort to construct a new synthesis of the War for Independence as an inseparable influencing agent in the establishment of a republican nation in the New World. We have not ignored important military engagements (the flow of guns and battles). Rather, we have attempted to widen the scenario by relating the war to the search for a stable and enduring republican order. We hope that our interpretation represents a more accurate version of America's national origins than has been presented heretofore.

In our efforts to present a succinct, fluid commentary, we have received invaluable assistance. Professors Richard H. Kohn of Rutgers University and Theodore Crackel of the Department of History, United States Military Academy, carefully scrutinized early drafts of the manuscript and made important suggestions for improvement. Other colleagues, including Ira D. Gruber of Rice University, Hugh F. Rankin of Tulane University, and Howard H. Peckham of the University of Michigan, commented incisively on various portions of the manuscript. Charles Royster of the University of Texas at Arlington provided material assistance along the way, as did the series editors, John Hope Franklin and Abraham Eisenstadt, and Arthur

S. Link, General Editor for History of Harlan Davidson, Inc. The authors alone are responsible for any errors in fact or judgment. We are also indebted to Maureen Hewitt and Karen W. Martin for editorial and stylistic advice; to Robert J. Babbitz, David J. Fowler, and Robert T. Miller for research support; and to Gail Heseltine and Wendy Yin for various versions of the typed manuscript. We each thank our families for their interest, patience, and concern, and we have dedicated this volume to Frederick William Martin, a loving brother and humane gentleman and friend.

James Kirby Martin
Mark Edward Lender

CONTENTS

One: Of Lexington and Concord, and the Myths of the War, 1763–1775, *1*
LEXINGTON AND CONCORD, *1*
OF STANDING ARMIES (POWER) AND MILITIA (LIBERTY), *6*
IDEOLOGICAL TRANSMISSION, *9*
THE PROVINCIAL MILITIA TRADITION, *15*
THE TYRANNY OF STANDING ARMIES, *20*

Two: The Republican War, 1775–1776, *30*
A REPUBLICAN ORDER AS THE GOAL, *30*
REGULARS VERSUS REPUBLICANS: THE BRITISH AT BAY, *34*
THE CREATION OF A CONTINENTAL ARMY, *40*
THE BRITISH MILITARY COUNTERTHRUST, *48*
THE NEW YORK CAMPAIGN, *53*
SUCCESS AND FAILURE, *60*

Three: Toward an American Standing Army, 1776–1777, *65*
THE NATURE OF THE CONTINENTAL ARMY, *65*
A NEW MODEL REBEL ARMY, *69*
WILLIAM HOWE'S CAMPAIGN OF 1777, *78*
THE SARATOGA CAMPAIGN, *83*
THE AMERICAN SEARCH FOR MANPOWER, *87*
THE OLD MYTH AND THE NEW SOLDIERY, *94*

Four: On and Off the Road of Despair, 1777–1779, *99*
VALLEY FORGE, *99*
MOUNTING ANGER IN THE OFFICER CORPS, *103*
TABLES TURNED: NEW LIFE FOR THE CAUSE, *110*
THE BRITISH DISPERSAL OF 1778, *118*
GROWING INTERNAL DIVISION: ARMY AND SOCIETY, *126*

Five: Moral Defeat and Military Turnabout, 1779–1781, *136*
DISPERSED WARFARE, *136*
PATRIOT NAVAL EXPLOITS, *142*
FINANCIAL MORASS ON THE HOME FRONT, *146*
THE WAR IN THE SOUTHERN STATES, *153*
TREASON, PENSIONS, AND MUTINIES, *158*
SUDDEN TURNABOUT: THE ROAD TO YORKTOWN, *165*

Six: Of War, National Legitimacy, and the Republican
Order, 1781–1789, *171*
THE YORKTOWN CAMPAIGN, *171*
FORMULATING A PEACE SETTLEMENT, *179*
THE NEWBURGH CONSPIRACY, *186*
TRANSITION TO A POSTWAR WORLD, *194*
MYTH AND TRADITION: A POLITICAL/MILITARY SETTLEMENT,
202
*A Note on Revolutionary War History and
Historiography, 210*
Index, 223

MAPS

The Northern Campaigns, *35*
The Southern Campaigns, *119*

Of Lexington and Concord, and the Myths of the War, 1763–1775

LEXINGTON AND CONCORD

At dawn on April 19, 1775, a select force of 700 British regulars under the command of Lieutenant Colonel Francis Smith approached the outer edges of Lexington, Massachusetts. The column had set out from Boston the night before under instructions from Thomas Gage, who was commander in chief of British military forces in North America as well as the new royal governor of the Bay Colony. Gage had ordered the column to capture and destroy patriot military stores at Concord, another six miles beyond Lexington. The redcoat operation was to have been secret, but many officers in Boston had been free with the details. Patriot alarm riders had alerted the countryside. As Smith's advance units under Major John Pitcairn marched into Lexington, they saw some 70 Minutemen assembling on the Green. Captain John Parker, the Minuteman leader, was no fool. Completely outnumbered, his intention that fateful morning was not to provoke a fight with the British regulars but to demonstrate whig resolve—to state through the presence of his small militia force that troops of the King's standing army had no legal right in time of peace to trample on the property of freeborn Englishmen.

Acting thus as an army of observation, Parker intended to leave the field once this symbolic martial protest had been made. Witnesses agreed that a British officer rode forward and ordered the Minutemen to disperse. Then, inexplicably, as Parker's men began to move aside, a shot rang out. No one knows who fired the bullet, but before the smoke cleared and Major Pitcairn had restored order, eight colonists had been killed and another 10 wounded. Some had been shot or bayoneted to death in their backs. It chagrined Pitcairn that his redcoats had lost control of themselves, but he could not turn back the clock. Perhaps he comprehended the grave reality that a civil war that would have profound short- and long-term repercussions throughout the western world had just begun.

Within minutes, the redcoats moved on toward Concord, their intended target. There they started to burn or toss into the village pond whatever military stores the patriots had failed to remove. Meantime, news of the mindless bloodshed at Lexington swept far and fast. Militiamen began moving toward Concord. Half a mile from town, across the North Bridge, one group of armed freeholders, seeing the rising smoke and fearing that Concord had been put to the torch, pressed forward. It was

8:30 in the morning. Fighting flared with a British light infantry company guarding the bridge, and soon the outnumbered regulars retreated. They left behind three dead comrades; another eight in their unit had been wounded. Blood now had been spilled on both sides.

Lieutenant Colonel Smith, a portly gentleman not known for quick decisions, slowly began to realize that his units were in a precarious position. Irregular colonial forces were gathering on all sides. After some vacillation, Smith ordered his men to pull out. Citizen-soldiers raked the retreating royal column from behind trees, stone fences, and any other available cover. "We were fired on from all sides," explained a dispirited British lieutenant after the action. There was no way his comrades could effectively counter the sniping provincials because the patriots "were so concealed there was hardly any seeing them." Such action went on all the way back to Lexington, with American "numbers increasing from all parts, while ours was reducing by deaths, wounds, and fatigue; and we were totally surrounded with such an incessant fire as it's impossible to conceive."

Fortunately for them, Smith's beleaguered redcoats linked up with a relief column at Lexington. General Gage, having suspected the worst, had sent out Hugh, Lord Percy, with another 1,100 men. Yet even with reinforcements and flanking parties directly challenging the Minutemen, the British continued to suffer heavy casualties as they retreated from Lexington to Charlestown and Bunker Hill, which they reached at sundown. Of the 1,800 British regulars engaged on that day, 273 had been killed, wounded, or were missing. Counting the Lexington slain, the provincials had lost 95. What had begun as a sortie to destroy supplies had become a full-scale military confrontation, and British regulars had fared very poorly by comparison to armed American amateurs who stood in defense of family and property.

The battles of Lexington and Concord set a civil war in motion that would last for eight years until 1783. Along with other events soon to follow, the martial clash on April 19, 1775, also has served to give credence to an enduring historical mythology about the Revolutionary era. Down to our own time, this mythology has affected the fundamental ways in which Americans have conceived of their national origins and of their nation as an agency of peace in a sordid, warlike world.

Drawing lifeblood from the battles of Lexington and Concord, the dominant strands in the mythology about the War for Independence may be enunciated as follows: 1) that provincial Americans were reluctantly forced into civil war by an overbearing, if not tyrannical parent state of Great Britain; 2) that the determined colonists willingly displayed moral commitment and public virtue, rushing into combat as citizen-soldiers and steadfastly bearing arms through eight long years of military travail; and 3) that, united as one family in the cause, they overcame the enemy after hundreds of battles, thereby assuring through their virtuous behavior that a republican order would flourish and endure in post-Revolutionary America.

As with any national mythology, there is some truth (perhaps better stated as accurate observation) in each of these strands. If there were not, the mythology would have long since been dismissed as literary or patriotic conceit, worthy of study because of metaphorical form and symbolism but not because of factual substance. Indeed, there is just enough content in each of the strands to make them plausible—to a limited point. Then they begin to weaken and unravel, as the material presented in this study demonstrates.

One of the objectives of this volume is to separate popular mythology, aspects of which professional historians have too often enshrined in their writings, from the new historical reality that has been uncovered in recent years about the era of the American Revolution, of which the War for Independence was an integral part. Another purpose is to present a synthesis of the fragments of the new reality. As such, the authors analyze how the experience of the war affected the establishment of republican values and institutions in Revolutionary America. Too often the war has been studied as a "guns and battles" phenomenon and has been treated in isolation from the larger currents of nation making that enveloped the era. That pattern has been unfortunate. The actual experience of the war, with all its hope, idealism, conflict, and dissension, was central to the process of constructing a specific form of well-ordered republicanism, as ultimately expressed in the Constitution of 1787. This study proposes that the military origins of America in the years 1763–1789 must not only be assessed but also must be given their rightful place in reconstructing the history of Revolutionary America.

At the outset, the story must begin with Lexington and Concord, simply because the salient characteristics of the opening clash lent persuasive form to the mythology that has become so deeply entrenched. These characteristics may be summarized by pointing out that the British army ostensibly invaded a peaceful counryside, thereby provoking the initial provincial martial response. The British constabulary consisted of well-trained and disciplined *regulars,* representing a textbook *standing army* acting without apparent provocation in time of peace. In turn, swarms of free citizens bested the British regulars by using irregular tactics. *Citizen-soldiers* organized as militia found themselves in the position of fighting defensively to protect their liberties and property. What is especially important is that the beginning of the war fit neatly into the radical whig ideological mood of the era. For the colonists, the presence of Britain's standing army epitomized the abuse of power. The citizen-soldiers of Massachusetts stood out as the protectors of liberty.

What commentators, including some professional historians, have not understood is that the Lexington and Concord paradigm came apart quite early in the war. Yet reading it into the whole of the war experience, they have skewed their interpretations about the nature of the martial contest that followed, including central matters such as the tenacity of patriot commitment, the actual nature of the American military effort, the issue of who actually accepted the burden of combat for rebel society, and the effect of the military confrontation on the creation of a sense of national legitimacy, nationhood, and republicanism. To move beyond mythology, then, this study must begin with the ideological roots of the controversy, which did reflect the experience of Lexington and Concord.

OF STANDING ARMIES (POWER) AND MILITIA (LIBERTY)

To get at the mythology and to separate it from reality, the ideological framework that influenced the world view of eighteenth-century provincials must be spelled out. Of prime importance was the overarching assumption of an ongoing struggle between power and liberty, based on the view that human beings naturally lusted after power and would resort to any form of corruption to gain their petty, personal ends. Bernard Bailyn, in his seminal study *The Ideological Origins of the American Revolution* (1967), has pointed out that Americans, as inheritors of England's radical whig opposition tradition, believed that power "meant the dominion of some men over others, the human control of human life: ultimately force, compulsion." Power, indeed, was constantly juxtaposed to liberty, which was "its natural prey, its necessary victim." While power "was brutal, ceaselessly active, and heedless," liberty "was delicate, passive, and sensitive," in the history of human civilizations more often the victim of power rather than the victor.[1]

According to whig ideology, property-holding citizens organized as militia would naturally stand up to those who would resort to military force as a means of despoiling liberties. An exceedingly significant personage in the struggle between power and liberty, then, was the citizen-soldier, the type of individual who came forth as a Minuteman at Lexington and Concord. From the mid-seventeenth century on, whig opposition writers in England had extolled the citizen-soldier. In particular, they were reacting to Oliver Cromwell's "New Model" army. According to these writers, Cromwell's forces had shown little concern for popular rights after they had swept the royalist supporters of King Charles I before them during the 1640s. The

New Model army became a repressionist instrument, and the reason seemed to be that Cromwell's soldiers hardened into regulars, whose loyalty in time of flux devolved onto a tyrannical Puritan leader—all at the expense of liberty.

Modern commentary in condemnation of standing armies and in praise of the citizen-soldier may be traced to early sixteenth-century Florence and the writings of Niccolò Machiavelli. Familiarity with Machiavelli's thought in combination with the threatening reality of Cromwell's army resulted in Englishman James Harrington's broadly influential opposition tract, *Commonwealth of Oceana,* published in 1656. Machiavelli had warned in *The Prince* (1513) "that no state is safe unless it has its own arms. . . .Your own arms are those composed of your subjects or citizens or dependents, all others are either mercenaries or auxiliaries." Harrington, in turn, carefully defined the independent citizen as the individual who held property, such as a freehold estate. Such a person, by virtue of property holding, had a clear economic stake in the preservation of society. Likewise, it was a fundamental duty of the citizen to keep and bear arms in defense of public liberty and personal property.

To Harrington and other seventeenth-century opposition pamphleteers who followed, "the . . .ideas of propertied independence and the militia" were inextricably tied together, as political scientist J. G. A. Pocock has observed. Since "independent proprietors," those with a demonstrable stake in society, should naturally provide for "the public defense," they would never become a "threat to the public liberty or the public purse." If they did, they would be attacking the very polity in which their property gave them a clear stake, which would have been contradictory behavior.[2]

Political and societal stability thus depended upon those who had property and, therefore, were citizens. For citizens to protect liberty, argued Harrington and many others, they had to be ever vigilant against those who might be power hungry. They had to display public *virtue,* the quality considered axiomatic in good citizenship. In *The Creation of the American Republic, 1776-1787* (1969), Gordon S. Wood has described such behavior as "the willingness of the people to surrender all, even their lives, for the good of the state." Public virtue "was primarily the consequence of men's individual private virtues."[3] Without citizen virtue, according to those following Harringtonian logic, the state would never be safe from the rapicity of the few who, for the sake of power, would enslave the many. "In free countries, as People work for themselves, so they fight for themselves," explained radical whig pamphleteer Thomas Gordon in *Cato's Letters* (1721). Any virtuous freeholder would willingly struggle to his own death to defend property and liberties; for if these were lost, "he loses all the Blessings of Life."[4]

Yet English opposition writers worried constantly about independent citizens who would not remain virtuous and vigilant. Those mad for power could always corrupt the system. They could bribe freeholders into passivity with titles, sinecures, and other meaningless emblems of privilege. Or luxury and excessive prosperity could lull propertied citizens to sleep. An example of this is found in Robert Molesworth's widely read *An Account of Denmark* (1694), in which he told the story of a standing army's destroying a constitutional order because pleasure-seeking aristocrats refused to act as a check on the army's truculence. Individual human greed and the desire for luxury had replaced public virtue as the highest value among citizens in Denmark, as it had in the ancient republics of Athens, Carthage, and Rome. The outcome was invariably disastrous for liberty, resulting directly in political tyranny.

The most noxious tool of impending tyranny, argued the radical whig writers, was a standing army. To them, a standing army was a military organization *separate* from the citizenry and not committed to the service of society. Unlike the militia, it did not consist of citizens; it was made up of trained regulars, soldiers for hire who had no necessary propertied stake in society. Attacking property and liberty was something that only rootless economic ne'er-do-wells would do. After all, such individuals had nothing to lose and very likely something to gain.

Indeed, the presence of a standing army in any society was both a measure and an agent of corruption, argued the whig writers. Paid hirelings suggested that property holders, usually wallowing in luxury, had lost their notion of public virtue and forgotten the obligations of citizenship by turning over defense to hired substitutes. Luxury could also weave a web of corruption, in that those who grasped for power could use the many offices, places, and contracts needed for maintaining an army as a resource for rewarding those compromising citizens willing to condone the actions of potential tyrants. Standing armies were part of a spreading cancer, destroying society from the inside. Their support demanded heavier and heavier levels of taxation, ultimately threatening the right to property itself as the foundation of independent citizenship. Before citizens knew it, they were facing political slavery, often described by the opposition writers as a state worse than death. If a standing army did not cause cancerous rot from within, it could always become a praetorian force in the hands of an aspiring tyrant to be turned against the people, as had been the case in Denmark or with Cromwell.

The presence of a standing army in any country thus connoted to whig ideologues that luxury, corruption, power, and tyranny were to various degrees threatening property, liberty, and life itself. An active militia, by comparison, connoted that citizens were taking their obligations seriously and that they were behaving virtuously. How well the Lexington and Concord confrontations fit this schema is especially interesting. Brute military power on the part of Gage's regulars had not overcome the vigilant militia of the Massachusetts citizenry. Liberty, even if all but snuffed out in Britain (as provincial whig leaders so often proclaimed before and after 1775), still had a fighting chance in America—and had prevailed on April 19, 1775.

IDEOLOGICAL TRANSMISSION

For the past several years, numerous historians have been analyzing the ways in which the opposition political writing of seventeenth- and eighteenth-century England influenced the values, ideals, and outcomes of the American Revolution. In 1959, Caroline Robbins published *The Eighteenth-Century Commonwealthman,* which delineated the full intellectual range of England's "real" whig writers, as she referred to them.[5] Another milestone came in 1967 with Bailyn's *Ideological Origins.* Whereas Robbins analyzed the thought of James Harrington, Algernon Sidney, Henry Neville, Robert Molesworth, John Trenchard, Thomas Gordon, and several others, Bailyn studied the pamphlet literature of the American Revolution. He concluded that England's opposition writers dramatically influenced the ideological world view held by the Revolutionary generation. These writers, argued Bailyn, transmitted to the provincials "a world regenerative creed," based on the need to preserve liberty at all costs in the face of the conspiring forces of tyranny in a darkened world.[6]

Provincial Americans (or perhaps more accurately, those favored few who were well educated and had access to opposition pamphlets) thus imbibed, argues Bailyn, English "radical" whiggism. Provincial leaders, who increasingly found themselves in the position of challenging Britain's imperial policies, seemingly took to the viewpoints of those who worried about the abuse of power from above.

One dominant concern of provincial leaders was very much related to virtuous citizenship, and it had to do with *balance* in government. A balanced government was one in which the three acknowledged social estates—the monarchy, aristocracy, and democracy—mixed and blended their particular interests as represented by the King, the House of Lords, and the House of Commons in government. If any one of the three estates gained too much influence over the other two in the governmental hierarchy, it could threaten the political liberties of the others. Whig opposition writers interpreted much of seventeenth-century English history as a problem of containing the absolutist desires of the Stuart kings. Charles I paid with his head in 1649. James II had to flee the realm during the "Glorious Revolution" of 1688–1689, and Parliament finally emerged as a body capable of dealing with capricious monarchs.

Yet the alleged machinations of the Stuart monarchs had not ended power-hungry willfulness. As the eighteenth century unfolded, radical whig opposition writers became increasingly virulent on the subject of the King's ministers, or the fourth hand in government. Sir Robert Walpole, who led the King's cabinet between 1721 and 1742, came to personify these corrupting individuals. The task was now to counteract the ministry, which reputedly used electoral bribery, patronage, and other forms of political influence to manipulate Parliament. The King's ministers thus replaced the Stuart absolutists as the chief conspirators against liberty. Certainly after 1763, with the reinvigorated imperial program, such an ideological perspective helped to explain to provincial Americans why they felt the hand of oppression descending upon them.

In England, as Bailyn, Robbins, and others have pointed out, radical whig pamphleteers had little influence on governmental activities. Parliament maintained and supported a peacetime standing army, despite persistent opposition whig cries. It could do so because of language contained in the Bill of Rights, the grand document of the Glorious Revolution. The Bill of Rights mandated that any regular military establishment must be clearly subordinate to civil authority. Specifically it stated: "That the raising or keeping of a standing army within the kingdom in time of peace, unless it be with the consent of Parliament, is against the law." Likewise, all citizens were to have the right to bear arms in defense of the state.

Ideologues who cheered the demise of James II and the promulgation of the Bill of Rights hoped that virtuous citizens as militia would be central to national defense. Reality, however, was something else. Militia units did exist, yet Parliament relied most heavily on a well-trained standing army (along with superior naval forces). Parliament exercised civil control through yearly appropriations and the annual Mutiny Act, first adopted in 1689, which legitimized the military establishment and prescribed its code of discipline. Propertied citizens generally did not worry about the implications of a standing army in their midst, and the establishment remained the backbone of imperial defense, although with sharply reduced manpower when not at war.

One important reason that Britons did not seem to object to a standing military establishment, even in peacetime, was that the empire was rather consistently at war between 1689 and 1763, battling primarily with France and Spain over the hegemony of Old and New World territories. Besides contending with two powerful external enemies, there was also a conscious effort underway to limit the destructiveness of war, a pattern that Walter Millis (*Arms and Men,* 1956) has attributed to the rising spirit of "eighteenth-century rationalism." Since warfare came to be accepted as an inevitable concomitant of balance-of-power politics in international relations, Millis argues that the new notion was to separate civilians from the impact of organized human brutality, to make war "the king's rather than the community's business."[7] If Millis is correct, rationalism in the dawning Age of Reason simply lessened the role of the citizen-in-arms in martial affairs.

The desire to separate war and its destructiveness from society ties into another major reason for Britain's primary reliance on standing forces. The skills and training required for war were turning the soldier into a highly specialized craftsman. Whether the desire for separation spurred specialization, or vice versa, will probably never be determined. The two phenomena worked together. The result, as Millis has asserted, was that armies increasingly came to be "composed of a class apart: the professional, long-service soldiers and seamen who could be hired, cajoled, or pressed into doing the nation's fighting, with a minimum of interference in the civilian's pursuit of profit or pleasure."[8]

Although Millis treats the functional specialization and separation of the soldiery and war from society as an important characteristic of the new rationalism, that very specialization and separation worried the opposition whigs. Clinging to their conception of citizenship and the corrupting influence that such a standing establishment portended, they balked at the social complexion of Britain's regular military forces. Freeholding citizens were rarely to be found among the rank and file. Common soldiers were drawn from the poorer groups in society, described graphically by Millis as "the sweepings of jails, gin-mills, and poorhouses, oafs from the farm beguiled into 'taking the king's shilling,' adventurers and unfortunates who might find a home" in the ranks.[9] However, Millis may have overstated his point. More recent findings by Sylvia R. Frey, based on her sampling of soldiers under British arms during the War for Independence, indicate that "the majority of British conscripts and German mercenaries did not come from the permanent substratum of the poor, but were members of the working classes who were temporarily unemployed or permanently displaced, and thus represented the less productive, but by no means useless, elements of society."[10]

However low the social origins of soldiers, military life in peace and war was harsh. Some terms of service were for life, and discipline was severe (insolence toward officers and desertion often resulted in death sentences or penalties of 1,000 lashes well laid on). Yet such an existence was an alternative to filching in the streets, rotting in prison, or starving or freezing to death for want of food and clothing. The military establishment thus became another means of helping the British to care for their growing poor population in an age when the modern social service state had hardly been imagined.

Attracting or forcing individuals from the poorer classes into military service and, hence, cleaning the streets, was yet another practical reason for maintaining a peacetime standing army, especially when it is recalled that the officer corps was, by and large, drawn from the ranks of the nobility and gentry. Training in, and the practice of, the military art had long since become a legitimate calling for English sons who were not the firstborn and would not share in the inheritance of land from generation to generation. As an alternative, these sons could purchase commissions and move up the officer-grade ranks to colonel, so long as they had cash in hand. The price of commissions varied but was usually well beyond the financial means of the middle classes. Often, aspiring officers needed influential patrons in government who could help them secure commissions—usually for generous fees. Demonstrated military acumen, regardless of social background, thus played a diminished role in the promotion of officer-grade personnel, since service in the officer corps was a respectable source of employment (and advancement) for the elite sons of Britain.

In its organization, then, the standing army offered employment for the progeny of the very well-to-do and prepared lower-class expendables for the part of battlefield cannon-fodder. Rigorous training and discipline taught the rank and file loyalty, if not blind obedience and martial courage in the face of concentrated enemy fire. Furthermore, harsh discipline was assumed to be necessary to control down and outers in the ranks. The rigid disciplinary code governing military life was not for the ulterior purpose of creating mindless automatons which could be used against the citizenry by some monarchical tyrant crazed for power. The likelihood of such a threat to civil society was extremely remote, given that the army's officers had a clear stake in society.

Although radical whig pamphleteers persisted in issuing warnings about luxury, corruption, and irresponsible citizenship, Britain's eighteenth-century standing military forces became more firmly entrenched as time passed. During the Seven Years' War (known as the French and Indian War in the provinces), the military establishment demonstrated its effectiveness by defeating Spanish and French armies. By the Treaty of Paris of 1763, France renounced all claims to Canada, thereby removing what every good Englishman viewed as the "French menace" from the North American continent. Struggling Spain had to give up its claim to the Floridas to regain Cuba. In 1763, the British establishment could fairly claim that it was one of the mightiest in the world. Certainly its record was impressive.

Only in the provinces, it seems, were people paying much attention to the antistanding-army concerns of the radical whig pamphleteers. Also in America the fear of a ministerial conspiracy against liberty would soon fuse with the antistanding-army ideological strain and help to produce conditions pointing toward open rebellion and civil war between Britons and Anglo-Americans.

THE PROVINCIAL
MILITIA TRADITION

Until a decade before the triumphant high tide of the first British empire in 1763, British ministers had been contemplating cracking down on American provincials and bringing an end to the so-called era of salutary neglect. During the period between 1700 and 1760 the legislative assertiveness of provincial assemblies and an attrition in the prerogatives of royal governors had increased. Such trends suggested to the ministry that the colonists had lost sight of their subordinate status in the empire.

Even before the Treaty of Paris, the ministry of Lord Bute (youthful George III's mentor and confidant) had made the decision to maintain a regular force in North America. Thus, amidst all the bravado of victory came the startling announcement from London that there would be a peacetime lodgment of 8,000 to 10,000 royal troops. An astounded Philadelphia whig wrote: "While we were surrounded by the French, we had no army to defend us: but now they are removed, and [with] the English in quiet possession of the northern Continent. . .we are burdened with a standing army and subjected to the insufferable insults from any petty officer." The decision was enough to make any conspiracy-minded provincial suspicious about the ministry's true intentions, especially with the French menace removed from the landscape.

The redcoats, in reality, were to form a frontier constabulary to stand between aggrandizing white settlers and angry Indians being systematically exterminated or pushed off tribal tracts. The goal was to have the regulars keep the peace and to prevent the kind of general Indian uprising that Pontiac's Rebellion of 1763–1764 turned out to be. It was both a bloody and financially costly guerilla clash, precipitated in large part because of tribal fears that their lands could not be maintained without traditional French support. Don Higginbotham (*The War of American Independence,* 1971) has offered a balanced conclusion about the ministry's intentions as of 1763: "While defense against the Indians or a resurgence of Bourbon ambitions figured implicitly in the decision to keep an army in North America, the chief function of the redcoats was actually to prevent war, not to wage it."[11] Most historians would agree with Higginbotham. The royal army was not being brought in through the back door with the ulterior purpose of deploying it against recalcitrants in eastern settlements who might resist other imperial policies.

Clearly, the ministry was not plotting slavery. Rather, its concerns in the early 1760s focused on achieving efficiency and economy in the administration of the vastly expanded postwar imperial domain. During the Seven Years' War the English national debt had jumped from £75,000,000 to about £130,000,000 sterling. No imperial leader wanted to see that figure, staggering for its time, rise any higher. To keep the settlers separated from the Indians would be cost effective because it would aid in avoiding the expense of prolonged local Indian wars. Over the long term, the ministry reasoned, the presence of the troops would save money, even if someone had to feed, house, and pay for them in the meantime.

The task of maintaining frontier harmony, furthermore, could not be entrusted to provincial militia because most units were in a state of general disrepair, if they were still functioning at all. Colonial militiamen were as likely as anyone to spark a general conflagration, based on their traditional support of white land claimants. Regular troops were the only alternative, the ministry thus concluded, even if that necessitated a standing army present in the American provinces during peacetime.

Despite the disheveled state of most provincial militia units, Americans took great pride in their system of armed defense built on the concept of the virtuous citizen-soldier. As early as

1632, points out historian John Shy, the assembly of Virginia had ordered every fit male to carry a weapon to church so that "he might exercise with it after the service."[12] During the next 130 years the militia system kept adapting to problems of the moment. Although early militia, especially those in New England, had been essential in defense against Indians, militia units during the 1730s and 1740s in the South played a large part in guarding the white populace against individual slave depredations and group uprisings. Over time the militia became the exclusive province of free, white, adult, propertied males, usually between the ages of 16 and 60. Thus Indians, slaves, free blacks, indentured servants, apprentices, and indigents came to be excluded from militia service. In actuality, a primary function of the militia turned out to be protecting the propertied and the privileged in colonial society from the unpropertied and unprivileged.

Although militiamen developed a record of sorts in tracking down recalcitrant slaves, wiping out discrete Indian bands, and entertaining an admiring populace with drill routines on muster days, citizen-soldiers did not earn much of a record in full-scale wartime combat. During the imperial wars of 1689–1763, there were few encounters that brought the militia glory. Indeed, most propertied colonists seemed to forget that extraordinary efforts were required to get provincial citizens to fight the Spanish and the French. Virginia, for example, in supporting regular army regiments during the French and Indian War, chose not to move its militia out of the province; rather, the planter-elite assembly passed legislation that placed the burden of service on "such able bodied men, as do not follow or exercise any lawful calling or employment, or have not, some other lawful and sufficient maintenance." Local candidates for front-line combat, as opposed to home defense, were to be those who came from the poor and indigent classes, those who ironically had been excluded from militia service. They would be the field substitutes for more favored, property-holding militiamen. What is so striking is that the pattern of service obligation was coming to resemble that of eighteenth-century England. In both societies the horror of actual, open-field combat had been set aside as an appropriate calling for the poorer sort (with upper-class leadership), while the middle classes filled the ranks of militia.

The middle-class character of the militia rank and file has led some historians to view the institution as another seedbed for future democratic flowerings. Since militiamen were invariably men of some substance, property holding must have been widespread. What has been forgotten is that militia law by the early eighteenth century rather systematically excluded the indigents and the unprivileged (a mushrooming proportion of the population by the 1750s) from service. Furthermore, the common practice of having militiamen elect their own officers has abetted impressions about the institution's egalitarian character. What evidence there is, however, suggests that the majority of the highest officers were men of at least modest wealth and distinction, when compared to their neighbors. As befitted the deferential character of the late colonial society, the rank and file accepted the leadership of their socioeconomic betters in the officer-grade ranks. Preference for the well-to-do did not change one fact, however. Whether or not the militia system was a source of incipient democracy, the lack of solid training and combat experience on the part of popularly elected officers and rank-and-file freemen was one reason for the militia's uneven record.

Indeed, concerning oneself with the presence or absence of democratic characteristics may be a misplaced concern. Richard H. Kohn (*Eagle and Sword,* 1975) has perceptively argued that "the militia was not a system at all." "In reality," he contends, "it was a concept of defense: the idea of universal obligation for defensive war, a people in arms to ward off an invader."[13] The function of the militiaman was to protect hearth and home, not to engage in regular warfare. "Pervasive localism," points out Lawrence Delbert Cress, was at the heart of the concept. Those who were expendable in society—the down and outers— were deemed to be the appropriate persons to be sent off to engage in full-scale combat at some far distant point on the map.

That was the reality of American participation in the French and Indian War, if not in earlier colonial wars.[14]

The failure to make this critical distinction served to confuse regular army officers about American fighting prowess. General James Wolfe, whose brilliant tactics resulted in the fall of Quebec during September 1759, described provincial soldiers as "the dirtiest, most contemptible, cowardly dogs you can conceive. There is no depending on them in combat." To another officer, they were "nastier than anything I could conceive." Regular army officers repeatedly characterized American soldiers as lazy, shiftless, hardly even fit for latrine duty. As John Shy has reminded us, however, these provincial soldiers were not militia, but rather outcasts from middle-class society, unfortunates who had been lured or legally pressed into service through promises of bounty payments and decent food and clothing. New England supplied the vast bulk of provincial troops engaged in conquering Canada. "It was the Yankee," concludes Shy, "who came to be regarded as a poor species of fighting man. This helps explain the notion of the British government in 1774 that Massachusetts might be coerced without too much trouble."[15]

General Gage, another French and Indian War veteran, wrote shortly after Bunker Hill in 1775: "In all their Wars against the French, they never Showed so much Conduct, Attention, and Perseverence as they do now." As with other army officers and the British ministry, Gage did not distinguish between militia and expeditionary service and those who made up the respective rank and file. At Lexington and Concord, Gage's regulars were not fighting against unfortunates who had been dragooned into service and whose primary goal was to stay alive. They had run into propertied freeholders operating locally, actually defending hearth and home. That was the unique strength of the militia system. Whether it could be equally effective on a broader scale, however, was yet to be seen.

Several salient points thus stand out about the provincial militia tradition. The ideal was universal military obligation, training, and service. That implied knowledge of, and the right to bear, arms in defense of liberty and property. In actuality, the military component of the concept of citizenship in late colonial America extended as far as the outer limits of property holding went. Heavy combat and major offensive operations, such as those conducted during the French and Indian War, had not drawn so heavily on militia as on the unprivileged and down-trodden who had been converted into quasi-regulars in arms (for the duration of the war instead of for life). Stated differently, military practice in the late colonial period was being Anglicized or Europeanized, as were so many other facets of provincial life.

The merging of British and American practices represented an important trend, given the strength of the antistanding-army ideology in America. Despite reality, provincial spokesmen clung with loyalty to the precepts of the militia tradition after 1763. They talked as if militia were the sole unit of defense while constantly juxtaposing the virtuous citizen-soldier with the standing-army regular of the parent state. In the spirit of the opposition whig writers, they proclaimed the superiority of armed militiamen as agents of war, never conceding the point that well-trained regulars might be more than a match for vigilant citizen-amateurs. Like the British generals, they had overrated themselves and underrated their opponents. Unlike the British, Lexington and Concord seemed to prove them right. However, it was going to be a long, enervating, and disillusioning war. By late 1776, patriot leaders would be consciously reverting to the French and Indian War pattern of seeking out the unpropertied in their quest to defend liberty and implant republicanism in America for the propertied citizens of society.

THE TYRANNY OF STANDING ARMIES

In 1774, one disturbed American writer gave ample summary to a whole lexicon of provincial perceptions about why there was serious trouble in the empire. He stated that it was "the MONSTER or a standing ARMY" in America that symbolized what was wrong. The army's presence was but one element in "a plan. . .systematically laid, and pursued by the British ministry, near twelve years, for enslaving America." The standing army was that which had been lodged as a frontier constabulary in 1763. In a number of ways, that army, in conjunction with vessels from the Royal navy patrolling vigorously for smugglers in American waters, had been a thorn in colonial flesh, assisting in the rapid demise of healthy imperial relations. The question of who was to pay for that army in the face of the mounting national debt of the home government had been one of the major reasons for Parliament's Stamp Act of 1765 and Townshend duties of 1767. In response to these taxation schemes, Americans had made clear that they would resist taxes not specifically levied by their local assemblies. To do otherwise would be to succumb to taxation by a legislative body in which provincial Americans were not directly represented.

Another vexing problem centered on the issue of billeting the British regulars. Parliament adopted a new Quartering Act in 1765. It allowed troops to be housed in public and uninhabited private facilities when barracks were not available. The act was silent on the subject of using private inhabited homes, although everyone agreed that this practice was illegal. The real point of contention was that of indirect taxation. The colonists were to absorb the costs of quartering the troops, based on appropriations made by their assemblies. American leaders loudly objected to the plan on the grounds that it represented forced taxation, as mandated by Parliament.

The dispute took a particularly virulent turn in New York, a colony in which many troops were stationed because of its central geographical location. In defiance of Parliament, the New York assembly passed its own Quartering Act, prescribing the province's financial liabilities and limiting them to a year. In turn, Parliament, sensing yet another slap at its vaunted legislative sovereignty, suspended the New York assembly until it conformed to the 1765 Act. The legal fight became particularly entangled, with Parliament finally backing down in 1769 by amending its original decision to allow individual provinces to legislate for themselves in providing billets for the regular army. The dispute left bad feelings on both sides, all of which fed the growing provincial sense of alienation from the parent state.

One of the most dramatic incidents involving the standing military forces occurred in Boston on March 5, 1770. The contretemps quickly earned the title "Boston Massacre." It involved regular soldiers firing on the working populace of that port city. The roots of the Massacre may be traced to the unusual turbulence characterizing Massachusetts political life during the 1760s. There was heated resistance to imperial legislation, such as the Stamp Act, and local mobs often made it impossible for royal officials to implement Parliament's will. During August 1765, a long night of crowd turbulence forced the local Stamp Act distributor to resign that post. Mob action continued in the days and months ahead, sometimes directed against royal officers assigned the responsibility of executing imperial legislation, sometimes against local customs officers charged with collecting trade duties, and sometimes against press gangs off British naval vessels out searching for "forced" crew members.

By the late 1760s, the Bostonians had earned quite a reputation among the heads of government in London as a disrespectful and lawless people. This city seemed to serve as a festering source of turbulence which, in turn, influenced anti-imperial behavior in many other American communities as well. The beleaguered Massachusetts royal governor, Francis Bernard, summarized such perceptions when he wrote home to England that since 1765 Boston had been "under the uninterrupted dominion of a faction supported by a trained mob." He believed that only the presence of regular troops could "rescue the government" and restore stability. Fear of local reprisals, however, kept him from specifically calling for standing military intervention.

As it turned out, Bernard's desire eventuated in 1768. The new Secretary for American Affairs, the Earl of Hillsborough, also subscribed to the dictum that provincial political stability depended on bringing the Boston "rabble" under control. In the late spring, General Gage received orders from Hillsborough to send four regiments to the Bay Colony port. Much to the enraged but controlled dismay of the local patriots, the regulars began disembarking on October 1, 1768. For those who believed in plots, it now looked as if the real purpose of the British constabulary had been revealed. In their minds, it was the suppression of American rights.

Between 1763 and 1768, there had not been much commentary from provincial writers about the peacetime lodgment of British regulars in America. Since the troops were out of sight for most eastern settlers, except in New York City, they were also largely out of mind. As of October 1, however, the regulars were intimidatingly present in the major port city of New England. Their red coats and muskets served to symbolize the threat of an insidious plan and to infuse antistanding-army ideology with vibrant meaning. A local minister, Andrew Eliot, caught the tenor of the moment when he exclaimed: "Good God! What can be worse to a people who have tasted the sweets of liberty! Things have come to an unhappy crisis; . . .all confidence is now at an end; and the moment there is any bloodshed all affection will cease."

Eliot wrote as if the letting of blood was inevitable. He presumed that well-trained, highly disciplined troops represented brute power, waiting to be unleashed upon an innocent populace who wanted nothing more than to preserve political liberty. The populace, however, was not that innocent, nor were the troops that brutal. Local whig leaders disdained such objective thought. They kept a "Journal of the Times," which made the most of isolated confrontations between hard-nosed, off-duty soldiers and taunting civilians. While some of the wealthier merchants seemed pleased with the specie that the soldiery infused into the local economy, the vast majority of citizens did not have one good word to say about the redcoats, despite what was a pattern of relatively good behavior under trying circumstances. Rather, they agreed with the local whig who saw in these "new guardians of liberty" only puppet-like automatons who would gladly "scatter with the [French] pox some of their loose money."

When the troops were not out whoring, charged the local opposition, they were accused of being perpetually drunk and ready for a brawl. To Bostonians, the swaggering, mindless redcoats seemed to violate every canon of the Bill of Rights of 1689, even though the troops were completely under civil authority and operating under strict orders never to use their weapons unless ordered to do so after a civil magistrate had first read the Riot Bill. (In English law the only time that officers could order up volleys without a prior reading of the Riot Bill was when the populace had been declared by the King-in-Parliament to be in a state of open rebellion.)

Given all the nervousness and fear, it would be easy to conclude that a clash was inevitable. But that was not the case. That bloodshed came when it did surprised and shocked many inhabitants. It was certainly clear by early 1770 that the ministry was divided in its own thinking about maintaining regulars in Boston during peacetime, since two regiments had been withdrawn in 1769. From the day of the arrival of the army, however, troop baiting had emerged as a popular local sport. One reason for irritating the soldiers had to do with the direct competition for jobs between off-duty redcoats and civilian day laborers. In Boston the struggling poor represented rapidly growing numbers of people who lived economically at or below the poverty line.

Economic competition or the collection of customs duties lay behind many isolated clashes, all of which came to a head on the chilly evening of March 5, 1770, when small bands of apprentices, day laborers, and merchant seamen began to congregate in discrete parties. At first they just milled about; then they began to move, seemingly without overall guidance, toward the Customs House on King Street. There a small detachment under Captain Thomas Preston was guarding the area of the Customs House. The angry bands pressed in on the soldiers, pelting them with snowballs and garbage. A redcoat apparently panicked and, before Preston could stop him, fired into the crowd. Other soldiers joined in the shooting. Preston finally got his men under control, but several civilians lay in the street wounded, dead, or dying. All told, five civilians lost their lives as a result of this incident. These individuals immediately became symbols as the first fallen martyrs in the struggle of liberty against tyranny.

Short-run effects of the Massacre may not have been as important as long-term developments. First, the regiments were removed from Boston. Then Captain Preston and his men came to trial. Through two hearings, one for Preston and one for his subordinates, the prosecution tried to prove that the troops had fired with malice aforethought, despite mitigating circumstances. Even in the alienated atmosphere of Boston, such a case did not have much legal merit. The court acquitted Preston and all but two of his men, who paid the modest penalty of having their thumbs branded.

In the long run, the most consequential effect related to the perceived specter of ministerial tyranny associated with anti-standing-army ideology. March 5 became an annual holiday in Boston, a time for remembering the martyred victims of Britain's wanton political plotting. Each year until the mid-1780s, when Bostonians opted for July 4 as a more fitting holiday, citizens gathered together to remember the slain and to hear a Massacre oration. The main speakers, in their turn, usually conjured up all the negative images of standing armies crushing innocent peoples.

None was more vivid than the oration of 1772, delivered by Dr. Joseph Warren, who later died at the Battle of Bunker Hill. Warren implored the throng never to forget *"the fatal fifth of March, 1770. . . .* Language is too feeble to paint the emotions of our souls, when our streets were stained with the blood of our brethren; when our ears were wounded by the groans of the dying, and our eyes were tormented with the sight of the mangled bodies of the dead.'' Warren also warned the populace to be on guard against future depredations. His "imagination presented" the imminent likelihood of "our houses wrapped in flames, our children subjected to the barbarous caprice of a raging soldiery; our beauteous virgins exposed to all the insolence of unbridled passion.'' The cause of liberty demanded citizen vigilance. The hope for Warren and other popular leaders was that such memorializing and image-building over the dead would ensure more commitment and citizen virtue, should the ultimate form of resistance—rebellion and civil war—ever become necessary against what they viewed as a plotting, willful home government.

An incident such as the Boston Massacre serves to epitomize how the fear of Britain's standing army developed after 1768 and helped to accelerate the breakdown of communications in the empire. After that crisis, there was a period of calm, but it ended with Parliament's decision of May 1773 to force Americans to buy East India Company tea and thereby pay the trade duty on that product. Events now pointed toward Lexington and Concord. The Boston Tea Party of December 1773 resulted in Parliament's Coercive Acts, passed during the spring of 1774. Included was legislation modifying the charter basis of Massachusetts government, and Thomas Gage was given the assignment of managing the Bay Colony with quasi-autocratic authority. There was something in the Coercive Acts to upset nearly everyone in all 13 colonies, which helped to spur the calling of the first Continental Congress in September 1774. The first Congress, in turn, adopted a plan of general economic boycott, which was to be put into effect across the land by local committees, sometimes with militia support.

George III and his ministers responded to the work of the first Continental Congress with increased disdain and inflexibility. Regarding the Americans as ill prepared for a military confrontation and viewing them as having been stirred up by designing, evil men, the King-in-Parliament decided to isolate and humiliate Massachusetts by declaring that province to be in a state of rebellion in early 1775. Lord Dartmouth, who had replaced Hillsborough as the American Secretary, was given the task of ordering Gage to use the 4,000 troops recently made available to him. ''The first essential step to be taken toward reestablishing Government, would be to arrest and imprison the principal Actors and Abettors in the [Massachusetts] Provincial Congress," stated Dartmouth. He could not imagine why Gage was hesitating to use more decisively the standing units at his command. "Any efforts of the people, unprepared to encounter with a regular Force, cannot be very formidable," he concluded.

Obviously, Dartmouth was wrong. The old stereotype about the lack of American martial prowess, so firmly planted during the French and Indian War, was there in the Secretary's orders. Like so many other ideas that passed for reality, it was inaccurate, at least immediately. Receiving Dartmouth's instructions in mid-April, Gage knew that he had to do something or be called home in disgrace. Since there was little prospect of running down elusive patriot leaders, the alternative target became the military stores at Concord. Gage hoped that the foray into the interior would awe the Americans into submission—and do so without bloodshed. He was being naive on both counts.

In the end, both sides blundered toward the civil war that was to come. Both served as protagonists. The home government wanted a more efficient and responsive empire. The colonists desired more freedom of action in economic, social, and political matters. As Britain attempted to tighten the reins, talk of conspiracy emanated from both sides. The presence and use of a standing army in America during peacetime abetted the final breakdown in communications. Ultimately, rebellion and war became all but inevitable.

It would be a serious mistake to conclude that Great Britain caused the war because of tyrannical designs. To do that would be to confuse the provincial ideological world view with the actuality of historical conditions in the years between 1763 and 1775. Such a statement does not deny the point that how provincials perceived reality and responded to it was much more important in moving them toward rebellion than reality itself. Citizens in and around Boston in April 1775 believed that they had been entrapped by political slavery. For them, the standing army marching toward Lexington and Concord was visible proof of the validity of their perceptions.

With the advantage of historical hindsight, it makes more sense to conclude that both sides drifted toward a state of civil war because they could not comprehend the intentions of the other. Such being the case, there was little chance of reversing the course of recent history after the bloodshed of Lexington and Concord. The time had come for republican war with the avowed goal of preserving liberty in a darkened world. The real question was whether American citizens could evidence enough virtue to sustain the momentous martial challenge now facing them.

NOTES

[1] Bernard Bailyn, *The Ideological Origins of the American Revolution* (Cambridge, Mass., 1967), pp. 56–58.

[2] J. G. A. Pocock, "Machiavelli, Harrington, and English Political Ideologies in the Eighteenth Century," *William and Mary Quarterly,* 3d Series, 22 (1965), p. 566. *See also* Pocock, *The Machiavellian Moment: Florentine Political Thought and the Atlantic Republican Tradition* (Princeton, N.J., 1975), pp. 333–505.

[3] Gordon S. Wood, *The Creation of the American Republic, 1776–1787* (Chapel Hill, N.C., 1969), p. 69.

[4] Thomas Gordon, *Cato's Letters,* no. 65 (February 10, 1721).

[5] Caroline Robbins, *The Eighteenth-Century Commonwealthman: Studies in the Transmission, Development and Circumstance of English Liberal Thought from the Restoration of Charles II until the War with the Thirteen Colonies* (Cambridge, Mass., 1959), *passim.*

[6] Bailyn, *Ideological Origins,* p. 138. For other important studies dealing with the nature of opposition ideas and the transmission process, *see* the works cited above and *also* studies listed in Robert E. Shalhope, "Toward a Republican Synthesis: The Emergence of an Understanding of Republicanism in American Historiography," *William and Mary Quarterly,* 3d Series, 29 (1972), pp. 49–80. *See also* John Phillip Reid, *In Defiance of the Law: The Standing-Army Controversy, the Two Constitutions, and the Coming of the American Revolution* (Chapel Hill, N.C., 1981), *passim.*

[7] Walter Millis, *Arms and Men: A Study in American Military History* (New York, 1956), p. 13.

[8] *Ibid.,* p. 14. *See also* Michael Roberts, *The Military Revolution, 1560–1660* (Belfast, Ireland, 1956), which dates the revolution in military practice to an earlier period in time.

[9] Millis, *Arms and Men,* p. 15.

[10] Sylvia R. Frey, "The Common British Soldier in the Late Eighteenth Century: A Profile," *Societas: A Review of Social History,* 5 (1975), p. 126. *See also* Frey, *The British Soldier in America: A Social History of Military Life in the Revolutionary Period* (Austin, Tex., 1981), pp. 3–21.

[11] Don Higginbotham, *The War of American Independence: Military Attitudes, Policies, and Practice, 1763–1789* (New York, 1971), p. 33.

[12] John Shy, "A New Look at the Colonial Militia," in *A People Numerous and Armed: Reflections on the Military Struggle for American Independence* (New York, 1976), p. 24.

[13] Richard H. Kohn, *Eagle and Sword: The Federalists and the Creation of the Military Establishment in America, 1783–1802* (New York, 1975), p. 7.

[14] Lawrence Delbert Cress, "The Standing Army, the Militia, and the New Republic: Changing Attitudes toward the Military in American Society, 1768 to 1820," (Ph.D. dissertation, University of Virginia, 1976), p. 5. In particular, consult Cress's first chapter, "The Military in Colonial Society," pp. 1–32. For evidence that provincial Americans tapped the poorer classes heavily for manpower to fight in the colonial wars, *see* Gary B. Nash, *The Urban Crucible: Social Change, Political Consciousness, and the Origins of the American Revolution* (Cambridge, Mass., 1979), *passim.*

[15] Shy, "A New Look at Colonial Militia," p. 32.

The Republican War, 1775–1776

A REPUBLICAN ORDER AS THE GOAL

Republicanism was the central concept giving both form and meaning to what Americans sought through the act of civil war. Their goal was the creation of a republican society. Then, as now, definitions of that term varied. The central thrust, however, was toward a socioeconomic and political order predicated on liberty and harmony in human relationships. In his *Thoughts on Government* (1776), John Adams argued "that there is no good government but what is republican." In succinct fashion, the Massachusetts patriot explained that "a republic is 'an empire of laws, and not of men.'" To Adams, republicanism transcended particular governmental forms. It was an attitude demonstrating respect for the law and human liberty, working to eliminate tyranny and unnecessary privilege. As historian Bernard Bailyn has explained in recent years, republicanism represented to the Revolutionary generation a "faith. . .that a better world than any that had ever been known could be built where authority was distrusted and held in constant scrutiny; where the status of men flowed from their achievements and from their personal qualities, not from distinctions ascribed to them at birth; and where the use of power over the lives of men was jealously guarded and severely restricted."[1] To achieve republicanism was to establish an even handed and impartial sociopolitical order in which citizens might prosper and enjoy the blessings of life, liberty, and property.

The central subject in the search for a republican order, according to whig ideologues, was the virtuous citizen, who had to be fully and morally committed to the worthiness of the quest. In 1775, especially after Lexington and Concord, the qualities of virtue and commitment appeared to stand out everywhere. Historian Charles Royster (*A Revolutionary People at War,* 1980) has accurately characterized this period by the phrase *rage militaire,* based on what a Philadelphia citizen described as a "passion for arms" that "has taken possession of the whole continent."[2] Except among the indifferent (no one has effectively estimated the size of this group) and those who maintained traditional loyalties and earned the epithet of tory (this group fluctuated in size throughout the war but probably never represented more than one-fifth of the American population), a spirit of determined enthusiasm in resistance to tyranny pervaded the landscape. Testaments to the glory of the republican quest poured forth, as evidenced by militia companies finding renewed vigor.

At the outset of war, most patriots simply accepted by faith that militia could stand up to regulars and thereby secure a republican polity. Public virtue and moral commitment was all that was necessary for militia to enjoy success. During May 1774, the Maryland Provincial Convention explained "that a well-regulated Militia, composed of the gentlemen, freeholders, and other freemen, is the natural strength and only stable security of a free Government." Hence it urged the local population to proceed with haste in organizing itself. Charles Lee, a retired regular British officer living in Virginia (soon to become one of Washington's most notorious lieutenants), assured those inhabitants who may have doubted the fighting efficacy of militia that citizen-soldiers could be more tenacious than regulars. "A Militia, by confining themselves to essentials," Lee observed, "may become, in a very few months, a most formidable infantry." If civilians were just willing to turn out for service, opined Lee, "this continent may have formed for action, in three or four months, an hundred thousand infantry." Even if better trained, Britain's army could not cope with such numbers. "History tells us," concluded the former regular, that free states in ancient times were all "subjugated by the force or art of tyrants. They almost all, in their turns, recovered their liberty and destroyed their tyrants" through effective militia action. New Englander Elbridge Gerry was more direct; he wrote, "On the Discipline of your militia depends your liberty."

Popular confidence in militia organization and the citizen-soldier as essential to achieving republicanism ran high through most of 1775. Success, of course, depended on the depth of commitment of citizen-soldiers—best described by their willingness to sacrifice themselves and their immediate interests, even if it meant the loss of their lives, for the benefit of posterity. Commentators repeatedly noted that Americans-in-arms were not only virtuous but ready for the long fight. One address, written in February 1776, expressed it this way: "Our Troops are animated with the Love of Freedom—We confess that they have not the Advantages arising from Experience and Discipline. But Facts have shown, that native Courage warmed with Patriotism, is sufficient to counterbalance these Advantages." Similarly, a French spy reporting back to the court at Versailles from Boston late in 1775 exclaimed that "Everybody here is a soldier; the troops are well dressed, well paid, and well commanded. They have 50,000 men under pay and a large number of volunteers who desire none. . . .They are stronger than others thought. It surpasses one's imagination. . . .Nothing frightens them." Despite obvious hyperbole with respect to numbers, the French observer clearly conveyed the feeling that dedication, vigilance, and virtue were the qualities most accurately describing the first patriots in arms.

In poetry and prose, rebellious Americans thus exhorted one another to action. One poet, leaving behind his "dear Clorinda," poured forth his soul this way:

> My bleeding country calls, and I must go.
> Distress'd it calls aloud, to arms, to arms;
> The trumpet sounds, I now must go and leave your charms:
> I've drawn my sword, I'll go forth with the brave,
> And die a freeman, ere I live a slave.

Melodramatic verse, indeed, perhaps only to be outdone by the far more prosaic advice of "an elderly lady" to "young men" about to enter wartime service in New Jersey. "Let me beg of you, my children, that if you fall, it may be like men," she exhorted them, "and that your wounds not be in your back parts."

As Charles Royster has stressed, American citizen-soldiers of 1775 felt more than courage, moral confidence, and virtue. Many of them believed that the republican quest in America represented a special mission in the eyes of God. Typical was the New Jersey soldier who rejoiced "that the ALMIGHTY Governor of the universe hath given us a station so honorable and planted us the guardians of liberty." To such men, tyranny was more than synonymous with political slavery; it was the work of Satan. The contest truly was between sin and the forces of darkness and liberty and God's righteousness. As Royster points out, numbers of citizens saw in the impending military contest "the greatest test of the chosen people. In it they bore the weight of both their heritage and God's promise for the future."[3]

Whether by Christian precept, whig doctrine, or some combination of these two important strains in conjunction with Enlightenment rationalism, the concept animating most provincial Americans in 1775 was republicanism. Theirs was a special trust, since citizens firmly believed that liberty was being snuffed out across the face of the globe. Standing orders of the day issued to the patriot army surrounding Boston summarized the mood and the calling best: "Let us therefore animate and encourage each other, and show the whole world that a Freeman contending for LIBERTY on his own ground is superior to any slavish mercenary on earth."

In this missionary sense, the patriot enthusiasts of 1775 decided to test the very vitals of republicanism and their worthiness in aspiring to that ideal. The War for Independence was to be the measuring rod of the moral commitment that free states demanded of dedicated and virtuous citizens. The question was whether the provincials had the fiber to endure the strain of sustained war against Britain's armed forces—to emerge bloodstained but triumphant. That they rather uniformly and willingly did has been the historical myth. Most did not.

REGULARS VERSUS REPUBLICANS: THE BRITISH AT BAY

Dr. James Thacher, a patriot witness to the events around Boston following the Lexington and Concord incidents, recorded this scenario in his diary: "Such was the enthusiasm for the cause of liberty, and so general and extensive the alarm, that thousands of our citizens who were engaged in the cultivation of their farms, spontaneously rushed to the scene of action, and the army was established without the effort of public authority." Another way to put the matter is to state that one of the most unusual armies ever gathered sprang up almost instantly and entrapped Gage on the peninsula of Boston. By the end of April, the rebel camp held over 10,000 enthusiasts. The Massachusetts Provincial Congress persuaded many of these militiamen to stay

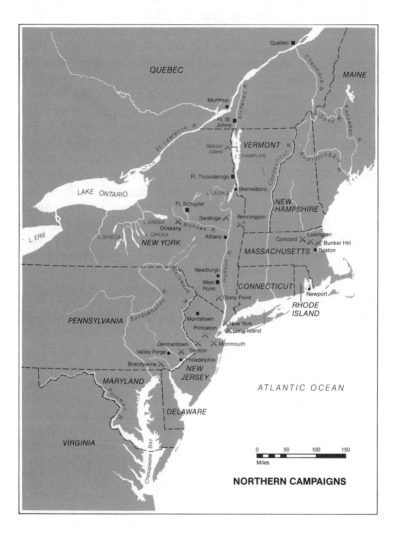

NORTHERN CAMPAIGNS

on until the end of the year. The assemblage was nominally under the command of Artemas Ward, described by ascerbic Charles Lee as "a fat old gentleman who had been a popular *church-warden.*" In actuality, Ward had seen some military action against the French and Indians, and he drew upon that experience in attempting to hold the irregular collection of patriots together.

Creating some semblance of an army was no simple task with 10,000 independent-minded volunteers. Discipline was lax, with citizen-soldiers coming and going from camp as they pleased and taking orders quite casually, if at all. Ward himself had only nominal authority over patriots from other provinces. He issued general orders only after meeting with a council of senior officers. Moreover, the citizen constabulary lacked tents and equipment, particularly muskets and field artillery. Also, these enthusiasts had little sense of camp sanitation. It was an enervating assignment, but Ward managed to keep enough units in some semblance of order to discourage any offensive movements by Gage's redcoats.

Most of the patriots in camp failed to see much wrong with the disorderly nature of New England's republican army. Indeed, these early citizen-soldiers seemed to revel in the contrasts between themselves and British regulars. They connoted to them that liberty was more vibrant than well-trained might. The general lack of discipline, the haphazard election of junior officers, and the continuing public response that further swelled the ranks all seemed to justify assumptions that tyranny was on the run. Indeed, many of these early soldiers were freehold farmers, artisans, and tradesmen who had left their homes and families to rush to the scene of action. Their numbers comforted each in the faith that regular troops could not stand up to middle-class, property-holding citizens of moral rectitude and virtue. The story of Israel Putnam's rush to the martial field further supported this mood. Putnam, a prosperous Connecticut freeholder and French and Indian War veteran, was reputedly behind his plow when he learned about the first shots at Lexington Green. Like the Roman Cincinnatus, the future Continental general cut his horse from the traces, armed his laborers, and rode off to defend the sweet fruit of liberty. Nothing, it seemed, could overcome such deep-felt commitment.

The righteous confidence born of high levels of enthusiasm served the cause well in the next few months, as the patriots chalked up an impressive early record. The capture of Fort Ticonderoga on Lake Champlain on May 10, 1775, was a case in point. Petulant and determined Benedict Arnold, then an officer in the Connecticut militia, suggested the venture in order to seize heavy ordnance badly needed around Boston. Massachusetts commissioned him to lead the raid; but tall, gangling Ethan Allen of Vermont, acting under Connecticut orders, got under way first. Catching up with Allen's Green Mountain Boys, Arnold disputed Allen's right to command, and there was an uneasy truce between the two when they stormed into the lightly garrisoned fort. Caught totally by surprise, the British offered no resistance. Ticonderoga yielded some 60 cannons. Enterprise and élan had secured the much-needed ordnance. Furthermore, despite all the bickering between Arnold and Allen over who outranked whom and who should get credit for the victory, the two of them reduced other enemy posts north of Ticonderoga, thus clearing the way for a possible invasion of Canada.

The action that truly underpinned the dominant assumption of 1775 that citizen-soldiers could withstand the withering fire of any regular onslaught occurred on Breed's Hill, across the back-bay from Boston. Toward the end of May, Gage received reinforcements, including Generals William Howe, John Burgoyne, and Henry Clinton. These three urged the British commander to take the offensive, the target being Dorchester Heights, located south of Boston and an excellent site for artillery placements, assuming the rebels could secure the ordnance to bombard the town. On the evening of June 16, however, the patriots diverted Gage's focus when they dug in on the Charlestown peninsula. The New Englanders planned to fortify Bunker Hill, but instead, for some inexplicable reason they threw up their most extended works on Breed's Hill, which was lower than Bunker and closer to the enemy in Boston. Seeing the works early on June

17, the British commanders prepared for action. They first wrangled among themselves about tactics. Instead of choosing flanking maneuvers and attempting to cut the rebels off by taking the narrow neck of land connecting Charlestown peninsula to the mainland, they opted for a massed frontal assault, with redcoats advancing in tightly formed ranks straight toward the American lines. Gage thought that such an assault would put some respect for the prowess of British arms into New England's citizen-soldiers, and the North American commander detailed 2,500 men under General Howe to take Breed's Hill. That afternoon, after the redcoats had been rowed across the bay, they found themselves advancing into what would be the bloodiest battle of the entire war.

On and around Breed's Hill, the Americans under William Prescott and Israel Putnam waited patiently. Well entrenched, they allowed the regulars to get within yards of them and then, at the last moment, they let loose a volley that shattered the first British advance. Reeling, the British columns reformed and came up the hill again, only to be thrown back with equal violence. Stunned by the carnage, Howe later admitted to *"a moment that I never felt before,"* the prospect of extermination in battle. With the outcome and British martial honor at stake, Howe ordered a third assault.

Much has been written about the iron discipline of the eighteenth-century regular soldier. It was such that the rank and file feared concentrated enemy firepower less than the certainty of discipline for disobeying orders. But the redcoats who rallied for a third attempt at that hill were more than disciplined: they were awesomely brave. And although it was inconceivable to committed whigs at the time, the redcoats probably took regimental pride and the cause of their King as seriously as the patriots took their own. Now the regulars moved up the slope again, this time without the extra weight of full field packs. They had to step on and over the bleeding, mangled bodies of their comrades. Again, determined patriot fire erupted and staggered them. Then American ammunition began to give out. The regulars bore in with their bayonets and drove the defiant patriots from their defensive works. Finally, it was all over; Howe's exhausted men had the bloodied landscape all to themselves.

The British had won in the technical sense of having forced the Americans to flee the peninsula, but they had not proved the superiority of well-trained and well-armed regulars. They had suffered 1,054 casualties, slightly over 40 percent of the force committed to battle. That was a staggeringly high casualty figure in an age of small-scale armies. American casualties totaled 411 (30 percent of the rebels engaged). It was "a dear bought victory," wrote a shocked Henry Clinton, "another such would have ruined us." Howe, who became the head of British forces in North America after the recall of Gage in October, never forgot the bitter lesson that he had learned about the fighting abilities of *entrenched* citizen-soldiers. Indeed, that lesson represents one explanation for his dilatory tactics in the field during the massive campaign effort of 1776.

The patriots, who at first were sullen about losing, soon added the engagement to the list of examples of the fighting prowess of the committed, virtuous citizen-in-arms. "Bunker Hill, along with Lexington and Concord," Robert W. Coakley and Stetson Conn have claimed in *The War of the American Revolution* (1975), "went far to create the American tradition that the citizen-soldier when aroused is more than a match for the trained professional."[4] Unfortunately for that tradition, the war did not end in 1775.

Over and above great confidence in themselves, there were other reasons why American volunteers stood up so well early on in the war. The British ministry and its military leaders, as John Shy has emphasized in *Toward Lexington* (1965), did not expect a full-scale regional revolt in 1775; nor were British forces strong enough or deployed well enough to meet an effective irregular challenge.[5] Like the vaunted British navy, the army, since the Seven Years' War, had grown rusty from lack of use. The British machinery of war had decayed, and it needed revitalization. Moreover, when the patriots fought in these early days, they generally dictated the terms. On the Lexington and Concord road, they harried needlessly exposed columns; at Ticonderoga, they picked off a weak and isolated post by surprise; and at Bunker Hill, they took advantage of terrain and a serious British tactical error (not cutting off the neck of Charlestown Peninsula). Yet in the first flush of victory, it appeared as if republican ardor was sweeping all before it. Indeed, success had come so easily that Americans would have greater difficulty in responding effectively when the tide of war suddenly changed.

THE CREATION OF A CONTINENTAL ARMY

The civil war could not be contained exclusively to New England forever, or at least patriot New Englanders hoped not. Broad-scale popular defense of liberty simply required the backing and involvement of as many colonies as possible. In May 1775, the Massachusetts rebel leadership thus asked the second Continental Congress to adopt the citizen's army around Boston, and on June 14 Congress agreed to the assignment. The delegates in Philadelphia also voted to raise 10 companies of Pennsylvania, Maryland, and Virginia riflemen to support the citizen-soldiers already in the field. By adoption, then, Congressional action had transformed the New England force, at least on paper, into a Continental army.

To proclaim the existence of an intercolonial army certainly did not assure that it would triumph over all. Congress, accordingly, put in place a new command structure to supplant the current one. As their first step, the delegates named George Washington, a dignified and reserved Virginia planter of great landed wealth, commander in chief. Although he had fought in the French and Indian War (Washington had survived the slaughter of General Edward Braddock's army in 1755), the 43-year-old Virginian had never commanded large numbers of troops. Yet Washington believed firmly in the rectitude of the American cause and was willing to do the best he could. His elevation resulted from the active support of New Englanders in Congress, such as John Adams, who favored having a southern commander. Through Washington, their idea was to ensure interregional support for what had begun as a fray in New England. Unbeknownst to them in 1775, they had selected an individual whose strength of character and depth of commitment to the goal of a republican order would have a major influence on the success of the cause.

The Congressional delegates also established the nucleus of a Continental general officer corps. They quickly issued commissions to four major and eight brigadier generals. Out of regard for the composition of the army at the time, most of the commissions went to New Englanders. Not surprisingly, Artemas Ward became a major general, as did Israel Putnam and wealthy landholder Philip Schuyler of New York, both of whom had considerable experience in the colonial wars. The fourth major generalship went to Charles Lee, a man of substantial intellect but irascible temperament. Lee had an excellent military record in Europe and was an ardent republican and a staunch advocate of the citizen-soldier as the central component of defense. During the early months of the American contest, he rendered valuable service. Of the original brigadiers, Nathanael Greene, the lame Quaker from Rhode Island who had intensively studied manuals on the art of war, became the most indispensable. Other appointments supplied the army with its first quartermaster, commissary, and adjutant generals. The first adjutant general was another British veteran officer and adopted Virginian, Horatio Gates.

Congress thus began the task of establishing a central army, but there were many problems yet to be solved. To whom the army belonged was still unclear. When Massachusetts asked the delegates to take charge of the forces before Boston, the Provincial Congress stated: that "the sword should, in all free states, be subservient to the civil powers." The Massachusetts leadership trembled "at having an Army. . .established here, without a civil power to provide for and control them." Since the objective was to have a Continental force consisting of troops from all the colonies, it simply could not be maintained and operated by rebel leaders in one province. Congress did represent all the rebellious provinces, yet it was to remain an extralegal body with unclearly defined authority throughout much of the war (until the final ratification of the Articles of Confederation in 1781). Out of expediency and the need for broad-scale planning, coordination, and participation, Congress agreed to take over. The issue of whether the army was of Congress or of the states, however, was never clearly resolved, and it caused the new commander in chief innumerable difficulties in the days and months ahead.

To have had 13 sovereign heads to report to instead of one would have made Washington's assignment impossible. In many ways, the Virginian resolved the broad issue early by placing higher priority on Congressional dictates than on requests for military support coming from the states. Even more important, he insisted on proper military deference to Congress as the source of civil power under which he and the army drew its life-blood. At times, as John Todd White has demonstrated, Washington's unstinting devotion to the principle of subordinating military to civil authority exasperated more than one Congressman, who in time tried to dump insoluable civil problems, such as logistical support, back onto the army. But Washington consistently sought to keep military power within prescribed bounds, even when politics in Congress and the states adversely affected the war effort and the army.[6] Above all else, Washington did not want to see the republican cause undermined by a military dictatorship, and that turned out to be one of his greatest contributions to the Revolution and its legacy.

Besides the question of what civil government should guide the army, there was the vexing matter of just dealing with Congress. The delegates, attempting to function as a deliberative, policy-making, and coordinating body, also tried to handle matters of administrative detail. At the outset of the war, Congress did routine army business by creating *ad hoc* committees to make recommendations and by asking particular states to attend to this or that item. Pressing requests for support and for policy thus had a way of getting bogged down, ignored, or lost. The establishment of a Congressional board of war in 1776 eased the pattern of interminable administrative confusion and delay somewhat, since there now would be one standing committee through which army needs and requests could be channeled. However, Congress did not seriously attempt to move beyond the stage of haphazard, inefficient administration (for which it had a well-deserved reputation) until 1781, when the delegates chose to establish separate executive departments relating to war, finance, and diplomacy. By that time, the worst days of the war had been nearly passed.

The Congressional maze of administraton seemed to have no end, nor did the wrangling among Continental officers over the issue of rank. The ink had hardly dried on the first commissions of June 1775 when disputes broke out over why this or that person should be outranking some other. Never-ending contention over status and rank thus besieged Washington and Congress about as much as did the British adversary, as Jonathan G. Rossie has shown in *The Politics of Command in the American Revolution* (1975).[7] In early 1777, Congress tried to settle this major source of contention once and for all with its Baltimore resolution: "In voting for general officers, a due regard shall be had to the line of succession, the merit of the persons proposed, and the quota of troops raised, and to be raised, by each state." If virtue meant subordination of self-interest to the greater good of the cause, many officers did not seem to comprehend its meaning. For their reasons, they put as high a priority on personal honor as on disinterested service, which adversely affected the ideal goal of unity in the cause.

Still another issue that caused significant disagreement, but only before Independence, had to do with the purpose and function of the Continental army. The establishment of an intercolonial military force clearly implied that the provincials had entered a new phase of heightened resistance and were preparing for full-scale civil war, should reconciliation prove impossible. During 1775, reconciliationists in Congress, individuals who hoped to settle differences with England short of declared independence, worried about what implications the British ministry might draw from the adoption of the New England forces. They did not want Congress's actions to stand in the way of imperial reunification, if reconciliation was at all possible. It was pressure from this large bloc in Congress that resulted in the "Declaration of the Causes and Necessity for Taking up Arms," promulgated in July 1775, which was to be forwarded to England. The petition stated that the reason for the military establishment was not "to dissolve that union which has so long and so happily subsisted between us." Rather, the new Continental army would function solely to *defend* American lives, liberty, and property until "hostilities shall cease on the part of the aggressors, and all danger of their being renewed shall be removed, and not before."

Through the Declaration, Congress provided ammunition for the myth of Americans being forced into war by an arbitrary and capricious enemy. Yet there is no escaping the fact that creating the Continental army was an aggressive, warlike act in itself, no matter how the reconciliationists sugar-coated the message for the home government. After all, the war had not got out of hand in the early summer of 1775, and Congress could have chosen less extreme methods to protect the provinces while still seeking reconciliation.

It did not take George Washington long to learn that, in accepting command, he had taken on a veritable host of difficulties. He was supposed to manage an army that was to maintain its citizen-soldier character and to act only to defend American rights (until Congress said otherwise). The civil authority that would have the most important voice in formulating military policy and actions was unclear; moreover, Washington could not be sure whether the army was to seek reconciliation or secure independence, at least until Congress and the 13 provinces made up their minds. Even more pressing, his officers were already wrangling over status and rank. Worse yet, when he reached camp at Cambridge on July 2, he found a cantonment of soldiers that came closer to epitomizing martial chaos than some form of basic regimen. That Washington was able to deal with these and numerous other administrative problems that beset the Continental army during the next eight years stands as a testament to his unusual strength of will. Serving as commander in chief of the new republican army would have very quickly broken most men.

Initially, the most serious problem of all, as the new commander viewed it, was the lack of order and discipline in camp. "Discipline is the soul of the army," he stated flatly. "It makes small numbers formidable; procures success to the weak and esteem to all." Indeed, as Marcus Cunliffe has cogently argued in *Soldiers and Civilians* (2d ed., 1973), Washington's ideal model for an effective army was the British standing force that he opposed.[8] From the outset, he insisted that everyone in camp respect the distinctions between officers and enlisted men. In this regard, Washington found the "leveling" tendencies of the New Englanders to be particularly vexing. He complained in one letter that "their officers generally speaking are the most indifferent kind of people I ever saw. I dare say the men would fight well (if properly officered), although they are an exceeding dirty and nasty people."

Regional prejudice aside, the Virginian committed himself to overcoming the informal, individualistic bravado that characterized so many units. If nothing else, the new commander was a realist. He doubted how long virtue and moral ardor would hold up in a full campaign of pitched battles against trained regulars. He probably suspected that the *rage militaire* of 1775 would quickly give out, if the enemy began to enjoy significant martial success. His immediate objective became that of turning the citizen-soldier into a well-trained and well-disciplined fighter—a functioning cog in the machinery of war rather than the strutting individualist of militia muster days. Sustaining the rebellion depended upon thorough training and good order, as much as anything else, in Washington's mind.

The new commander and his most trusted aides thus aspired to an army of regulars. Washington's personal involvement with the French and Indian War had convinced him that heavy reliance on amateur citizen-soldiers in long-term campaigns was folly. As he once boldly stated: "To place any dependence upon militia is assuredly resting upon a broken staff." He did not question the inherent character of the citizen-soldier, but past experience had convinced him that virtue and moral commitment were not so important in sustaining soldiers in combat as rigorous training, regimen, and discipline. Militia, with their short-term enlistments, could come out, fight, and go back home when they pleased. They could be (and often were) erratic and prone to run in battle. Their very independence made them an unsteady base on which to lean for a commander charged with combatting His Majesty's redcoats.

From a similar angle, Nathanael Greene perhaps summarized attitudes best among Washington's closest general officers when he wrote that militiamen represented "people coming from home with all the tender feelings of domestic life." As such, they were "not sufficiently fortified with natural courage to stand the shocking scenes of war. To march over dead men, to hear without concern the groans of the wounded, I say few men can stand such scenes unless steeled by habit and fortified by military pride." Only training, discipline, and combat experience (qualities setting off the regular from the amateur soldier) could make for an effective army, concluded Greene.

Historians have hotly debated the issue of whether regulars or militia were more essential to winning the war. Claude H. Van Tyne, whose classic *The War of Independence* (1929) won the Pulitzer Prize, argued that the war "proved the utter failure of the militia system."[9] More recently, Don Higginbotham has presented a less extreme viewpoint in stating that "the militia. . .for all its frailties, made its finest contributions to the nation in the Revolution."[10] Higginbotham's position makes more sense. The most significant problem facing Washington in 1775 was how to create an effective Continental fighting machine in the face of the colonial militia tradition and so many ideological pronouncements about the inherent tenacity of virtuous citizen-soldiers. He knew that he could not abandon the militia tradition; he would have to work with it. However, he and his advisers hoped to modify it by employing militia on the periphery while developing a core of trustworthy regulars, combining the best of both the amateur and regular traditions. As

Marcus Cunliffe has correctly phrased it, Washington "recognized that he would have to depend largely on scratch units and that he could not hope for more than a nucleus of seasoned Continentals. His aim was to make this nucleus as large as possible, and to enlist battalions for as long as Congress would allow and Americans would consent to serve."[11]

The critical point is that the new commander in chief was realistic enough to begin putting together an army out of the materials at hand. No matter how much free-wheeling citizen-soldiers might object, even to the point of going home, instilling camp discipline was the first vital step. During the summer and fall of 1775, prompted by general orders and court martials, the republican forces begrudgingly accepted a superficial sense of decorum. Soldiers, for example, who were found drunk or asleep while on duty had been winked at in the past. The winks became fewer and the floggings more frequent. The commander also came down hard on unsanitary camp conditions. Disease was by far the greatest enemy attacking eighteenth-century armies. Washington put particular stress on clean kitchens and proper waste disposal. As much as possible, he used tact and persuasion to guide the changes; failing that, he was not squeamish about the lash. (The Congressional Articles of War of 1775 allowed a maximum of 39 stripes, although Washington thought that many crimes, such as striking an officer, were worth at least 500.) By the late fall, the commander felt that he was making some headway in disciplining his citizens-in-arms. (Of course there were lapses—in October a captain was caught shaving one of his men!)

While Washington labored to establish "a respectable army," as he once phrased his greatest task, the British remained militarily inactive around Boston. Replacing Thomas Gage with 46-year-old William Howe made little difference. Dark-complexioned and handsome, Howe had a good military record, which included innovative leadership in training regulars in light infantry tactics. Yet he made no overt moves to break his army out of Boston. Indeed, Washington began tightening the ring around that port city in January 1776. He wanted to storm

Boston and drive the British host into the sea, but his council of war persistently opposed the idea. Then his talented Chief of Artillery, 25-year-old Henry Knox, brought the ordnance taken at Ticonderoga into camp after a harrowing overland trek in the dead of winter. The logical decision was to place the cannon on Dorchester Heights. Twelve hundred men worked through the night of March 4 to fortify the Heights. Now the guns could be unleashed against Boston at any time.

This feat demanded a response from Howe. After a severe late winter storm aborted a planned British attack on the Heights, Howe conceded that he was maintaining untenable ground. On March 17, a fleet of almost 200 vessels carried the redcoats away to Halifax, Nova Scotia, with some 1,000 solemn loyalists in tow. Without having fired a shot, the Continental establishment could claim triumph. Howe's retreat only added to the spurious sense among patriot soldiers that moral commitment and virtue would surely win out over discipline and training. The British, however, were already planning a massive campaign effort that potentially would permit them to reconquer the lost colonies by the end of 1776. The republicans of 1775 were about to face one of their most harrowing trials of fire.

THE BRITISH MILITARY COUNTERTHRUST

As official reports of Lexington, Concord, Ticonderoga, and Bunker Hill reached England, Lord North's ministry came to realize that it was facing much more than a whimsical challenge to imperial authority. Two points were clear: the ministry did not have a strategy for subduing the patriots; and while British military forces appeared formidable on paper, both the army and the navy were in a state of peacetime disarray. The military establishment had to shake off its cobwebs, and the ministry had to formulate a strategy for conquering the eastern edge of a continent by military force, since political accommodation became less viable with each passing week. Both assignments were far more difficult than could have been foreseen in 1775.

Great Britain might seem to have had most of the advantages going into war, especially with respect to available manpower. American population stood at 2,500,000 in 1775 (including 500,000 Afro-American slaves). Britain's population was closer to 11,000,000, with some 48,000 soldiers on the army's muster rolls in 1775 (the actual number available and fit for duty was considerably lower). Likewise, the navy on paper had 139 ships of the line; however, many were old and rotting, and few had enough sailors for extended service at sea. An enlistment campaign finally got under way late in the year, but Englishmen did not seem particularly interested in signing up. In fact, the ministry finally had to resort to pardoning criminals and reducing the terms of enlistments (the norm had been for life) to secure soldiers.

As a general rule, the recruiting experience of late 1775 held up throughout the war. The average Briton did not want to have anything to do with regular military service. The long tradition of reserving military duty for the poor and the harsh conditions of camp life militated against any popular rush to arms, certainly much more so than feelings of sympathy for the American cause. In reality, no one really expected the middle classes to come forward. The well-established practice of separating military concerns from society thus severely limited Britain's natural manpower base in 1775 and thereafter. Also, within the spirit of the age, the ministry sought to keep the effects of the war as removed from the home populace as possible. The goal was to make sure that the contest did not touch the general citizenry, and almost as a *quid pro quo,* the ministry expected that these same civilians would not turn against or attempt to undercut the war effort.

There was only one alternative in congregating an army with haste. As Don Higginbotham has described the process, "the Crown, refusing to call upon the productive elements in society, resorted to the familiar practice of hiring soldiers from the continent.''[12] All told, six German principalities ultimately supplied some 30,000 soldiers. Over one-half (17,000) came from Hesse-Cassel, where the local landgrave pressed these unfortunate souls into service in return for handsome subsidies paid directly into his treasury. It was little more than human slavery for those Germans dragooned into the ranks, but the British ministry was not concerned about the social implications. The Hessians, as they came to be called, represented what the Crown believed to be the needed margin in manpower to put down the American rebellion.

Virtually unprepared at the outset for the needed military buildup, the ministry responded aggressively with its campaign effort of 1776, the most gargantuan land and sea offensive undertaken by Britain during the eighteenth century—and not to be matched, as an overseas expedition, until the 1942 allied invasion of North Africa. The objective was to shatter rebel militance in one campaign season; this would avoid the expenses associated with long-term war and assure that the Americans would not have time to ally with traditional enemies like France and Spain.

Besides the King and Lord North, the principal figure in formulating policy and putting the campaign effort together was Lord George Germain, who replaced Lord Dartmouth as the American Secretary in 1775. Germain lasted in office until early 1782 and did a creditable job in the face of adverse conditions. Until recently, however, historians have had little good to say about him, largely because he had been court-martialed and cashiered from service on charges of cowardice in the face of the enemy at the Battle of Minden in 1759. However, Piers Mackesy, in his brilliant *The War for America, 1775–1783* (1965), has demonstrated that Germain was primarily the victim of petty political infighting that carried over into his court martial. Mackesy's assessment is that he was a solid administrator, a man who was thoroughly loyal to his patron George III and often effective as a civilian war minister.[13]

Germain's solid administrative acumen can be seen by looking at the preparations for the 1776 campaign. That effort stretched Britain's inefficient and generally corrupt bureaucracy to its limits. Effective coordination among the Admiralty, War, and American offices was precarious at best. Still, a flotilla of unparalleled proportions set sail for America by the early summer. It was an army and navy that was well-supplied, well-clothed, and exceptionally well-armed. The bivouac point was to be Staten Island, where William Howe (having sailed south from Halifax) landed with some 10,000 soldiers at the end of June. By mid-August, another 20,000 troops had been carried across the Atlantic on some 370 transport vessels and placed at Howe's disposal. In addition, Howe's talented brother Richard, Lord Howe, the Admiral, had more than 70 naval vessels and 13,000 sailors in the vicinity. With 45,000 soldiers and sailors confronting New York by August 1776, it is safe to conclude that Britain had overcome bureaucratic manpower problems and was now in a position to reestablish a foothold on the American continent.

Success depended on strategy, and there matters were, at best, confused. The grand problem was that of reasserting political control over the former provinces through the application of military power. The issue was how best to use the massive military force concentrating on New York in accomplishing that end. The task may very well have been beyond the standard military means of the day, given the characteristic separateness, diffuseness, and sheer geographical size of the rebellious colonies. Attempting to regain control of much of the eastern edge of a continent stretching some 1,500 miles from Maine to Georgia was beyond ordinary eighteenth-century assignments in this age of formalized warfare, especially because the erstwhile colonies lacked a strategic vital center which, if captured, would have destroyed the rebellion. Conquering one city, such as the nominal capital, Philadelphia, or even one region, such as rambunctious New England, would not guarantee total American submission. Pursuing the normal military strategy of capturing posts and territory did not seem to be a very feasible means for restoring political allegiance.

Indeed, Eric Robson's study *The American Revolution in*

Its Political and Military Aspects, 1763–1783 (1955) was among the first to have effectively raised the issue of whether Great Britain ever had a realistic chance of winning the war, given the nature and scale of eighteenth-century military activity. Robson framed two fundamental questions: Why did the British lose? Why did the Americans win?[14] What he found was that the parent state faced nearly insuperable bureaucratic, strategic, tactical, and logistical obstacles. On top of all this was the problem of condescending attitudes toward the rebels, which the experience of waging war against the patriots did not significantly alter. As one British officer explained in 1779: "The contempt every Soldier has for an American is not the smallest. They cannot possibly believe that any good Quality can exist among them." British ministers, generals, and soldiers persisted throughout in their sense of military superiority; as a result, they failed to grasp that reconquering a continent was an awesome task for small-scale armies. The attitude of condescension may have represented the greatest problem of all, since it seemed to be a fixed part of the regular officers' minds.

Home officials, however, were not thinking in such broadly problematic terms in 1776. The basic strategy, essentially sound, was to concentrate troops in and around New York City, an excellent base port from which operations could emanate. New York would thus initially serve as the point from which the surrounding countryside could be reconquered. In time, the King's minions could move northward and take the Hudson Highlands region, severing New England from the other states and isolating for conquest the area that had been the hotbed of prewar patriot defiance. The British host could also move southward and westward across New Jersey, providing a regional land base, not only for food supplies but also for loyalists who could come forward and help to reinstate civilian authority under the Crown. Then it would be a matter of casting the net ever wider, until the patriot will to resist had become completely ensnared.

Still, a major issue, the intensity with which the campaign was to be conducted, was unclear. Germain preferred a virtual scorched-earth policy with the paramount goal being the early entrapment or annihilation of Washington's army. He reasoned that the rebellion would not be dead until the main rebel force no longer existed. The Howe brothers preferred a more cautious approach to the 1776 campaign. They accepted the ground rules of formalized war, which treated combat more as a chess board experience. The Howe brothers, moreover, can be identified with the whig leaders in England who had some sympathy toward American grievances. The Howes believed that calculated brutality, even if it ended the rebellion, would only further alienate the Americans and set the stage for yet another civil war in the years ahead. They preferred the use of persuasion in conjunction with military might, employing their martial resources to prod Americans into signing loyalty oaths and renewing allegiance to the Crown.

Indeed, when the Howes arrived in the New York vicinity, they carried instructions with them to act as Crown-appointed peace comissioners. Even though they lacked the power to negotiate a settlement until the colonists surrendered, they hoped that the presence of their massed forces would be enough to bring submission. To pursue peace and war at the same time was inevitably clumsy for commanders in the field. Yet there is reason to believe that the Howes tried to do just that; and Germain, back in England, could do nothing to push them into a military reign of terror, which may have been the only tactic that would have ended the rebellion in the 1776 campaign season.

THE NEW YORK CAMPAIGN

After William Howe's evacuation of Boston in March 1776, the patriot command moved its republican army to New York City, the logical point for the beginning of the British counterstroke. If the Continental army's manpower was not so great as Washington would have liked, enthusiasm for the cause was still quite high, as Allen Bowman has effectively demonstrated in his study of *The Morale of the American Revolutionary Army* (1943).[15] Philip Vickers Fithian, a chaplain on duty with the New Jersey militia in New York, wrote home about soldiers eager for serious combat. Nothing, he claimed, was too much to endure for liberty, not even army food. In Pennsylvania, Private Aaron Wright personified the continuing spirit of virtuous commitment. He detested strict discipline, arbitrary officers, and citizens uninterested in or only lukewarm in the cause. Once, when a junior-grade officer resigned, then asked for reinstatement, Wright bristled: "You shall not command us," he told him, "for he whose mind can change in an hour, is not fit to command in the field where liberty is contended for."

Amidst the preparations for the British counterthrust, soldiers continued to claim steadfastness in the republican cause. William Young of Pennsylvania referred affectionately to "our American land" and begged Jehovah to afflict the unrighteous enemy with evil. Private Joseph Plumb Martin probably summarized best the attitudes of the soldiery prior to the start of the 1776 land offensive. He recalled that he had formed "pretty correct ideas for the contest between this country and the mother country. . . .I thought I was as warm a patriot as the best of them." Martin disliked "arbitrary government." His "correct ideas" did not go beyond this point, except that he and his comrades heartily approved of the signing of the Declaration of Independence. Now they knew what they were fighting for; and in their enthusiasm, they had no doubt that they could stand up to anything.

Comparisons between whig virtue and imperial tyranny, in fact, had started to become too neat, adding to unnecessary overconfidence among rebels in and out of the army. Committed patriots reveled in the words of the Declaration of Independence and its indictment of the King. After all, the Crown had kept among them "in Times of Peace, Standing Armies, without the consent of our Legislatures." The King had rendered "the Military independent of and superior to Civil Power" in America. Worse yet, he had "abdicated Government here" by "waging War against us." Then there was the reality that George III was "transporting large Armies of foreign Mercenaries to complete the Works of Death, Desolation, and

Tyranny," which he had started so many years before. For those citizen-soldiers who cheered so mightily at the first public readings of the Declaration, all that stood in the King's tyrannical path was their republican army, a military force that was not for hire—units consisting of short-term enlistees, militia, and volunteers who believed that they could stop anything because of the urgency and righteousness of their cause.

George Washington was less sanguine. Not only had reenlistments for the 1776 campaign come very slowly, but the Continental army lacked even a small hard core of well-trained and seasoned veterans. Although Washington had a force of nearly 28,000 in mid-August 1776, only 19,000 were fit for duty. Most of these troops were raw militia or half-trained Continentals.

Washington's tactical position was not much better. Since New York City was surrounded by water, the British fleet could land Howe's army anywhere it pleased. Thus the commander in chief had to deploy his soldiers knowing that he could be easily outflanked. As it was, Washington had little choice except to split his units between Manhattan and Long Island, divided by the East River. The strongest fortifications had to be on Brooklyn Heights. Washington understood that control of the Heights was essential to the defense of New York. The presence of enemy artillery there could reduce that port city to submission or to ashes (much as critical ordnance placements on Dorchester Heights had rendered the defense of Boston all but impossible). In making these tactical deployments, it would be difficult for Washington's reserves on Manhattan to back up the advanced forces. Moreover, General Howe now had an unparalleled opportunity to wreak havoc upon the divided American army, should the Royal navy under Admiral Richard seize control of the East River. That maneuver could effectively crush Washington's main units on Long Island between British naval and land forces, leaving the reserves to be taken later in mopping up operations. Hence the rebel disposition, mandated because of Congressional insistence that New York be defended (no matter what the tactical perils), was fraught with grave risks.

After a year of military delusion—during which it can be

argued that the British had been off balance—the myriad weaknesses of the patriot military establishment became all too apparent when William Howe finally got the summer offensive rolling. The British landed at Gravesend, Long Island, on August 22. Sweeping north, Howe launched a multipronged attack on the morning of the 27th. Although the patriots fought with intensity and held well in the center, a surprise flanking maneuver smashed the whole of the rebel line, driving it back to the Heights. The retreat quickly turned into a rout with the Hessians brutally bayoneting trapped American soldiers begging for quarter. The day's devastation revealed that rebel casualties had approached 1,500, as compared to fewer than 400 for the British.

Washington, with his back against the East River, drew more soldiers from New York City into the patriot entrenchments when he should have ordered a general evacuation to reunite his army. The American commander was not yet ready to concede New York. Even more curious, given the rebel army's untenable position, the Howes showed no military dash whatsoever. Pressure by land and water could have resulted in the surrender of thousands of Continental troops. Rather than storming the Brooklyn entrenchments, however, Howe dawdled and, in uninspired fashion, prepared to commence formal siege operations. Admiral Richard also failed to maneuver his naval vessels into the East River. Ultimately realizing that entrapment would be his army's fate, Washington called a council of war in which the decision was made to evacuate. With the assistance of John Glover's Marblehead (Massachusetts) mariners and under cover of a heavy evening fog, the Americans managed to extricate themselves late on the night of August 29.

Why the Howes failed to bag their prey—and threw away the best chance that Great Britain had during the war to do irreparable damage to rebel resisters—has been a source of much historical speculation. Writers have cited as probable explanations for Admiral Richard's dilatoriness, unfavorable winds, tides, and/or blindness in sensing the immediate advantage. As for William's lack of aggressiveness, some historians have claimed that his Bunker Hill experience dissuaded him from pursuing the Americans into their trenches. Others have suggested that Howe worried incessantly about manpower and feared the impact of heavy casualties if the general engagement became too spirited. The very presence of so many Hessians demonstrated that troops who became casualty statistics could not be easily replaced. Indeed, Howe did feel that maintaining a numerical advantage in forces at all times was essential to wearing the Americans out. In an important study of British planning and strategy, Ira D. Gruber (*The Howe Brothers and the American Revolution,* 1972) has emphasisized the whiggish predilections of the brothers. Acting as much as men of peace as of war, they may have "been following a strategy of careful advances, designed to create the impression of British invincibility, destroy the colonists' faith in the Continental army. . .and produce a genuine reconciliation."[16] Whatever the appropriate set of reasons, the Howes had let Washington escape. The American commander never again allowed his forces to get into such a tactically dangerous posture.

In the days and weeks that followed the Battle of Long Island, Washington kept retreating while William Howe, characteristically slow in pressing his advantages, only nipped at the heels of the rebels. Manhattan clearly offered little safety, as successive British landings forced Washington to withdraw progressively north toward Westchester County. As the struggling patriots marched and ran, they left behind some 6,000 comrades in Forts Washington and Lee, perched high on the palisades on opposite sides of the Hudson River. After inflicting an inconclusive beating on the main rebel units at White Plains on October 28, Howe doubled back, thus gaining control of the ground between Washington and the rebel forts. On November 16, a determined force of Hessians overwhelmed the defenders of Fort Washington on the New York side. The British sustained 452 casualties; however, 2,000 Americans fell into enemy hands, many of whom would later die in the squalor of British prison ships in New York harbor. Two days later, a large detachment under Charles, Lord Cornwallis, caught rebel forces under

General Nathanael Greene virtually off guard at Fort Lee. Greene got most of his men out in the nick of time, but he lost the bulk of his materiel. For the confident citizen-soldier, the patriot defense of New York had turned into what amounted to virtual Armageddon.

When Fort Lee fell, Washington was already in New Jersey. After White Plains, he had crossed the Hudson with 5,000 men, leaving another 8,000 in the lower Hudson Highlands region under Charles Lee. All the commander in chief could do then, however, was direct a harrowing retreat. Still moving slowly, Howe had decided to follow up on the Fort Lee debacle with a full-scale invasion of New Jersey. Washington's forces had already taken a tremendous pounding. The burden of the sick and wounded, as well as the problem of massive desertions, took a distressing manpower toll. So full of moral commitment just a few months before, the fleeing remnants of the Continental establishment were thoroughly dispirited. The sense of superiority in virtuous behavior simply wilted in the face of disciplined regulars. Personally frustrated when frightened New Jersey militiamen failed to turn out in adequate numbers, Washington led his battered columns through New Brunswick, Princeton, and across the Delaware River, managing to stay just ahead of Howe's pressing columns. What remained of the rebel army got across the Delaware and into Pennsylvania in early December.

Howe stopped the pursuit at the Delaware. He was unable to obtain boats for a crossing, since Washington's army had confiscated all vessels in the area. Concluding that enough had been accomplished for one campaign season, he ordered his triumphant army into winter quarters. Mopping up could wait until springtime. The rebellion, from Howe's perspective, was moribund. The republican army seemed to be all but shattered. The Continental Congress was fleeing from Philadelphia to Baltimore. Many in the harassed New Jersey populace seemed quite willing to renew their allegiance to Britain through loyalty oaths. Symbolic of British overconfidence was the decision of Colonel Johann Rall, who headed three regiments of 1,500 Hessians, not to waste time in digging in or preparing fortifications at his advanced outpost at Trenton on the Delaware River.

In one sense, Howe's assessment of the patriot situation was accurate; in another, it was incredibly wide of the mark. Washington would have agreed with him that the rebellion was teetering. On December 18, he wrote to his brother: "I think the game is pretty near up. . . .No man, I believe, ever had a greater choice of difficulties and less means to extricate himself from them." Yet Howe failed to consider Washington's persistent temperament, even against overwhelming odds. That Howe did not pursue the plan of 1776 to its logical end by attempting to wipe out Washington's army would soon be haunting the British commander. Washington instinctively understood that, so long as he had an army in the field, however small and ill-supported, he and other diehard rebels could claim that the cause was still alive. Washington also knew that a great many of those soldiers who were still with him would melt away on December 31 when their enlistments ran out. As never before, bold action was necessary, if he wanted to keep some semblance of an army together—and the republican cause alive. The target thus became the Hessian outposts of Trenton and Bordentown.

Before something dramatic could be accomplished, one fundamental problem had to be addressed. Washington's available manpower had reached low ebb. His own forces down to a mere handful, he anxiously awaited the arrival of Charles Lee's regiments. Lee, however, was moving lackadaisically through northern New Jersey, spending about as much time criticizing his commander in chief as moving toward the Delaware. It is very possible that Lee was not cooperating on purpose. His correspondence reveals Lee's expectation that, if Washington failed to mount some form of a counteroffensive, Congress would sack him and name the former British major to the highest post. But a British patrol intervened at Basking Ridge when it stumbled upon and captured Lee in a local tavern. General John Sullivan of New Hampshire took command and promptly linked up with Washington. Several hundred Pennsylvania militia also came forward, all of which gave the commander nearly 6,000 effectives—more than enough for a quick-hitting foray across the River.

The Americans moved out stealthily on Christmas night. Only Washington's main body of 2,400, one of three planned invading groups, got across the icy Delaware with the assistance of John Glover's mariners; but one body of soldiers was enough. The attack caught Johann Rall's Hessians, laden with drink from their Christmas celebration, completely off guard. With no trenches or fortifications, they could not defend themselves. About 400 got away, but nearly 1,000 were captured (with some 30 casualties). Then, after resting and disposing of the prisoners back in Pennsylvania, Washington crossed into New Jersey again on December 30. Near Trenton, he skirmished sharply on January 2 with Lord Cornwallis on the Assunpink Creek. The fighting broke off in the evening, with the Earl sure that he would "bag the fox" at daybreak. Washington, in response, left his campfires burning brightly and slipped away toward Princeton, where, on the next morning, he smashed a British brigade marching to join Cornwallis. Only exhaustion stopped the rebels from descending on New Brunswick and the lightly guarded British paychest there. Instead, Washington and his redeemed army pushed north toward the cover of the Watchung Mountains and Morristown, New Jersey, where the patriot force could spend a safe winter and attempt to regroup.

SUCCESS AND FAILURE

So close to having reached the enunciated goal, the British had failed. So close to collapse, the Americans had survived. Through its massive campaign effort, Great Britain had nearly surmounted the obstacles that blocked them from ending the rebellion. Failure to pursue Washington until he was beaten beyond revival had brought them up just short. Trenton and Princeton proved that a rebel army, however desperate it had become for manpower, was still in the field and capable of inflicting biting wounds. Moreover, there was every likelihood, that should sufficient manpower somehow be found, some sort of a force would be there for future campaigns. In that sense, Britain's campaign effort, predicated on the concentration of forces at New York, had failed, and for one fundamental reason: the unwillingness or inability of the British general officers to follow through to total victory when annihilation was possible.

Also of long-term significance was William Howe's decision to abandon his distant Jersey outposts and draw into a much narrower ring around New York, which effectively undercut hundreds of New Jersey neutrals and loyalists, great numbers of whom had identified themselves in public by having taken loyalty oaths to the King. Their military protection was gone, and they would find themselves subjected to the less than temperate justice of local patriots. As Paul H. Smith has carefully documented in *Loyalists and Redcoats* (1964), as the war progressed, the British field generals time and again undermined the loyalists or used them ineffectively by not holding the ground that the army had taken.[17] Britain, with so much potential support among the divided Americans, simply did not use this vast reservoir of manpower with intelligence. By not capitalizing effectively on people who were willing to bear arms, grow foodstuffs, or reinstitute civilian government, the British did little more than further weaken their effort by having to maintain a heavy dependence on human and logistical resources from home. Over the long haul the pattern helped to add up to failure.

As was so often the case, rather than learning from mistakes and correcting them, there were excuses. "Now as to the Hessians, they are the worst troops I ever saw," complained a British officer in excusing the Trenton setback. Rather than worrying too much about it, William Howe settled into his comfortable quarters in New York and reveled in the honor of the knighthood that the Crown bestowed on him for his Long Island victory. He started to plan the 1777 campaign and enjoyed the pleasures of his pert blonde consort, Mrs. Joshua Loring. (Her understanding husband did not seem to mind; he was enjoying the financial rewards of his post as commissary of prisoners.) Like the incredulous officer who faulted the Hessians, Howe simply did not accept the point that the objective of bringing the Americans back into the empire rested upon much more than just winning an occasional battle with massed forces. It depended on making effective use of those triumphs, of going for the jugular; and the British high command in America had not done that. As a result, the former parent state had little to show for its great effort, except for control of New York and its immediate environs and Newport, Rhode Island, which had been captured by Clinton in December 1776 for a naval and foraging base.

For Washington, the climax of the 1776 campaign in Trenton and Princeton may be described as a dazzling display of creative generalship. Outmaneuvered and outfought from August until December, and with the patriot army disintegrating around him, the American commander had come back with a tactical masterpiece that left the enemy stung and frustrated. In Europe, no less than Frederick the Great concluded that Washington had engineered one of the most astonishing campaign turnabouts of the century. Militarily, months of British planning and effort had come undone, "destroying," as Ira D. Gruber has summarized it, "the illusion of British invincibility, . . .and spoiling the Howes' hopes for an end to the war and a start toward a lasting reunion."[18] The British never again came so close to snuffing out the rebellion as they did in 1776; never again the Americans so close to losing.

Washington, however, had little time to celebrate his success. The campaign of 1776 had simply confirmed what the commander in chief feared. It had demonstrated that enthusiasm and brave talk of virtue were not enough to sustain the military effort, that the patriot army, resting so squarely on the militia tradition, had reached the limits of what a highly motivated but short-term, half-trained, insufficiently organized, partly disciplined, and poorly equipped force could accomplish against seasoned regulars. Indeed, Washington had long since concluded that fighting and winning a war for the sake of human liberty through republican forms and means was a fool's consistency. Virtue and moral commitment were simply not enough. Some form of a well-trained, standing American army had to be created and made to be consistent with republican forms, if the cause was to endure, or so reasoned the undaunted American commander in chief and his closest aides.

Popular morale and support for the cause, so seriously undermined during the New York campaign and consequent retreat across New Jersey, would also have to be revived. No doubt Washington would have agreed with the Pennsylvania soldier who proclaimed after the Trenton sortie that only divine intervention would save the cause. "If Salvation comes to our guilty Land, it will be through the tender mercy of God," the soldier lamented, "and not through the virtue of her people." Widespread ardor for the war did not burst forth again after Trenton and Princeton. It never again reached the lofty levels of enthusiasm that had been prevalent before the Battle of Long Island. Too many eager patriots had learned that enemy bayonets were profoundly indifferent to the fact that they thought their cause just, their motives sincere, and their sense of posterity pure. The real question in early 1777 was how Washington intended to endure, given that so many sunshine patriots were now more interested in staying home from the war than in rushing to arms. With that attitude as the new reality, the republican phase of war, characterized by the citizen-soldier in arms as the centerpiece, had come to an end.

NOTES

[1] Bernard Bailyn, *The Ideological Origins of the American Revolution* (Cambridge, Mass., 1967), p. 319.

[2] Charles Royster, *A Revolutionary People at War: The Continental Army and the American Character, 1775–1783* (Chapel Hill, N.C., 1980), p. 24. *See also* Royster, "'The Nature of Treason': Revolutionary Virtue and American Reactions to Benedict Arnold," *William and Mary Quarterly*, 3d Series, 36 (1979), pp. 163–93.

[3] *Ibid.*, p. 9.

[4] Robert W. Coakley and Stetson Conn, *The War of the American Revolution: Narrative, Chronology, and Bibliography* (Washington, D.C., 1975), p. 29.

[5] John Shy, *Toward Lexington: The Role of the British Army in the Coming of the American Revolution* (Princeton, N.J., 1965), pp. 375-424.

[6] John Todd White, "Standing Armies in Time of War: Republican Theory and Military Practice during the American Revolution," (Ph.D. dissertation, George Washington University, 1978), pp. 147-290.

[7] Jonathan G. Rossie, *The Politics of Command in the American Revolution* (Syracuse, N.Y., 1975), esp. pp. 135-53. *See also* Richard H. Kohn, "American Generals of the Revolution: Subordination and Restraint," in Don Higginbotham, ed., *Reconsiderations of the Revolutionary War: Selected Essays* (Westport, Conn., 1978), pp. 104-23.

[8] Marcus Cunliffe, *Soldiers and Civilians: The Martial Spirit in America, 1775-1865,* 2d ed. (New York, 1973), pp. 147-49. *See also* Cunliffe, *George Washington: Man and Monument* (Boston, 1958), pp. 70-113.

[9] Claude H. Van Tyne, *The War of Independence: American Phase* (Boston, 1929), p. 115.

[10] Don Higginbotham, "The American Militia: A Traditional Institution with Revolutionary Responsibilities," in Higginbotham, ed., *Reconsiderations,* p. 103.

[11] Cunliffe, *Soldiers and Civilians,* p. 148.

[12] Don Higginbotham, *The War of American Independence: Military Attitudes, Policies, and Practice, 1763-1789* (New York, 1971), p. 130.

[13] Piers Mackesy, *The War for America, 1775-1783* (Cambridge, Mass., 1965), pp. 46-57.

[14] Eric Robson, *The American Revolution in Its Political and Military Aspects, 1763-1783* (New York, 1955), pp. 93-174. *See also* Walter Millis, *Arms and Men: A Study in American Military History* (New York, 1956), pp. 22-33.

[15] Allen Bowman, *The Morale of the American Revolutionary Army* (Washington, D.C., 1943), pp. 45-56. *See also* Mark E. Lender, *The New Jersey Soldier,* New Jersey's Revolutionary Experience, no. 5 (Trenton, N.J., 1975), *passim.*

[16] Ira D. Gruber, *The Howe Brothers and the American Revolution* (Chapel Hill, N.C., 1972), p. 156.

[17] Paul H. Smith, *Loyalists and Redcoats: A Study in British Revolutionary Policy* (Chapel Hill, N.C., 1964), pp. 10-43, 168-74.

[18] Gruber, *The Howe Brothers,* p. 156.

THREE

Toward an American Standing Army, 1776–1777

THE NATURE OF THE
CONTINENTAL ARMY

Since the days of the Revolution, the myth has persisted that provincial Americans, like the great Cincinnatus of republican Rome, fully exercised their obligations of citizenship by voluntarily leaving the plow or bellows, shouldering muskets, and following Washington in defense of liberty and property. Afterward, having humbled the tyrannical British legion, they meekly returned to their civilian callings, expecting no more than thanks from what was a grateful new nation. Even as the war ended, these citizen-soldiers became idealized as the legendary "embattled farmer" or the enduring and proud "ragged Continental." To this day, the legend of the dedicated citizen-soldier epitomizes for most Americans the spirit of the Revolutionary generation. Perhaps, the strength and endurance of the image may explain why many historians, until recently, have not contradicted but have accepted and enshrined the legend.

The roots of the myth may be traced to several sources. These include the antistanding-army ideology of the eighteenth century, historical commentary written during the war itself and thereafter, and the loquacious musings of Fourth of July orators. Politicians through the generations, likewise, have borrowed selectively from the past in exhorting their followers to support some program, cause, or putative truth, often in the name of the dedicated and committed Revolutionary generation. Historians themselves have repeated ingrained tradition, seemingly more willing to endorse national legend than to subject it to scrutiny and analysis and accept the interpretive consequences, whatever they may turn out to be.

During the nineteenth century, for example, no historian had greater influence than George Bancroft. His *History of the United States from the Discovery of the American Continent* (10 vols., 1834–1874) was a massive treatise in praise of national destiny. Like many of the Revolutionary generation, Bancroft viewed the enshrinement of liberty in America as part of God's "grand design" for redeeming the earth. The citizen-soldier was essential to that design. Leaving "behind. . .their families and their all," they "came swift as a roe or a young hart over the mountains" to the fields of battle. Troops from all the states displayed a love of human rights that reached deeply into the freemen's well of voluntarism. "The alacrity with which these troops were raised," Bancroft concluded, "showed that the public mind heaved like the sea from New England to the Ohio and beyond the Blue Ridge."[1]

Several years later, in 1902, Charles K. Bolton published his influential monograph, *The Private Soldier under Washington.* Still considered a classic survey of the military world of the soldiery, Bolton's work insisted that the rank and file "were not a rabble recruited from the low ranks from which a city mob is drawn." Although some may have fought for reasons other than patriotic ardor, idealism infested the bulk of these freeholding freedom fighters. A suggestion by a French officer with Washington that American Continentals really amounted to paid mercenaries, the author stressed, was not worthy of a serious reply.[2] However, Bolton did not look very critically into the social composition of the Continental ranks before formulating his generalizations.

Bancroft and Bolton typified those early patriot writers who lent credence to the popular image before an establishment of professional historians came into being in the United States. That image, however, has not changed very much since an identifiable professional group appeared in the early twentieth century. In recent times, Howard H. Peckham in his well-received survey volume, *The War for Independence* (1958), concluded:

The American in arms was a citizen-soldier. He had volunteered because he had an idea of how his political life should be ordered. He introduced a new concept into war: patriotism. . . . The American's own honor was at stake. He was fighting to determine the destiny of his country and therefore of his children. Once he received some military training, he usually could defeat the professional soldier and the mercenary because he had higher motivation, more initiative, and greater hope. These embattled farmers and artisans fought as men possessed—possessed of a fervent and ennobling desire to be free men.[3]

Joining this prominent patriot strain in historiography has been Edmund S. Morgan, whose widely read study, *The Birth of the Republic, 1763-89* (rev. ed., 1977), claimed that it was "doubtful that the British could ever have won more than a stalemate'' because the Revolution was decidedly "a people's war." "It was this experience at Concord and at Bunker Hill," opined Morgan, that "would tell again whenever a British army attempted to sweep through the country."[4] More recently, Charles Royster (*A Revolutionary People at War,* 1980) has admitted that popular participation fell off dramatically in the wake of the New York campaign. However, the reason seemed to be that "Revolutionaries outside the army assumed that they could rely on popular defiance throughout a vast continent when their army was not near or even if there were no Continental army." This represents a curious rationale. Royster seems to be saying: Broad-scale participation was very important; yet even if it had all but collapsed by the end of 1776, it did not matter, since citizens would again become involved if they had to, since they understood that "the absence of an army would have conceded the collapse of public virtue."[5] By implication, their apparent willingness to be involved meant that they really were, even if the historical record demonstrates that innumerable patriots disdained direct service, once the glory days of war had been left behind.

In this context, it is important to recall that Thomas Paine, in his first *Crisis* paper, written in 1776 while the Continental army was in desperate flight across New Jersey, denounced "the summer soldier and the sunshine patriot" as the bane of the Revolutionary cause. "These are the times that try men's souls," Paine wrote urgently. "Tyranny, like hell, is not easily conquered; yet we have the consolation with us, that the harder the conflict, the more glorious the triumph." Paine employed biting language in urging his wavering brethren to remain virtuous and not to eschew the fundamental military obligations of citizenship. He reminded them that the success of the republican quest depended on citizens who were willing to make personal sacrifices over and over again. Near the end of 1776, Paine knew that the *rage militaire* had passed—or been beaten out of the confident patriots by the huge campaign effort of the British. The purpose of his biting prose was to stem the tide. Yet even Paine's immortal words made little difference in the days and months ahead. The last thing that the vast bulk of propertied, middle-class citizens wanted to do, especially after all the reverberations of the 1776 campaign had been felt, was to become a soldier in Continental military arms.

Indeed, the overwhelming problem facing George Washington, even as early as the late fall of 1775, was to assure that enough soldiers would be in the field so that the Continental establishment would have the appearance of more than a shadowy likeness of an army. Enthusiasm for direct and sustained participation had been fading even at the height of the *rage militaire,* possibly because of Washington's emphasis on camp discipline, possibly because of boredom. This lack of committed involvement was one of the essential reasons why, in the end, the British came so close to winning the war (when they should not have) and why the Americans came so close to losing (when the geographic size, diffuseness of population, and lack of a strategic vital center made the conquest of the 13 provinces a virtually impossible military task for armies designed to wage formalized, linear war). The dimensions of that paradox can be comprehended only by looking at the related problems of manpower and popular commitment that Congress, Washington, and his generals faced and the ways in which they attempted to address these critical issues.

A NEW MODEL REBEL ARMY

The challenges that confronted Washington at the Cambridge camp during the summer and fall of 1775 were fundamentally interrelated. Discipline, hygiene, training, and dedicated rather than wrangling officers were all necessary qualities of a well-regulated and respectable military machine. As has been pointed out, Washington strove to bring about orderly conditions from the moment he arrived in Cambridge. That would not be possible, however, unless Americans could be convinced that it was their duty to serve in the army's ranks for more than short periods of time, if at all. In Washington's mind, short-term citizen-soldiers undercut the ability of any army to perform capably in the field. Indeed, he believed that erratic service as a function of short-term enlistments was what was fundamentally wrong with militia. Worse yet, an army unsure of its size, strength, or fighting capability at any given time was not the kind of establishment around which effective long-term campaigns could be planned or executed.

Washington was disturbed that citizen-soldiers came and went from Cambridge, virtually as they pleased. Moreover, he was angered that so few citizens wanted to reenlist for the 1776 campaign season. Although recruiting went on throughout the colonies and Washington (in October 1775) commenced an extensive effort to secure one-year enlistees from among those in camp, not many came forward. By early December, fewer than 4,000 of the early enthusiasts had signed up for the next year, and entire militia units had marched home. If the British had possessed a clear sense of how unstable Continental army manpower really was, they would have been wise to make every effort to break out of Boston.

Ennobling appeals to the patriot populace, moreover, did not seem to have much impact. In and out of camp, recruiters reminded potential enlistees of "the bountiful rewards of the industry of our worthy forefathers" and "the future grandeur of the western world." They asked "whether we will see our wives and children, with everything that is dear to us, subjected to the merciless rage of uncontrolled despotism." They reminded the populace that "we are engaged. . .in the cause of virtue, of liberty, of *God*." It would take only "a few more noble exertions, . . . a few more spirited struggles, and we secure our liberties; a few more successful battles, and we are a free and happy people." With the great deed accomplished, "happy" would be "the man who can boast he was one of those heroes that put the finishing stroke to this arduous work," hence bequeathing this "estimable patrimony to his grateful children."

Other recuritment appeals made during the fall of 1775 stressed that "never was a cause more important or glorious than that which you are engaged in." The fate of mankind, claimed these writers, depended on the outcome: "For if tyranny should prevail in this great Country, we may expect liberty will expire through the world." The message was simple: "Persevere, ye guardians of liberty." However, few guardians signed up, even in the midst of the *rage militaire.*

Why the citizen-soldiers of 1775 preferred to go home rather than to reenlist related to a host of individual explanations. Every potential enlistee, no doubt, had sound reasons in his own mind. For some, it may have been relatively low pay, compared to what they could be earning in the civilian marketplace. For others, it may have been unattended responsibilities at home or the stringencies of camp life. Many of these early soldiers were middle-class property holders. Many had crops that needed harvesting. They faced the prospect of personal financial disaster if farming operations were not maintained, if stock was not cared for properly or fields left unploughed and unplanted in the spring. They could be seasonal soldiers, and some willingly performed irregular militia service after 1775. That way, the "glorious cause," as many called it, would not interfere too directly with the accepted seasonal rhythms of eighteenth-century life, yet some contribution could be made to the martial effort.

David Ramsay, the well-known South Carolinian and contemporary historian of the era, offered a variety of explanations in his *History of the American Revolution* (2 vols., 1793). For some, "they were . . . soon tired of military life.—Novelty and the first impulse of passion had led them to camp; but the approaching cold season, together with the fatigues and dangers incident to war, induced a general wish to relinquish the service." These and others who had not known the travail of army life before were "but feebly impressed with the military ideas of union, subordination, and discipline." Washington's emphasis on discipline and regimentation, argued Ramsay, drove many away. Ramsay stated it this way: "Even in European states, where long habits have established submission to superiors as a primary duty of the common people, the difficulty of governing recruits. . .is great; but to exercise discipline over freemen, accustomed to act only from the impulse of their own minds, required not only a knowledge of human nature, but an accommodating spirit, and a degree of patience which is rarely found among officers of regular armies."[6]

Washington's frustration in trying to reenlist patriot citizens became even more intense after he learned about the initial results of the abortive campaign against Canada. During the summer of 1775, the Continental Congress sanctioned a two-pronged invasion of Canada. The expedition was clearly a blatent violation of the "Declaration" against offensive warfare—in hopes of reconciliation. Yet Congress wanted Quebec to throw in its lot with the patriots (a fact that seemed strange to many of its French-speaking citizens, who remembered the strong anti-Catholic phobias of their more southerly brethren). Securing Canada as the fourteenth colony would also have enlarged the American phalanx against Great Britain, making it more difficult for his majesty's armies to invade the colonies through the Hudson River-Lake Champlain corridor. For some Congressional delegates, too, taking Canada would have resulted in a broader base from which to launch the dawning dream of a new world phoenix rising up out of the ashes of the old.

The determined patriot invaders marched forth in the late summer of 1775. One group moved over the border from New York under the capable guidance of General Richard Montgomery, while Colonel Benedict Arnold launched his epic march to Quebec through the wilderness of Maine. In December, with Montreal in hand but with short-term enlistments about to expire on December 31, the two commanders decided that an all-out attack on the walled town of Quebec was necessary before too many troops left for home. Late on the evening of December 30, the rebels advanced under the cover of a driving snowstorm. Forthwith, everything went wrong. Montgomery was shot dead; Arnold was seriously wounded in the leg; and dozens of other men became casualties or prisoners, including the roughhewn but talented leader of Virginia riflemen, Daniel Morgan. Even though Arnold persisted in a hopeless siege of Quebec, the plan for taking Canada never really recovered from this staggering blow. Patriot forces, decimated by a smallpox epidemic, were driven out of Canada once and for all by a large assemblage of British regulars in the late spring of 1776.

All committed rebels mourned Montgomery and praised Arnold for their heroic deeds. Arnold became the American Hannibal. Whigs proclaimed Montgomery, a former British regular officer who had settled in New York and married into the wealthy Livingston family, to be a martyr of classic proportions. He became yet another of the rebellion's sainted farmer-soldiers. The slain general was "An American Patriot! . . . A General from the Plough! Such was Cincinnatus, in the best days of Roman virtue." Like the oft-mentioned Roman hero, Montgomery had "bid farewell to his peaceful retirement" and taken up the sword in the cause of liberty. Here again was patriot imagery at its best, dwelling on glory rather than defeat—and ignoring Montgomery's background as a regular army officer.

George Washington and members of Congress, although deeply chagrined about Montgomery's death (he was one of the most promising generals in the Continental establishment), clearly understood one of the reasons the Quebec assault had turned into a fiasco. Facing expiring enlistments, Montgomery and Arnold had rushed into battle and may not have acted at the most propitious time. As Washington stated after recalling Montgomery's death, "the evils arising from short, or even any limited enlistments of the troops, are greater, and more extensively hurtful than any person. . .can form any idea of." "It takes you two or three months to bring new men in any tolerable degree acquainted with their duty," the commander explained. It took even more time to establish "such a subordinate way of thinking as is necessary for a soldier; before this is accomplished, the time approaches for their dismissal, and you are beginning to make interest for the continuance for another limited period." To woo the perpetual short-term enlistee, then, Washington argued, "you are obliged to relax your discipline," all of which made it impossible to maintain a well-trained, effective fighting establishment. The Americans could not have it both ways; winning the war against British regulars required discipline and, in Washington's mind, a core of malleable, long-term enlistees. Yet discipline and long-term enlistments did not suit the style of many patriots, despite brave words and easy talk about the need for moral commitment to the cause.

Washington had to find a way out without undercutting the war effort itself. The impact of the Quebec campaign, along with the failure to gain many enlistees for the 1776 campaign, convinced him, carrying forward on his thoughts of 1775, that Congress must agree to a full "new modeling" of the Continental army. Trying to instill discipline and subordination in free spirits was not enough. Congress would have to approve policies supporting a regular military establishment—the nucleus of a standing army that would serve for the duration of the war, would be well paid, and would not buckle under to either harsh camp life or concentrated enemy offensives. Furthermore, officers needed to have reason for pride in command as well as incentives for staying in the service. The latter problem became more pressing in 1777 and 1778; the former was paramount even before the full brunt of the British offensive of 1776 had been felt.

In the minds of a few republican ideologues more interested in consistency than in matching the impending British martial challenge, Washington's thinking represented a frontal assault on antistanding-army ideology and the concept of a virtuous citizenry fully capable of overcoming any martial threat. Yet Washington, the supreme realist, firmly grasped the long-term challenge that British men-in-arms posed. He needed a cadre of soldiers that could be counted on day in and day out, that could be deployed when they were needed, not when they felt like fighting.

Reports from Quebec had also mortified Congressional delegates, including many who would normally have preferred relying on militia. In 1776, bespectacled James Wilson typified the latter. As John Todd White has pointed out, Wilson saw the nation as having "a choice between two evils." Besides being expensive, an army of short-term soldiers provided no continuity or stability, and service (especially with rigorous camp discipline) would never be attractive enough to assure sufficient manpower. That had already been demonstrated in the midst of the *rage militaire*.[7] Yet an American standing army could threaten the very liberties that the rebel leadership hoped to ensure. As a worried Samuel Adams explained, in "a Standing Army, . . . Soldiers are apt to consider themselves as a Body distinct from the rest of the Citizens. They have their Arms always in their hands. Their Rules and their Discipline is severe. They soon become attached to their officers and disposed to yield implicit obedience to their Commands." "Such a Power," concluded Adams, "should be watched with a jealous Eye."

Adams, Wilson, and others worried openly about what new modeling the Continental army might lead to. They recalled Oliver Cromwell's active, highly efficient, thoroughly disciplined Puritan fighting force which had, in time, become an agent of oppression in maintaining Cromwell and his minions in power. Cromwell's war machine had helped to inspire James Harrington's *Oceana* and a handful of other opposition whig tracts speaking out against the dangers of standing armies. The Congressmen thus faced an essential dilemma. With the citizen-soldier more interested in going home (or staying there) than in coming out for war, the choice became that of attempting to create a standing military force (and insuring Washington stable manpower) capable of contending with Britain's war machine or deciding to trust everything to evanescent numbers of citizen-soldiers who did not want to stay in the field for a long-term war. Ultimately pushing fears of societal corruption or the potential for an internal military coup aside, Congress finally adopted Washington's reasoning.

The commander in chief and his closest generals kept writing to and putting pressure on Congress. Yet it was the weight of events in the first nine months of 1776 as much as these appeals that influenced the delegates to lean toward the approval of a standing regular force. John Todd White points out at least four factors that moved Congress toward Washington's position: 1) news that the King was hiring thousands of Hessian mercenaries; 2) the arrival of a sizable royal force in Canada which had pushed the Americans out in June 1776; 3) the massive British concentration of forces on Staten Island; and 4) the overall failure of short-term enlistment appeals, in combination with the relatively mild military code of 1775, to attract even close to what was considered sufficient manpower for the Continental army.[8] The delegates finally faced reality during the late summer and fall of 1776, when Great Britain's New York land offensive was beginning to take its heavy toll.

Besides putting greater teeth into the Articles of War (Congress raised the legal limit on lashes from 39 to 100 and increased the numbers of crimes for which the death penalty could be exacted), the delegates voted the commander virtually the contours of the "respectable army" that he wanted. There were to be 88 battalions of 738 officers and men each, to serve for a minimum of three years or for the duration, even if more than three years. The delegates also assigned state troop quotas according to population distribution. Thus more populous Massachusetts was to enlist 15 battalions, while Delaware and Georgia were to supply one each. In December 1776, Congress empowered Washington to recruit 16 more battalions, without state affiliations, and a number of cavalry, artillery, and support units. The projected army numbered 75,000 on paper, which contrasted sharply with Washington's 6,000 effectives on the eve of the Trenton counterthrust.

Hindsight, of course, has demonstrated the naivete of patriot hopes for (or the ability to support logistically) an army of this size. It should be recalled, however, that Congress framed the essentials of the legislation in September, before the full effects of the 1776 campaign had been felt. Furthermore, the delegates had rough estimates of the American population available to them. Accepting the base of nearly 2,000,000 whites, allowing for as many as 500,000 loyalists, and conservatively figuring that one in every four or five of the remainder were adult males between the ages of 16 and 50, there may have been as many as 350,000 potential soldiers in the population. (During the 1760s

Benjamin Franklin had estimated the number of white males in the same age group to be 250,000 on a smaller population base.) Even if the figure of 350,000 is slightly high, an army of 75,000 would have called upon no more than one fourth to one fifth of the eligible males at any one time. This would have left the remainder available for civilian occupations, including the production of food, and the manufacture and procurement of war materiel and other related goods.[9]

Yet even Congress recognized that an army of 75,000, or even one half that size, was unlikely, unless there were sufficient financial inducements. Specifically, the inclusion of bounty provisions in the recruiting laws was an admission that appeals to virtue had not spurred enough enlistments. That had already been proved by the end of 1775, at the height of the *rage militaire*. Even though potential enlistees listened to patriotic appeals "with patience," as Washington phrased it after the 1776 campaign, the numbers who actually signed up were "no more than a drop in the Ocean." The commanding general saw only one way to solve the shortfall problem: "The allowance of a large and extraordinary bounty." Unpalatable as it was to republican sensibilities, Congress conceded Washington's argument that "such People, as compose the bulk of an Army," would not be "influenced by any other principles than those of Interest." The delegates thus voted each potential recruit a bounty payment of $20 (that sum climbed steadily during the war) upon enlistment, a yearly clothing issue, and a hundred acres of land for those who served for the duration. After much debate, the standard minimum term of service was set at three years, although individuals would be encouraged to sign up for longer periods. Washington continued to press for full duration commitments, but he readily conceded that three years was far more desirable than the shorter terms with which he had been contending.

It might be argued that the British offensive of 1776 frightened Congress into accepting the concept of a standing army for hire as opposed to a republican force. The reality of military conditions certainly was an important factor, as was the

necessity of a response to the astonishing collapse of citizen enthusiasm for direct participation. Likewise, the crushing blows
that Washington's forces sustained in the fall of 1776 established
the point that a disciplined army carried more sustained punch-
ing power than one depending on public virtue and zealous commitment. The commander now had the authority to build a
military establishment that could approach the Old World
model, to seek out and hire those who could be trained as a
steady core of regulars on behalf of the cause of republicanism.
Indeed, Washington was doing more than building on practices
that had become common during the French and Indian War.
He was seeking to Europeanize the Continental military
establishment, ironically for the purpose of ensuring the liberties
of all citizens. The questions that were uppermost in early 1777
were: Could Washington find enough manpower and, if he did,
would he be creating a military monster in the Cromwellian
mold that would come back to haunt the very cause and citizenry
for which it was being hired to defend?

WILLIAM HOWE'S CAMPAIGN OF 1777

John Taylor was the kind of a man that the patriot cause needed
in its darkest hours. He was solid—a good whig, a respected
faculty member of Queen's College (now Rutgers) in New
Brunswick, New Jersey, and a man with convictions about
the military obligations of citizens in a republic. He willingly
strapped on his sword as a militia colonel and participated in the
attempted patriot military revival in New Jersey during 1777.
Yet he was not a happy man. In April, while on duty near
Princeton, he watched the training of some of the army's new
regulars. What he saw appalled him. The "yeomanry," Taylor
wrote despondently to a friend, the country's "original
safeguard," were staying home; Continental regiments were being filled with people he did not trust. They were "mostly
foreigners," he claimed. They were "really mercenaries" with
"no attachment to the country except what accrues from the

emoluments of service." The rebellion and, therefore, the republican cause were in trouble. "Hope for the best," he concluded, "but at the same time fear the worst."

What Taylor had seen at Princeton was part of the process of building and training the new American army. Primarily at Morristown, but at other locations as well, rebel officers were hastily attempting to bring together a force capable of withstanding another major British offensive, one that the British ministry hoped would complete the goals of 1776 and end the civil war once and for all. Washington had few reasons to be optimistic. During the early winter of 1777, soldiers in camp had dwindled to below 3,000. In May his following was back up to 10,000, with 7,363 present and fit for duty. His total manpower, concentrated mostly in the Watchung Mountains northwest of William Howe's major outposts at Perth Amboy and New Brunswick, did not represent much more than one-third of the effective troop strength available to Howe.

Although Washington lacked numbers, he had the clear advantage of the hilly and mountainous terrain; moreover, there was no disagreement over what his army should do in the campaign season. Its objective was to stay alive as a fighting force in the field while strengthening itself, hurting the enemy as much as possible in the meantime. As Russell F. Weigley has pointed out, Washington understood that he must maintain "the strategic defensive," parrying and thrusting when necessary but avoiding full-scale engagements that might threaten the army's continued existence. The New York campaign had taught the American commander that large battles with a "tactically superior enemy" were ill advised, especially when his troops were not so numerous or well-trained in open-field maneuvers and close-order movements.[10] However reluctantly, Washington wittingly had come to accept the part of Fabius Cunctator, the Roman Delayer who wore out the Carthaginian enemy by simply maintaining a defensive presence in the field. During the spring of 1777, Washington allowed small-scale raiding parties to peck away at the British in the New Brunswick-Perth Amboy vicinity. Besides pestering the enemy and maintaining the high ground, the commander simply had to wait for the British to make the major moves.

Indeed, the burden of proof during the 1777 campaign effort was on the British, especially if they wanted to hold down further additions to the national debt or avoid the prospect of an enlarged war, should the rebels secure fighting allies. Success depended on coordinated operations, specifically between Howe's main force in New York and His Majesty's forces in Canada, now under the command of General John Burgoyne. The logical objective would have been securing control of the Hudson Highlands corridor and cutting New England off from the remaining states. But William Howe, vacillating endlessly about what course to follow, made up his mind that Philadelphia had to be taken; and in the process he hoped to destroy Washington's forces through a decisive engagement.

Why William Howe chose Philadelphia as his prime target when he knew that Burgoyne would be pushing south out of Canada has remained a perplexing question for historians. Possibly Howe could not imagine that Burgoyne would face such strong irregular resistance, or Howe may have viewed the well-connected, dandyish Burgoyne as a potential rival for New World military glory, should the latter be too successful. On the positive side, Howe clearly wanted another crack at the main Continental army after the telling embarrassments of Trenton and Princeton. He, too, had learned from previous errors that a nearly shattered army was not *ipso facto* moribund. Even if Howe were not successful in wiping out Washington, he would still have Philadelphia, a base from which to subdue the surrounding countryside. Also, seizing the rebel capital might signal the beginning of an overall patriot collapse—much as taking a European capital would all but resolve an Old World conflict. In the end, Howe may have considered all or only some of these possibilities. What is clear is that he did not do what Germain and the ministry assumed. He did not work in synchronized fashion with "Gentleman" Johnny Burgoyne.

In May 1777, Washington moved the bulk of his forces south from Morristown to Middlebrook, holding to the high ground a few miles northwest of New Brunswick. Try as Howe might, he could not lure the Continentals out of their mountain-side stronghold and into a general engagement. Memories of Bunker Hill no doubt dissuaded the British commander from attempting an assault on the Middlebrook site. Washington's tactical positioning was masterful. Not only did Howe not dare attack him, but with the Continental army intact and with militia units working actively in support, Sir William perceived that there would be many risks in marching overland to Philadelphia. The rebels could nip at his flanks or, worse yet, beat him to the Delaware and cause havoc in any attempted crossing. Also, the patriots might choose to slip behind the British forces and disrupt communications and supply lines back to New York. Eighteenth-century generals rarely took such risks, and Howe was not a very imaginative tactician. Because of the positioning of Washington's army, the British commander concluded that the only safe way to get to Pennsylvania was to move his army by sea. So, frustrated and delayed by his own indecision and attempts to lure the rebels into a major battle, Howe evacuated New Jersey in late June and set sail on July 23 with 15,000 redcoats, leaving a reserve force of 7,300 in New York under Henry Clinton.

All of this surprised Lord George Germain, back in London. When he received Howe's letter describing the Philadelphia plan, he easily discerned that the North American commander was no longer concerned about having units ascend the Hudson to support Burgoyne. Reluctantly, the American Secretary approved the plan. Yet, he responded by urging Howe to take Philadelphia quickly enough to send substantial help to Burgoyne. This was futile advice. Now committed fully to his own plan, Howe debarked his men on August 25 at Head of Elk at the top of Chesapeake Bay, some 50 miles southwest of Philadelphia. Adverse winds and difficult channels had kept this army at sea for a critical month in the middle of the campaign season. Even if he had felt some desire to aid Burgoyne, crucial time had been lost, and Burgoyne's army was too far away.

In the meantime, Washington, who at first could not believe that Howe was going south rather than north, arrived in Philadelphia with 11,000 soldiers. Obligated and pressured by Congress to defend the patriot seat of government, the American commander diverged from his Fabian posture and got ready for a general engagement. Howe also prepared; and the two armies clashed on September 11, when Washington moved to block the British approach to the city at Chadd's Ford on Brandywine Creek. Howe had one wing of his army demonstrate across the ford, keeping the center of the Continental line occupied, while a second wing swung wide, as on Long Island the year before. Those units smashed through the American right under luckless General John Sullivan and carried the day. The Continentals sustained an estimated 900 casualties, compared to Howe's 550.

Outgeneraled again, Washington was still game. Some of his units had held together and fought well at Brandywine, a sign that intensive training and vigorous discipline were making his army more competitive. Having temporarily stripped off the mask of Fabius, Washington also wanted to continue the fight. A torrential rainstorm that soaked the Continentals' powder destroyed one attempt. Before the rebel counterattack could come, however, Sir Charles Grey, one of Howe's subordinates, executed a surprise night raid on Anthony Wayne's division on September 20. The redcoats used their bayonets well, leaving behind nearly 300 victims in what has become known as the Paoli Massacre. Within another few days, Howe had got his opponent out of position northwest of Philadelphia, which caused Congress to flee to York, Pennsylvania. The British marched triumphantly into the city on September 26.

Not backing off, Washington soon dashed any British hopes that the loss of the rebel capital would bring peace overtures. Early on October 4, he struck back at Germantown, a thriving community north of Philadelphia where Howe had stationed many of his troops. Washington's plan, as it turned out, proved to be too complicated. The rebels were to attack in four columns, converging from several directions, but a dense morning fog confused them and, at one point, they started shooting down one another. Although caught by surprise, the British rallied and drove off the Continental forces. Howe's dead and wounded amounted to 520; Washington lost 650 men. To make matters worse, the enemy captured over 400 rebel troops.

The American commander was terribly disappointed by the results of Germantown; Howe was elated. In retrospect, the moods should have been reversed. From a strategic point of view, Howe had frittered away a most critical campaign season in which he had nothing concrete to show for his efforts, except for losses to his army and numbers of elated loyalists in eastern Pennsylvania. In taking Philadelphia, the British had captured an empty shell. Its fall had not deterred rebel resistance. Indeed, the Continentals fought on, raiding Howe's communications outside the city, and grimly holding on to Forts Mercer and Mifflin, which blocked the Delaware River below the town. In fact, even after Germantown, Washingon hoped that clinging to these forts would prevent the Royal navy from freighting supplies to Howe, letting his redcoats starve in the prize. The British finally secured the river and thus assured their safety in Philadelphia, but only in mid-November after weeks of fierce combat.

The costs of Howe's delays and Washington's willingness to fight were incalculable for the British cause. Howe had conducted his campaign at the expense of Burgoyne's northern army, thus making possible a series of formal diplomatic gestures with France that rendered it all but impossible for Great Britain to win the war. Although Howe had enjoyed much success in particular battles during 1777, he still lacked strategic imagination. Philadelphia did little more than provide his army with comfortable winter quarters. That was a staggering price to pay for the loss of Burgoyne's army and France's formal intervention on behalf of the Americans.

THE SARATOGA CAMPAIGN

Far to the north in September 1777, Burgoyne's struggling units faced unremitting patriot harassment. Growing hordes of New

England militia had backed up sparse numbers of regular Continentals under Horatio Gates, who had just taken over command of the army's Northern Department from Philip Schuyler. The rebels smelled blood, and they had almost entrapped Burgoyne's slow-moving force of 9,500. Gentleman Johnny still held out hope that he could punch through to Albany before winter. But he desperately needed help from the south. The relief expedition that did finally materialize moved north from New York City under Henry Clinton, but it was too small, came out too late, and never got near Burgoyne's beleaguered force.

Actually, the Burgoyne debacle was an ironic culmination to the Canadian campaign of 1775-1776. The Montgomery/Arnold assault on Quebec resulted in a ministerial decision to rush 10,000 regulars to Canada. During the spring of 1776, the rebels countered by sending hundreds of soldiers northward. They were no match for the British. By mid-June, while under the overall command of John Sullivan, they had been driven from Canada as smallpox ravaged these luckless but courageous souls. As summer turned to fall, it looked as if nothing could deter the redcoats, Canadians, and Indians under Guy Carleton, who planned to sweep as far south as Albany before brutal winter weather set in.

Carleton decided to float his army down Lake Champlain, his major military target being Fort Ticonderoga. However, he wasted a good portion of the summer putting together his fleet, which included dozens of small crafts and three large vessels that were disassembled at Montreal, carried overland, and reassembled at St. John's. Meantime, indomitable Benedict Arnold hastily constructed a small patriot flotilla to defend Lake Champlain. The two fleets clashed on October 11 at Valcour Island. Arnold's outnumbered and outgunned gondolas fought daringly before slipping away under cover of darkness and fog. The determination of Arnold's resistance and the lateness of the season convinced Carleton that pressing the advantage would be unwise. He retreated to Canada to wait out the winter season.

Direct lobbying in England during that same winter (1776-1777) netted Burgoyne overall command of the Canadian army.

His forces left St. John's on June 15, 1777; soon he had taken Fort Ticonderoga, beaten a patriot rearguard at Hubbardston, Vermont, and swept on to Skenesborough, where he rested for three weeks. To Burgoyne's right in the Mohawk Valley, a flanking column under Colonel Barry St. Leger was also doing well. With 1,700 regulars, Indians, and loyalists, the British colonel had Fort Schuyler under siege by early August, where 750 rebels desperately attempted to hold out. The American situation looked perilous; and Washington, positioning himself to defend Pennsylvania, could not help, except for a few reinforcements sent northward.

Suddenly, the scales of war shifted. As the main British southward advance resumed, Schuyler had his soldiers fell trees across roads and block fords with boulders. Burgoyne's rate of movement slowed down to a crawl. The royal column had some 2,000 women and children with it, plus an excessively large baggage and artillery train. Burgoyne's personal "necessities," which included his silver dining service, fresh uniforms for all occasions, and many cases of his favorite champagne, filled 30 wagons. After Horatio Gates replaced Schuyler, many more New England militiamen, who seemed to be put off by Schuyler's aristocratic bearing, flocked to the scene. Unwittingly, Burgoyne further aided the patriot rally when, out of fear that he would lose his Indian allies, he did not punish those who participated in the murder and mutilation of Jane McCrea, the fiancée of one of his loyalist officers. Word spread quickly among the potential rebel militia that Burgoyne actually condoned and encouraged such atrocities, all of which further swelled Gates's ranks.

The British advance thus began to collapse in mid-August. On the 16th, New Hampshire militia under General John Stark crushed two Hessian columns sent to capture rebel stores at Bennington. The action cost Burgoyne 900 men. St. Leger also ran into serious trouble. Although his Indian allies had stopped a militia attempt to relieve Fort Schuyler at the bloody battle of Oriskany on August 6, American General Nicholas Herkimer and half of his men lay dead or wounded to prove the point.

Then Benedict Arnold, heading another relief column, shook the Indians when he sent a half-witted loyalist into St. Leger's camp, spreading stories about awesome numbers of rebel soldiers sweeping in their direction. The Indians panicked and fled, leaving St. Leger only with regulars and loyalists. Rather than confronting Arnold, he raised the siege on August 22 and withdrew to Canada. Burgoyne was now alone.

The first of the two-part Battle of Saratoga occurred on September 19. Burgoyne found his southward march blocked by rebel entrenchments at Bemis Heights, six miles north of Stillwater, New York. He tried to push through, but the thrust faltered short of the entrenchments. Instead, Benedict Arnold and Daniel Morgan met him at Freeman's Farm, well in front of the patriot line, and mounted a savage attack. The British sustained 556 casualties, compared to 280 for the Americans. Licking his wounds, Burgoyne pulled back and regrouped for another challenge.

In the interim, the most dramatic action occurred between Arnold and Gates. Temperamental Arnold exploded in rage when he learned that Gates, in official reports, had neglected his subordinate's prominent role in the Freeman's Farm engagement. Gates, who apparently wanted the glory for himself (although he had not been near the battle), relieved Arnold of command for insubordination. When Burgoyne finally came forward again on October 7, the rebel forces sallied forth once more. When the current battle had still not taken a decisive turn, Benedict Arnold mounted his horse and rushed to the front line, even though specifically ordered by Gates to stay away. He rallied the patriots and led them toward the redcoat redoubts. When the day had ended, it was clear that Arnold's charge had carried positions that made Burgoyne's overall position all but helpless. This time Gates reluctantly gave Arnold, who had been seriously wounded in the leg for a second time, proper public credit.

Burgoyne, who had lost over 600 in casualties on October 7 compared to 130 Americans, retreated seven miles north from Bemis Heights to Saratoga. His depleted command found itself surrounded by ever-growing numbers of New England rebels. Thoroughly dejected, Burgoyne asked for a parley with Gates and formally surrendered on October 17, 1777. A British officer noted poignantly in describing that scene that "we marched out, according to treaty, with drums beating and the honors of war, but the drums seemed to have lost their former inspiring sounds, . . . then it seemed by its last feeble effort, as if almost ashamed to be heard on such an occasion."

Unknown to this officer, Saratoga turned out to be a very solemn drum beat for Great Britain in its martial attempt to reconquer America. The lack of coordinated planning and field action by Germain, Howe, Burgoyne, and Clinton, among many others, had turned the campaign of 1777 into a British shambles. If there was one hope left for them, it was that the Americans still had to prove whether some in their number could endure militarily in the cause. At the end of 1777, whether that would happen remained to be decided.

THE AMERICAN SEARCH FOR MANPOWER

Two important characteristics of the Saratoga battle related directly to the Continental manpower problem. First, militia had turned out in substantial numbers. They clearly played a vital role in sealing Burgoyne's fate, although the Continentals carried the brunt of the fighting on September 19 and October 7. Militiamen were always critical as harassing auxiliaries, if they chose to come out. In 1777, for example, Washington had not been so lucky as Gates. The Pennsylvania militia gave the Virginian only minimal support against Howe. Indeed, strong loyalist feelings among southeastern Pennsylvanians, as well as the strongly held doctrine of pacifism among Quakers, were primary reasons for such scanty support, making Washington's situation that much more perilous when compared to Gates's. The problem, of course, was the inconsistency of militia support, which did vary significantly by region.

Second, Gates worked out a controversial arrangement with his British adversary, whereby Burgoyne's troops would be marched to Boston and shipped back to England, all in return for unconditional surrender. Once home, it was agreed that they were to sit out the remainder of the war. It did not take much intelligence to figure out that their return to England would free other soldiers assigned to duty in Britain for service in America. Congress, on Washington's advice, rejected Gates's terms of capitulation. Ultimately, the "convention army," as it came to be known, marched from Boston to the interior of Virginia. Along the way, recruiters convinced many British and Hessian veterans to enlist in Continental ranks.

Indeed, the reality of the matter was that Washington, Gates, and others fought the campaign of 1777 with minimal popular support, even with militia in the field. If it had not been for bounties and promises of regular pay, decent food, new clothing, and free land after the war, Washington may not have had an army with which to challenge Howe and his minions. Throughout the war, the American commander struggled to build up and maintain a central core of long-term regulars, and the task of doing so was continuous and enervating.

Recruiting campaigns represented the basic means of seeking out long-term manpower. Although Washington and Congress issued instructions on who might serve (they preferred healthy freemen between the ages of 17 and 50), they could not afford to be fussy. The actual process of recruiting was dispersed between the army and the 13 states. The army employed the traditional European practice of "beating up" for enlistees. A sergeant or a junior officer whose commission depended on raising his own unit would move through an area with a detachment of drummers to attract a crowd. Often he would set up a table at a tavern, where he regaled potential recruits with liquor and the glories of army life. It was a laborious procedure, suited to armies that could spare soldiers and take unlimited time to find manpower. The Continental army could afford neither.

Civilian recruiting efforts tended to be even more complex. State officials conducted their own appeals, and a number appointed their own state recruiting officers. Many states also offered bounties, over and above Congressional allocations, and they frequently angered neighbors by "poaching" for enlistees across state boundaries. State bounties also upset troops who had enlisted without them, which ultimately forced Congress in 1779 to vote these Continentals a gratuity payment of $200 per person. State authorities often had recruiting problems when funds designated for bounties ran low. Thus, while state-directed efforts did produce a trickle of recruits, as did "beating up" on the part of the army, the results were generally disappointing.

It is doubtful, especially after the campaign of 1776, that any recruiting system based on voluntarism could have produced a Continental establishment at even half of authorized strength. Memories of hardship, defeat, rigid discipline, and disease remained too vivid. Stories circulated widely among the population and scared off thousands of potential recruits. At Morristown in early 1777, many officers openly questioned whether the newly planned regiments, so fine in theory, would ever exist. In the first weeks of the new year, only about 1,000 of the veterans of 1776 chose to reenlist. The recruiting situation was so chaotic in early 1777 that Washington despaired, even as late as May, about whether he would even dare to confront Howe in the tactical way that he did. As Charles H. Lesser's invaluable compilation of Continental manpower reports (*The Sinews of Independence,* 1976) has shown, Continental strength, based on returns from all departments, did not reach a peak for 1777 until October, when 39,443 (including militia) were in the ranks.[11] This was 35,000 fewer soldiers than Congress had projected, as well as more than 8,000 short of peak strength the year before (48,017 in October 1776). Even with the new financial incentives, voluntarism had begun to wither well before the war was two years old. The pattern continued, moreover, as the rebellion dragged on. Each year, as a general rule, fewer and fewer people wanted to have anything to do with Continental service.

The manpower dilemma placed an intolerable burden on Congress, the states, and the army command. All began searching for any and all recruits. Instead of accepting only propertied freeholders of the ideal republican type, they moved quickly to enlist any "able-bodied and effective" civilian. Early in 1777, for instance, New Jersey granted exemptions from militia service to all men who hired substitutes for Continental duty and to masters who would enroll indentured servants and slaves. In the following year Maryland permitted the virtual impressment of vagrants for nine months of regular service. Indeed, the majority of recruits who fought with Washington after 1776 represented the very poorest and most desperate persons in society, including ne'er-do-wells, drifters, unemployed laborers, captured British soldiers and Hessians, indentured servants, and slaves. Some of these soldiers were in such desperate economic straits that states had to pass laws prohibiting creditors from pulling them from the ranks and having them thrown in jail for petty debts. Very few of the new Continentals were independent farmers and tradesmen. Their service after 1776 came as militia on the periphery of the Continental establishment.

A number of recent quantitative studies have verified that Washington's new regulars were largely from the poor and dependent classes in Revolutionary America, which had been growing dramatically for at least two decades before the rebellion. These soldiers were not normally engaged in the defense of home and family because they rarely had either. They were most often in their teens or early twenties, although a small handful were boys of 14 and younger. The army considered the young "very proper for the service," as one South Carolina recruiter viewed it, because "they have little, and some no property," and thus had few economic ties or marital bonds in the civilian world. Lack of property and economic standing, however, was not just a function of age; the families of most recruits were also quite poor. Edward C. Papenfuse and Gregory A. Stiverson have found that "poverty was endemic" among Maryland troops of 1782, with half of those with traceable economic status coming from family units holding less than £45 in assessed wealth.[12] In New Jersey, Mark E. Lender discovered that at least 90 percent of the Continentals with available socioeconomic data represented the poorest two-thirds in society and that 46 percent of the soldiery or their families for those underage owned no taxable property whatsoever. Fifty-seven percent were landless, not an attractive condition in that state's largely agricultural economy.[13] Case studies by John R. Sellers of the Continentals of Massachusetts and Virginia have revealed distinctly similar patterns, especially in confirming the poverty-stricken family backgrounds of Washington's new regulars.[14] Among the post-1776 Continentals, poverty—before, during, and after Continental service—was a unifying characteristic. What is certainly clear is that when Continental enlistees marched off to war after 1776 they left behind them little in the way of property to defend.

Besides the unemployed and transient groups, the unfree also became fair game for Continental service. Going beyond indentured servants, hundreds of black slaves eventually found themselves placed in the ranks. Massachusetts led the way in 1777 by declaring blacks (both slave and free) eligible for the state draft. Shortly thereafter, Rhode Islanders set about the business of raising two black battalions, which served with distinction. Other states soon followed, mostly by permitting slaves to become substitutes for their white masters. The South, however, remained somewhat obdurate in adopting such practices. While Maryland and Virginia did come to permit slaves to substitute for whites, the lower South persistently refused to do so, even in the face of a successful British invasion of Georgia in 1778. To let slaves fight for liberty was simply too threatening to the social fabric of that region. Despite the lower South, General Philip Schuyler perhaps best summarized the pattern when he asked why so many "Sons of Freedom" were so willing "to trust their all to be defended by slaves." Irony aside, the answer was simple: Increasingly after 1776, when middle- and upper-class property holders felt pressure from recruiters or from state-legislated conscription programs, they turned to those who did not always have the right to decide for themselves whether military service was an appropriate test of disinterested citizenship.

Besides servants and slaves, Washington and his closest advisors also reluctantly accepted the presence of women in the army. So-called camp followers were to be found traveling with almost all eighteenth-century armies. Usually marginally poor, they came along with husbands or lovers, or because they could not find other ways to survive economically. Popular lore aside, they were not just followers or prostitutes. Indeed, women as well as men were "on the ration"; in return for half-rations, armies assigned these women a variety of duties, which included cooking, caring for the sick and wounded, washing and mending clothes, scavenging the field for clothes and equipment, and burying the dead after battle. In the British army, there was an accepted ratio of one woman for every 10 men on the ration; the ratio was one to 15 in the Continental army. Washington personally never approved of the presence of women in camp, but he never drove them out either. He knew that he would also probably lose their husbands or consorts, which would adversely affect overall troop strength. Thus women came along and participated, even if the commander in chief preferred to keep them out of sight whenever the army paraded in public.

Enemy deserters and prisoners of war were more welcome. Early Congressional pronouncements barred such persons from the ranks; but manpower shortages remained so acute after 1776 that even Washington warned that if the army "suffered to moulder away. . .we must look for Reinforcements to other places than our own states." The commander in chief personally pardoned at least one English prisoner on the condition that he join a Continental unit. Apparently, this practice was common. How many enemy deserters and prisoners were in the ranks has not been established, and the records are too incomplete for a precise estimate. The safest summary is to recall that Nathanael Greene claimed that he used a number of British deserters in the Southern army during 1781, and they evidently took perverse delight in turning their fire upon their former employers. Moreover, recruiters regularly enrolled Hessians, such as those from the convention army, and Congress started to issue ongoing appeals to these German mercenaries, promising them land and a new start in life. Over time, these soldiers came to form an important part of Washington's forces.

Loyalists arrested on charges of treason, especially in the middle states, often received a choice of accepting Continental service or going on trial for their lives. Patriot courts in Morristown, New Jersey, for instance, sentenced at least 105 loyalists to hang; although four of them held to principle and went to the gallows, the court reprieved all who consented to "enlist in the American army for . . . the war." The pattern was similar in criminal dealings, epitomized by the story of John Saunders, who received a sentence in 1777 of two public floggings for stealing horses in the Morristown vicinity. After the first beating, the dazed Saunders agreed to enlist in the Continental army; the judge, a generous man, eliminated the second flogging.

By the spring of 1777, it was more than clear to rebel leaders that manpower quotas resting only upon abstract notions of public virtue would largely go unfilled. General Washington called openly for conscription: "The Government must have recourse to coercive measures; for if the quotas required of each State cannot be had by voluntary enlistment, in time, and the Powers of Government are not adequate to *drafting,* there is an end of the Contest, and opposition becomes vain." Congress recommended the draft to the states on April 14, 1777. However, the states that adopted conscription laws also provided huge loopholes in the form of substitute and fine provisions, which protected the most economically favored from Continental duty. Hundreds of well-to-do property holders paid fines rather than face service. Drafting days also saw a brisk trade in willing substitutes, most of whom came from the poor or unfree classes. Hence there were citizens of lesser economic standing like Joseph Plumb Martin of Connecticut who enlisted for the duration as a substitute. When a group of reputed patriots learned that he was available for hire, they quickly had a bidding contest for his services. "I forgot the sum," Martin recalled later. However, "they were now freed from any further trouble, at least for the present, and I had become the scapegoat for them. . . . I thought, as I must go, I might as well endeavor to get as much for my skin as I could."

Hundreds of others, apparently trapped by straitened personal conditions, felt the same way. In New Jersey, at least 20, perhaps as many as 40 percent of the state line of 1778 consisted of substitutes for draftees. In New Hampshire, the town of Epping sent only substitutes forward when the local militia held its draft in 1777. Thus the manpower pattern unfolded. The draft, inherently at odds with the concepts of citizen virtue and moral commitment to republicanism, did little to reverse the dramatic movement away from the presence of middle-class yeomen in the post-1775 Continental army.

THE OLD MYTH AND
THE NEW SOLDIERY

It is hard to escape the conclusion that, as Washington continued to maintain a military presence in the field during 1777 and beyond, he did so by ignoring the dictates of republican ideology with respect to citizens-in-arms. Middle-class farmers and tradesmen, John Adams observed in passing, seemed to have better things to do than go soldiering for years at a time. That did not surprise Adams and his colleagues. Why should such "men who could get at home a better living, more comfortable lodgings, more than double the wages, in safety, not exposed to the sickness of camp" enlist for three years and/or the duration? "I knew it to be impossible," the sage of Braintree concluded.

From the point of view of social characteristics, the new Continental rank and file increasingly took on the appearance of a traditional European army while looking less and less like a republican force. Out of necessity, Washington simply had to accept what manpower he could get, whether as a product of voluntarism, recruitment, or conscription. In the growing pool of poor and unprotected peoples in Revolutionary society,

Washington and Congress found some individuals who were willing to serve long enlistments and who would stand the brutal rigors of life in the field, including its harsh discipline and the ever-present specter of disease, starvation, and death. Myth to the contrary, these were the "hardy" Continentals, the "rabble" which endured to the end. Their more socially acceptable Revolutionary brethren were most willing to let them do the hard fighting; then, after the war, selective memory returned the legendary citizen-soldier to the center stage of history, where myth has kept him in place ever since.

Despite the concept of virtuous citizenship and republican ideology, the freeholding American populace, beginning by late 1776, was hiring, for all practical purposes, a regular army to fight for it. That does not mean, however, that these new model soldiers viewed themselves as mere mercenaries. Many of them were simply trapped by the circumstances of their lives, and Continental service offered them positive alternatives. Black slaves, as Benjamin Quarles has reminded us in *The Negro in the American Revolution* (1961), usually found the army less oppressive than a civilian world that held them in chains and viewed them with unthinking prejudice.[15] For many slaves there was the tentative promise of freedom after the war, in return for long-term service; for the criminal, an end to prison; for the debtor, an avoidance of creditors or a settlement of burdensome debts; for the Hessian, a new start in the freer New World environment. Most recruits also had the prospect of free land at the end of the war. Their dreams were of a better life, if only Continental service could be survived. And their dreams, while intensely personal, paralleled and complemented the broader societal quest for liberty and republicanism, all of which made the bargain between civilians and the new regulars possible. The initial financial inducements, likewise, were of paramount importance for individuals with little or nothing in life. The army meant personal socioeconomic mobility or outright freedom, but only if the new nation kept its part of the financial and moral bargain.

Lest other myths be created, it must be stressed that not all luckless citizens rushed forward to join the Continental ranks. For many, the toll of long-term military service and its multifold dangers was too dear a price to pay, even if not signing up meant continued economic and/or legal bondage. Moreover, some of the down and outers who filled Washington's ranks were just plain scoundrels. They were variants of M'Donald Campbell, a sometime New Jersey militiaman and Continental soldier who also found it convenient to serve with the British (he claimed afterward that he was spying for the Americans). At one point, he recalled, he "had formed an acquaintance with a young woman. . .of a very creditable family, with whom I had been too intimate." Her father insisted upon marriage, and Campbell obliged. However, he did not particularly care for his new bride and fled to the Continental ranks. After the war, he highlighted his notorious career by prospering temporarily as a counterfeiter. Men like Campbell and John Saunders typified those who joined the war simply because it happened to drift into their way. But for most of those who formed Washington's small band of hard core regulars after 1776, the dirty work of fighting the civil war meant something much more—the dream of postwar prosperity and a new beginning in life.

Still, there was a lurking danger in amassing such a regular force within the framework of antistanding-army ideology. Don Higginbotham has stated part of the proposition: "So long as American soldiers were little more than a reflection of American society, the Continental army posed no threat to free institutions."[16] The fact of the matter was that, in terms of social composition, the post-1776 Continental was a very distorted reflection. The latent possibility was developing that Washington's new modeled army, once it evolved into a thoroughly effective fighting machine, might turn and attack the very republican edifice that it had been hired to help bring into existence, should an ungrateful citizenry not remember its contractual promises and obligations. To state the matter differently, Washington's army held the potential of becoming very dangerous to civil society, if it gained the impression that more respectable civilians did not intend to allow these new regulars to enjoy the full benefits of a freer, more open republican world at war's end. Indeed, precipitate conditions portending real trouble between army and society were very much in the making as the war effort deepened and lengthened after the unsuccessful British campaign effort of 1777.

NOTES

[1] George Bancroft, *History of the United States from the Discovery of the American Continent,* 10 vols. (1834–1874; Boston, 1860), 8:62–64.

[2] Charles K. Bolton, *The Private Soldier under Washington* (New York, 1902), pp. 13, 235, 238.

[3] Howard H. Peckham, *The War for Independence: A Military History* (Chicago, 1958), p. 204.

[4] Edmund S. Morgan, *The Birth of the Republic, 1763–89,* rev. ed. (Chicago, 1977), p. 79.

[5] Charles Royster, *A Revolutionary People at War: The Continental Army and the American Character, 1775–1783* (Chapel Hill, N.C., 1980), p. 116.

[6] David Ramsay, *History of the American Revolution,* 2 vols. (New York, 1968 reprint), 1:233–34.

[7] John Todd White, "Standing Armies in Time of War: Republican Theory and Military Practice during the American Revolution," (Ph.D. dissertation, George Washington University, 1978), p. 140.

[8] *Ibid.,* pp. 144–45.

[9] For an argument that one state had stretched itself to the absolute limit by September 1776 with respect to available manpower in military service, consult Richard Buel, Jr., *Dear Liberty: Connecticut's Mobilization for the Revolutionary War* (Middletown, Conn., 1981), pp. 53–80. Buel also notes that this was the peak of manpower output from Connecticut. After that time, Connecticut civil officials were pressed to get individuals into service.

[10] Russell F. Weigley, "American Strategy: A Call for a Critical Strategic History," in Don Higginbotham, ed., *Reconsiderations of the Revolutionary War: Selected Essays* (Westport, Conn., 1978), pp. 48–50. For a different point of view, *see* Dave R. Palmer, *The Way of the Fox: American Strategy in the War for America, 1775–1783* (Westport, Conn., 1975), *passim.*

[11] C. H. Lesser, ed., *The Sinews of Independence: Monthly Strength Reports of the Continental Army* (Chicago, 1976), pp. 2–56.

[12] Edward C. Papenfuse and Gregory A. Stiverson, "General Smallwood's Recruits: The Peacetime Career of the Revolutionary War Private," *William and Mary Quarterly,* 3d Series, 30 (1973), pp. 117–32.

[13] Mark E. Lender, "The Enlisted Line: The Continental Soldiers of New

Jersey," (Ph.D. dissertation, Rutgers University, 1975), pp. 110-39. *See also* Lender, "The Social Structure of the New Jersey Brigade: The Continental Line as an American Standing Army," in Peter Karsten, ed., *The Military in America: From the Colonial Era to the Present* (New York, 1980), pp. 27-44.

[14] John R. Sellers, "The Common Soldier in the American Revolution," in S. J. Underdal, ed., *Military History of the American Revolution: Proceedings of the Sixth Military History Symposium, USAF Academy* (Washington, D.C., 1976), pp. 151-61; *idem,* "The Origins and Careers of the New England Soldier: Noncommissioned Officers and Privates in the Massachusetts Continental Line" (paper delivered at the American Historical Association Convention, 1972). For additional insight, consult Robert Middlekauff, "Why Men Fought in the American Revolution," *Huntington Library Quarterly,* 43 (1980), pp. 135-48.

[15] Benjamin Quarles, *The Negro in the American Revolution* (Chapel Hill, N.C., 1961), pp. 33-50, 182-200.

[16] Don Higginbotham, *The War of American Independence: Military Attitudes, Policies, and Practice, 1763-1789* (New York, 1971), p. 93.

FOUR

On and Off the Road of Despair, 1777–1779

VALLEY FORGE

Washington's army had been battered in Howe's Pennsylvania campaign, but it had not been beaten. Its most pressing concern in December 1777 was to find a suitable winter encampment. The commander chose Valley Forge, some 18 miles northwest of Philadelphia. Because the terrain was hilly with the Schuylkill

River at its back, the location afforded the bedraggled army a natural defensive site. If Howe fell out of character and became aggressive during the winter season, the army would be able to defend itself. Yet the American commander made no pretenses about his ability to protect the whole region around Philadelphia. When local patriot leaders insisted on that, Washington replied sharply: "It would give me infinite pleasure to afford protection to every individual and to every Spot of Ground in the whole of the United States. Nothing is more my wish. But this is not possible with our present force."

On December 19, the army moved into Valley Forge. The soldiers were in miserable shape. Of those 11,000 hardy warriors, at least 2,000 had no shoes. Many more lacked decent clothing in weather that was cold, wet, and windy. Private Joseph Plumb Martin noted that the soldiers' path to Valley Forge could "be tracked by their blood upon the frozen ground." Equally demoralizing, the army had not been paid since August. "Unless some great and capital change takes place," Washington wrote nervously, "this Army must inevitably . . . starve, dissolve, or disperse."

If the expectation was for modest comfort in winter camp, that expectation did not eventuate. Just about everything that could have gone wrong did. The soldiery struggled to build huts in the face of intermittent blasts of snow and biting cold weather. The Marquis de Lafayette, only 20 in 1777 but already a major general and one of Washington's favorites, characterized these huts as "little shanties that are scarcely gayer than dungeon cells." By January 1, most of the men and women forming the army were finally getting some decent protection from the weather, but they had little food or drink to warm them on the inside. There was not enough rum on Christmas day for Washington to issue the prescribed holiday allotment of a gill per person. Firecake, when flour was available to mix with water, became standard fare. It had enough nutritional value, according to Dr. Albigence Waldo of the first Connecticut infantry regiment, to turn human "Guts. . .to Pasteboard." As early as December 21, many soldiers could be heard to be shouting in unison: "No Meat! No Meat!" Within days the chant had changed to: "No bread, no soldier!"

The lack of food and clothing has most often been attributed to a complete breakdown in the commissary and quartermaster departments just prior to the Valley Forge encampment. Certainly that standard explanation was an important reason. Inefficiency and corruption characterized both of these support departments. Unfortunately, rank-and-file soldiers were the victims. At one point during the Valley Forge winter, they went without meat for six days and, on three separate occasions, there were no provisions whatsoever. In December 1777, Congress, which had failed to correct commissary problems, finally ordered Washington to commandeer local foodstuffs to ward off the specter of starvation. (Local farmers in the vicinity of the competing armies preferred British gold to Continental paper currency.) Equipment, as with food and clothing, also remained in desperate supply, as Congress allowed the vital post of quartermaster general to remain open for three months after General Thomas Mifflin's resignation in November. By February 1778, some 4,000 troops were unfit for duty for lack of shoes, clothing, blankets, soap, medicines, and other basic items.

The impact of these shortages was disastrous. Between December 1777 and June 1778, some 2,500 human souls (nearly one-fourth of the army) perished, easy prey to exposure, malnutrition, typhus, smallpox, and other camp maladies. Droves more of the rank and file were deserting. Reflecting on the chant, "no bread, no soldier," they no doubt felt that the country was not keeping its part of the enlistment bargain. There was no reason for enduring such suffering to defend the liberties of civilians who were not reciprocating, and in some cases were profiting directly by selling rancid meat and moth-infested clothing to the army. That civilians in the vicinity would not even sell them straw to help prevent sick and emaciated comrades from freezing to death in bed had to make the soldiers angry. In fact, the soldiery received little more respect or concern from the civilian populace that winter than did the army's horses, some 500 of which perished for want of forage. So many dead animals only added to bad sanitation conditions and the spread of disease, since it was difficult to bury rotting carcasses in frozen ground.

One incident in particular epitomized the senselessness of it all. General Anthony Wayne, famous for his daring leadership in battle, tried to make arrangements to get 500 coats for the ill-clad men under his command. The Clothier General, James Mease, a Congressional appointee, insisted that only authorized civilian tailors could do the work. While Wayne's troops continued to suffer, Mease took a leave of absence, and there was no one who could process the order. When he returned to duty, the Clothier General refused to issue the uniforms because only yellow buttons were available and Pennsylvania's regimental design specified white buttons. Finally, an apoplectic Wayne had the specifications changed, and Mease released the coats. How many of Wayne's soldiers died from exposure while this farce was playing itself out has never been determined.

The food and supply situation only began to improve after the wealthy Connecticut merchant, Jeremiah Wadsworth, took charge of the commissary department, and Nathanael Greene reluctantly acceded to the quartermaster generalship. Help also came from an early shad run in the Schuylkill River, providing an abundance of fresh fish, while the severe winter weather broke early in the spring. All of this saved many lives. Popular lore aside, the encampment at Valley Forge was not the harshest in terms of weather or material conditions that Washington's army endured. That dubious distinction befell the Morristown encampment of 1779–1780. But that observation cannot mitigate the high level of unnecessary suffering that did occur.

In the end, what made Valley Forge so gruesome was the widespread indifference of patriot civilians toward an army so desperately in need of help. It is important to ask whether such suffering would have taken place had middle-class Americans made up the ranks of the army. That they did not may be a significant reason why there was such neglect of those down and outers who had agreed to fight for republicanism. Indeed, it was not just the commissary, quartermaster, and clothing departments (the traditional culprits) that caused the needless privation. Nor was it necessarily the result of popular ignorance about what was happening, as has been recently asserted by John B. B. Trussell in *Birthplace of an Army* (1976).[1] It was just as much that the general populace did not care (befitting social attitudes of the times), since so many of those who suffered were from the laboring and indigent classes.

The soldiers remembered what happened to them. They had already resorted to various forms of protest, which included desertion. However, the bulk stayed in the ranks and continued to endure further hardships in the months and years ahead. The alternatives were not necessarily any better outside the army, especially since their dreams of economic self-sufficiency, personal liberty, and human dignity had now come to depend upon long-term Continental service—as part of the societal quest for a republican order in America.

MOUNTING ANGER
IN THE OFFICER CORPS

As the first two years of warfare came to a close, Washington's officers were growing as restless and angry as the soldiery. Their discontent started to spill over into overt protest in the weeks preceding the move to Valley Forge. Grievances focused on two primary issues: appropriate rank and economic survival. As a group, the officers fretted incessantly about both matters, and they most often manifested their anxieties and frustrations in their talk of personal honor. As Charles Royster has cogently observed, "honor not only required a man to uphold his rank, keep his word, and demand the same of others; it also required that he resent any insult." For each officer, "honor kept. . .self-esteem inviolable; and, since he felt his own worth so keenly, the slightest indignity or affront struck him as an attack on his rights as a gentleman."[2] To receive a promotion for valorous service was to be treated with honor, to demonstrate respect. To pay the officer at a level representative of his personal sacrifice was to accomplish the same. However, Congress, always sensitive about recognition of its paramount authority in matters military, was rarely cordial about the psychological needs of the officer corps. The result was a deepening wedge of contention between civil and military bodies—with negative implications for the outcome of the Revolution.

The tribulations of Benedict Arnold in 1776 and 1777 over his rank typified the strained relations of many high-ranking officers with Congress. Because of his service at Quebec, Congress had commissioned Arnold a brigadier general early in 1776. A year later, the central body passed over him for promotion and named five new major generals, all previously junior to the American Hannibal. Washington was among those who felt strongly that Arnold deserved recognition, given his record of meritorious service. In response, the delegates argued that Connecticut already had its complement of major generals, based on its proportion of troops in rank. (The Baltimore resolution of 1777 stipulated that promotions at the general officer level would be based on order of succession, merit, and proportion of troops in service from each state.) In dismay and anger over what he described as besmirched honor, Arnold hinted strongly at resignation. Congress was obdurate, however, arguing that it was working within prescribed policy. Also, many delegates did not like Arnold personally, and they resented the fact that he was questioning civil authority.

Then events took an unusual turn. Late in April 1777, the former apothecary, visiting in Connecticut, rushed to the defense of his state to stop a foray by British soldiers that had resulted in the sacking and burning of Danbury. Arnold personally rallied the militia, threw himself into the thick of the fighting (in one heated exchange his horse was shot out from under him while another enemy bullet tore open his uniform), and was instrumental in driving the marauding British column back out to sea. Shortly thereafter, a red-faced Congress belatedly recognized his merit by promoting him to major general. To prove their superior hand, however, the delegates did not restore his seniority. A querulous Washington mused:

"General Arnold's promotion gives me great pleasure. He has certainly discovered in every instance. . .much bravery, activity, and enterprise. But what will be done about his rank? He will not act, most probably, under those who commanded him but a few weeks ago."

To deny him proper succession was a second needless insult. Arnold decided, perhaps unwisely, to take his case directly to Congress. He explained why: "Honor is a sacrifice no man ought to make, as I received so I wish to transmit [it] inviolate to Posterity." The delegates did not take kindly to his personal lobbying effort, considering it an affront to their prerogatives. In fact, not until the end of November 1777 did the delegates, acknowledging Arnold's vital role at Saratoga, award him seniority in line of command over the five who should not have been ahead of him. By that time, however, personal bitterness over such incidents had begun to fester. It eventually set Arnold on the path to treason. Had Congress acted less rigidly in this general's case, the Arnold story might well have ended somewhat more pleasantly.

Arnold's tribulations over rank and his sense of desecrated honor were not unique to him. While Congress played politics with the likes of Arnold, it also insisted that no one in the military establishment question its right to elevate well-connected foreigners to the highest general officer ranks. In July 1777, a celebrated dispute broke out over Philippe du Coudray, a stuffy Frenchman who supposedly had extensive experience with artillery. One of the American commissioners in France had promised du Coudray that he would be named Washington's Chief of Artillery at the rank of major general, should he come to America. When he arrived, du Coudray presented his credentials to Congress, thereby placing the delegates in a difficult position. They in no way wanted to anger Washington and downgrade Henry Knox, nor did they want to undercut the commissioners working for a formal Franco-American alliance.

Then, Knox, Nathanael Greene, and John Sullivan sent public letters to Congress, which implied that they would resign should du Coudray be placed in rank before them. Irate at such military insolence which threatened, as one perturbed Connecticut delegate phrased it, "the authority, Esteem, or dignity of Congress," the delegates insisted on apologies or resignations. The three generals ignored the demand. The matter finally ended without serious offense of anyone only because du Coudray, pompously insisting that he would ride instead of walk his horse onto a ferry, was thrown overboard and drowned in the Schuylkill River.

Such incidents helped to spread a festering sore in civil-military relations. To the officers, any needless tampering with rank became an attack on personal honor. Congress, enduring pressures from all sides and often succumbing to politics, did not always use good judgment and generally viewed the officers, in the words of John Adams, as "Mastiffs, Scrambling for Rank and Pay like Apes for Nuts." Such thinking, as Richard H. Kohn has persuasively written, was a major reason why the officers "grew to hate Congress for its weakness and its arrogance."[3] Washington's lieutenants wanted the respect they thought due them as propertied citizens who now held high military rank. Congress, however, treated them as if they were professional soldiers—and a possible threat to society. As Washington wrote at Valley Forge, "We should all be considered. . .as one people, embarked in one Cause, in one interest; acting on the same principle and to the same End." Yet the "very jealousy" of Congress over the army's proper "subordination to the supreme Civil Authority, is a likely means to produce a contrary effect."

That warning, in time, had more profound meaning than Washington could have imagined in 1778. Part of the tension over rank and personal honor may be explained in terms of the social origins of the officer corps. In his study of New Jersey Continentals, Mark E. Lender found that the officers, as a group, were drawn from the top level of society. Some 84 percent of the New Jersey officers came from the wealthiest third of the population—and none from the lowest third. Thirty-two percent of them fell into the wealthiest ten percent. Some, like William Alexander (Lord Stirling), owned thousands of acres of property, or they had excellent family connections, like Ensign John Ford Morris of Morris County, who received his commission at the age of 16.[4] As one observer in that state reported, the officers were the type of men "who would not pass unnoticed in the politest court in Europe."

Outside of New Jersey, the pattern was much the same. Officers were largely established local and provincial community leaders before the war or sons of the same. Some were economically successful in their own right, such as upwardly mobile upstarts like Benedict Arnold or Alexander McDougall. Others had close relatives in important Revolutionary political offices, such as General Jedidiah Huntington, who had married a daughter of Governor Jonathan Trumbull of Connecticut before the war, or Henry Knox, who had married into an elite, even if loyalist, family. Overall, they were no different in socio-economic composition and personal accomplishments from their fellow Revolutionaries in state legislatures and Congress.[5]

In fact, their well-developed concern about honor was a reflection of their generally high community status. To be treated in Congress as little more than grasping mercenaries, instead of as men of personal virtue and moral commitment, was particularly irksome, especially when they had demonstrated their fervor through military service when so many like them among prosperous civilians had not.

By the end of 1777, these men of prominence who now made up Washington's officer corps were getting increasingly sensitive, especially about the way society was treating them. To add further to their frustrations, the financial costs of maintaining themselves in the field had begun to hurt, and some of the officers were starting to get into serious financial trouble. Participation in the war had eliminated any prospect of income from agriculture or commerce within the civilian world. Rampant inflation had set in, and their salaries were being undermined. There were also the multifold expenses of purchasing personal clothing and equipage so that they could maintain themselves in the style expected of gentlemen in the field. While some civilians were amassing small fortunes as a result of the war effort, the wealth of many officers was eroding. Resenting civilian peculation, the officers borrowed from British practice and struck upon a solution—half-pay pensions for life to begin at the end of the war as just recognition for their sacrifices and lost income.

A small group of field-grade officers first approached Washington in November 1777. Initially, the commander was cool to the idea of pensions. He doubted whether the country could afford them; he also indicated that Congress would not take any such proposal seriously, especially one that contained such an unrepublican sounding notion as "some order of knighthood" over and above pensions for officers of unusual merit. Once at Valley Forge, Washington began to take the scheme more seriously. It was not just the rank and file who were deserting; officers had started to resign in great numbers. Many of them had made clear that the cause owed them more than financial penury, especially when the civilian population, from their perspective, did not seem to be very interested in the army's general welfare or survival. Thus Washington conceded before the end of 1777 and referred a plan to Congress that called for half-pay, saleable commissions, and pensions for widows of officers who fell in combat.

As could be expected, the immediate reaction of Congress was largely negative. Half-pay, especially among the New Englanders, seemed like a direct attack on republicanism. Massachusetts delegate James Lovell spoke about "a wish or design to put our military officers upon the footing of European." He wondered why it had been "forgotten that this *was* in its beginnings a patriotic war." Others worried about "a total loss of virtue in the Army," about officers who were not "actuated by the principles of patriotism and public spirit," about future pensioners who would become a privileged class "of People idle" not engaged in "useful industry" but "burdening the country." Worse yet, half-pay would "involve the idea of a standing army in time of peace. . .at the disposal of Congress," which would undercut "the rights of the states" to appoint "regimental officers" or have any influence over military matters whatsoever.

The concerns of the delegates thus had a definite ideological base. At the core, they feared that pensions were one step too far to go in new modeling Washington's army. The American officers were now asking for what British officers already had. That was precisely the problem. Whig ideologues explained that Britain's standing army, with its train of pensioners and contractors, had helped corrupt the polity of the former parent state. Purists among the delegates now openly feared that the Revolution might produce nothing more than the same putrid system in a different environment.

Once committed to pensions, Washington subordinated any ideological reservations that he previously held. Confronted with a mounting number of resignations, he needed something to raise officer morale and encourage further service. He was straightforward with Congress: "A small knowledge of human nature will convince us, that, with far the greatest part of mankind, interest is the governing principle." The commander further pointed out that "motives of public virtue may for a time . . .actuate men to the observance of a conduct purely disinterested." However, the days of "continual sacrifice" without an attention to "private interest" were long since gone. He thus concluded that "nothing. . .would serve more powerfully to reanimate their languishing zeal, and interest them thoroughly in the service, than a half pay and pensionary establishment."

By late spring of 1778, the alternatives were very clear: Maintain ideological purity and lose a substantial portion of the officer corps, or maintain the officers in the hope that a republican polity would still be viable, even with the "corrupting" influence of postwar pensions. Since the army was about all that stood between the cause and its collapse, Congress succumbed to reality. The delegates did so because they understood that a republican order was not possible without the army's commitment. In May 1778, Congress approved pensions, but restricted them to seven years. The central body, out of a sense of fairness to enlistees, who as a group were not in a position to lobby their concerns, voted a bonus of $80 for each person already in the ranks who would extend his enlistment for the duration of the war. At the same time, Congress rejected vendible commissions and pensions for widows. No pensioner, furthermore, could hold public office. Barring the officers from postwar political positions, as historian John Todd White has stressed, meant that "they would not be able to dominate legislatures and vote for such things as stronger central government and standing armies in time of peace."[6]

In the short run, the officers seemed to accept these restrictions. Something was better than nothing, but they also remembered that some leaders in Congress had treated them with unnecessary contempt and had denounced them as mercenaries extorting pay from a defenseless and helpless polity. That only exacerbated their sense of honor. Their anger would thus continue to grow, and they would be heard from again and again on the issue of pensions, even to the point of the threat of a military coup d'etat in 1783.

TABLES TURNED: NEW LIFE FOR THE CAUSE

The Continental army endured the winter at Valley Forge and survived. Sheer fortitude and the faded dream of a better postwar existence kept many foot soldiers in camp, and the prospect of pensions helped to assure that numbers of officers would be present for another campaign season. Three other matters put the army on a more solid footing than it had previously been. The first focused on what appeared to Washington and his immediate staff as a hidden campaign of innuendo and political action to replace the Virginian at the head of the army. The confrontation has come down to posterity as the "Conway Cabal." The second, relating to better training and discipline, had to do with one of the most colorful (and effective) foreigners to offer his services to the struggling American effort. His name was Friedrich von Steuben, a pretended Prussian nobleman. The third factor related directly to the creation of a formal Franco-American alliance. With the alliance came not only the distinction of a major European power's recognition of American independence; but, equally important, it altered the fundamental character of the war.

Until the past few decades, historians had interpreted the so-called Conway Cabal as an organized plot among disaffected generals and congressmen to remove Washington from command. That an actual cabal existed is quite doubtful, as argued first by Bernhard Knollenberg in *Washington and the Revolution* (1940).[7] However, Washington thought that such a plot was underway and that it involved Generals Thomas Conway and Horatio Gates. Moreover, he and his staff responded to it as if it were no mere phantom. It all began with an intercepted letter from Conway to Gates. Conway, an Irish-born Frenchman of little discretion but with a solid military record in Europe, reputedly wrote to Gates in the fall of 1777: "Heaven has been determined to save your country or a weak general and bad counselors would have ruined it." These words came at a time when Gates had triumphed over a British army in the North; when Washington had failed to subdue William Howe in the Middle Department. The obvious implication was that Gates deserved to be in charge of the whole army.

The fact that the letter was to Gates should not have, by itself, implicated him. Yet there were reasons for Washington to be suspicious. This favorite of New England militiamen, when reporting his Saratoga triumph to Congress, had not gone through prescribed channels by sending his reports to Washington first. Ignoring the commander in chief was enough to make him angry and testy. Then Congress reorganized its Board of War and charged it with monitoring daily military activities. The delegates not only selected the hero of Saratoga for the board but named him president, technically making him Washington's civilian superior even though still very much in uniform. Gates's elevation had been vigorously supported by a small group of delegates who were decidedly anti-Washington and held him personally responsible for Howe's presence in Philadelphia. This group had previously objected, for ideological reasons, to new modeling the army. Then, to complicate matters further,

Congress in December 1777 promoted Conway, who had done very little to deserve it, to a major generalship. It also named him inspector general of the army, to be in charge of all drilling and training and with the authority to report directly to the Board of War rather than through the commander in chief. These decisions, although unrelated, would have been enough to make almost any person suspicious.

Isolated at Valley Forge, Washington and his "family," as he affectionately referred to his immediate staff, began to worry that these actions were all preliminary steps to supplanting him with Gates. Well before December 1777, Washington had urged that Congress not promote Conway on the grounds that he was undeserving and that it would upset too many American general officers who were. On what can only be described as a note of hyperbole, Washington had claimed that Conway's promotion "will give a fatal blow to the existence of the Army." When newly appointed Inspector General Conway arrived at Valley Forge in late December to assume his duties, Washington received him with an air that was chillier than the weather. Within a few days, Conway left camp in a huff, explaining sardonically to Washington that "by the two receptions you have honored me with since my arrival, I perceive that I have not the happiness of being agreeable to your excellency." Conway also stated that he "was ready to return to France and to the army where I hope I will meet with no frowns." For Washington and his loyal aides, Conway's abrupt departure was a godsend.

The "scheme," as Washington called it, quickly fizzled out, all of which suggests that not much of a plot existed in the first place. In reply to a caustic note from Washington, Gates wrote in mid-February: "I solemnly declare that I am of no faction; . . .After this, I cannot believe your Excellency will either suffer your suspicions or the prejudices of others to induce you to spend another moment upon this subject." Washington accepted Gates's recantation and replied that he was "burying" the matter "hereafter in silence, and, as far as future events will permit, oblivion." However, the commander never fully trusted Gates from this point on, and that mistrust along with an unwillingness to help Gates when the latter's career fell into open disrepute later in the war, served to build the drama in the Newburgh crisis during the winter of 1782–1783.

The Conway Cabal, even if a product of imagination more than fact, did have other consequences, besides putting Washington on guard against Gates and a small group of republican purists in Congress. John Todd White has argued that the most significant effect was to force Congress to accept "the principle that Washington was essential to the Revolution." "Until the end of the war," White notes further, "the desire to support and not offend the commander in chief played a key role in congressional military policy."[8] The Virginian came out of the contretemps in a stronger position to manage military matters. Moreover, Congress would listen to him more carefully and would not be so quick, for example, to promote such ilk as Thomas Conway over the objections of the commander. The fact that Congress, despite strong feelings, caved in on the issue of pensions in May 1778 was a sign of its reinvigorated respect for Washington's opinions. Even though the army was to have less popular support with each passing year, it was to have better Congressional communications. In the long run, that may have made a critical difference in maintaining a proper balance in civil-military relations, especially since Washington could exercise firm control over his standing forces when he needed to and because he never failed to keep the coercive power of the army subordinate to the will of Congress.

On February 24, Washington wrote to Gates and accepted his apology; that was the day after General von Steuben arrived at Valley Forge. Unlike Conway and other foreign mercenaries, the "Baron" was well-liked from the very outset. In his early career, he had been a staff aide-de-camp to Frederick the Great of Prussia but had lost that post, possibly because his family had claimed *de facto* baronial status that had never been awarded by the state. Although Steuben's career had been checkered before coming to America, he had learned much in the process and behaved with great acumen upon arrival. Like Lafayette before him, he volunteered his services to Congress. The resulting agreement in Steuben's case was that, once he proved his worth to the army, he would receive appropriate pay and rank.

Steuben had a magnetic personality. He also had exceptional knowledge of Prussian training and drilling procedures. Within a month of arriving at Valley Forge, he began the formidable task of introducing the soldiers to a simplified set of drill procedures, as well as to train them in the use of the bayonet in battle. Furthermore, he began the task of preparing a uniform drill manual, which remained the basis for training American troops until the War of 1812. Heretofore, each company had more or less followed its own procedures, which meant that there was no standardized way to move troops or command them in battle.

Energetically, Steuben got himself in front of the regulars and set the tone for rigorous drilling. He did so by working with a model company. He pushed these troops hard. Speaking almost no English and barely recognizable French, he communicated through grunts and instantly understandable swear words. The soldiers quickly adapted to Steuben's prodding. Indeed, they seemed to revel in it, which heightened morale in the midst of human despair. Steuben also insisted that officers come forth and lead in training, rather than leaving fundamentals to the whims of noncommissioned officers. There is no doubt that a hardier, more resolute, and better-trained army emerged by the late spring of 1778—with renewed determination to stand up, fight when necessary, and endure until the dream of postwar freedom and prosperity could be realized.

His voluntarism earned Steuben both a major generalship and the post of inspector general. John Laurens, one of Washington's most talented aides, wrote affectionately: "The Baron Steuben has had the fortune to please uncommonly, for a stranger, at first sight. . . .All the general officers who have seen him are prepossessed in his favor, and conceive highly of his abilities. . . .The General seems to have a very good opinion of him." The last comment was a classic understatement. Especially when compared to Conway, to have a person who was truly capable in the inspector generalship was to bring the Continental army one large step closer to becoming an effective regular fighting force. In the months ahead, Washington came to depend heavily on Steuben, and the former German captain never disappointed him. To this day, historians agree that the enduring reputation of Baron von Steuben is largely merited.

Initially, Steuben had come from Paris at the urging of the American commissioners there. In 1776 Congress, desperately in search of foreign support (and allies), had sent Benjamin Franklin, Silas Deane, and Arthur Lee to Paris with the assignment of wooing the French. There, the Comte de Vergennes, serving as the French foreign minister, welcomed them to the calculating and whimsical world of European diplomacy. Vergennes was a skillful diplomat, and one of his highest policy goals was reducing Britain's imperial might. The Treaty of Paris of 1763, which ended the Seven Years' War, had cost France its North American empire and had swung the European balance of power heavily in Great Britain's favor. There were many in France who saw in the Anglo-American rift an opportunity to strike back and seriously injure an ancient and imperious foe. Vergennes was a leader among such individuals. They believed that there was unparalleled opportunity to strengthen France over Britain through the American War for Independence.

From 1775 through 1777, the French government followed a policy of covert assistance to the American rebels. It hoped to widen the breach beyond repair, making it possible to enter the war in safety and crush the hated Britons. One of Vergennes's many assistants, the dapper courtier Caron de Beaumarchais (the author of the *Marriage of Figaro* and the *Barber of Seville*) went to London in May 1775 to search out a wayward Frenchman who was reputedly selling state secrets to the North ministry. His other assignment was to seek out prominent Americans conducting business in England. He thus began meeting with acid Arthur Lee of Virginia, and the two of them struck upon a plan to facilitate informal French aid, should the government of Louis XVI concur.

In the spring of 1776, the ostensibly private mercantile firm of Roderigue Hortalez & Cie., which was a front for Beaumarchais, began operations. With handsome loans and financial grants from the French government, Hortalez & Cie. purchased war materiel destined for American soldiers. In something over a year, this operation collected an estimated 30,000 muskets, 100,000 rounds of shot, 200 cannons with full train, 300,000 rounds of powder, 13,000 hand bombs, 3,000 tents, and clothing for 30,000 men. Admittedly, much of the merchandise was old and shoddy, but such bulk goods were far better than nothing. Many of these items passed through New England to upstate New York, where the Continental army's Northern Department distributed them to regulars and militia involved in defeating Burgoyne. French loans, cash grants, and materiel hence were essential to effecting the circumstances that brought that autocratic state out openly into the republican war effort.

While providing covert aid behind the scenes, Vergennes cagily held the American commissioners at a distance in public. He had to maintain a posture of neutrality until the wedge had been driven deep enough for timely intervention. When the North ministry insisted that Frenchmen stop giving succor to American privateers by allowing them to refit their vessels in French ports, Vergennes complied. What Vergennes legitimately feared was a hasty reconciliation of differences with reunited Britons and Americans suddenly turning on an overextended France. His public posture thus made it appear that the American commissioners had to do a lot of convincing to gain formal French involvement. In reality, they did not. A willing Vergennes had been biding time at Versailles, looking only for the proper moment to consummate the flirtatious relationship. Meantime, the American military machine had to prove that it would not come apart when hit by concentrated British military strength. The Battle of Saratoga established that for Vergennes and Louis XVI.

From the American side, no better person than Benjamin Franklin could have represented his country's interests. The old man was well known in European intellectual circles. Many considered him America's premier creative genius. In 1772, he had been elected to the French Academy of Sciences, primarily for his work on electricity. Appearing in Paris and Versailles with his simple clothes, fur hat, unkempt hair, and spectacles, Franklin came to embody the uncorrupted, simple republican. And the Philadelphian thrived in his role, making friends for America wherever he went. Witty and urbane as a diplomat, he enjoyed his celebrity status in France and gloated over the reproduction of his republican-looking countenance on such objects as snuffboxes, handkerchiefs, rings, and watches. (Franklin did, however, question whether it was a compliment to have his likeness portrayed on the inside of porcelain chamber-pots!) All the public adoration shown him helped to strengthen Franco-American relations in the months preceding the formal alliance.

The alliance agreement, which came about through the signing of two treaties during February 1778, put trade between the two nations on a most-favored-nation basis and declared to the world that France recognized American independence. Louis XVI also agreed to renounce French territorial aspirations in North America, including Canada, in return for a free hand in attempting to conquer valuable British sugar islands in the West Indies. Each party stipulated that no formal peace terms could be drawn up without the consent of the other. This clause guaranteed that France would have a large voice in any peace settlement and some protection from double-dealing, should a concerted reconciliation attempt develop between England and America. The mutual consent clause eventually caused con-siderable embarrassment when peace negotiations began in 1782; but in 1778 no American minister could have avoided such a clause and got an alliance. It was Vergennes's protection against any lingering possibility of an Anglo-American trap.

This particular cycle of diplomacy reached a climax in June 1778 when a French/British naval battle erupted in the English Channel. Formal declarations of war followed quickly. A civil rebellion had now turned into a world war that, in the long run, would stretch British military resources too thinly across the globe. In the short run, formal French intervention (along with that of Spain in 1779 and the Dutch Netherlands in 1780) forced

Great Britain to modify its strategic approach to the war. The new pattern started to become clear with the British pullout from Philadelphia in June 1778.

When Congress and Washington learned about the French alliance, they were overjoyed. The commander designated May 6 as a day for "rejoicing throughout the whole Army." It was a wonderful time of celebration at Valley Forge. The army had survived the winter, and there were still enough soldiers to face the enemy and the cheering prospect of thousands more coming from France to supplement Washington's meager numbers. The army was better trained than ever before. The officers had expectations of postwar pensions, and the commander himself had better control in relations with Congress over the fate of his constabulary. There was much reason to justify the extravagance of giving each soldier a gill of rum and having all the rank and file participate in a *feu de joie* of musketry. Once it assembled on parade, the army was to cheer in unison: "Long Live the King of France. Long Live the Friendly European Powers. To the American States." That the army was still alive—and vital—explains the official attitude of giving the soldiers "more than the common quantity of liquor" and tolerating "some little drunkenness among them." Equally significant, the cause had been rescued, or so the celebrants hoped—not, however, by republican enthusiasts in the patriot population but by an autocratic European power eager to humiliate an ancient enemy. It was indeed fortunate for the republican aspirants that the former parent state had numerous enemies in the Old World.

THE BRITISH DISPERSAL OF 1778

Given that leading rebels had set as their goal a republican sociopolitical order in America, the alliance with France made little ideological sense. New Englander Elbridge Gerry caught the irony of it all when he wrote:

What a miraculous change in the political world! The ministry of England advocates for despotism, and endeavoring to enslave those

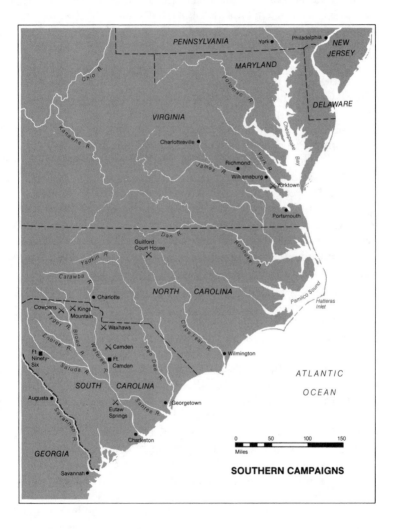

SOUTHERN CAMPAIGNS

who might have remained loyal subjects of the king. The govenment of France an advocate of liberty, espousing the cause of protestants and risking a war to secure their independence. The king of England considered by every whig in the nation as a tyrant, and the king of France applauded by every whig in America as the protector of the rights of man! . . . Britain at war with America, France in alliance with her! These, my friend, are astonishing changes.

Ideological inconsistencies aside, the alliance drastically altered Great Britain's approach to the war. For one thing, Lord North hurried a peace commission to America. Known as the Carlisle Commission, it was to offer the Americans everything they wanted, save independence. Congress chose to ignore the commissioners. For another thing, the commencement of war with France forced British policy makers to redeploy military and naval forces. More troops would be needed at home to guard against a possible French invasion. (In time, France did organize a massive expeditionary force; however, horrendous weather and other problems destroyed plans for an assault on the island kingdom.) Then there was what Piers Mackesy has called the North ministry's "obsession with the West Indies."[9] In 1778, French troops in the islands outnumbered English regulars by a ratio of at least four to one. French involvement made it necessary to defend the British sugar islands, which played a key role in the parent state's overall economic health. Likewise, there now was the legitimate opportunity to seize French West Indian islands, which could serve as significant compensation for the loss of the American provinces, should that be the outcome of the war.

What is decidedly clear is that British strategy shifted dramatically with France's entry into war. No longer could troops be concentrated at one critical point, such as they had been in the campaign of 1776. Rather, dispersal with the purpose of concentrating precious resources in different places became the operative norm. The most obvious indicator came in the form of instructions to Sir Henry Clinton, who had replaced Sir William Howe in the spring of 1778 as British North American commander. Clinton's orders were to evacuate the rebel capital, to retreat with all British soldiers to New York City and, if necessary, to evacuate New York, should pressures from the allies become too great. By the fall of 1778, the ministry would be siphoning off manpower from Clinton for campaigning in the West Indies and elsewhere. Indeed, strategy could no longer focus on trying to break the back of the Continental army. Henceforth, the allies, provided they got themselves working in unison, could contemplate offensive warfare. That moment finally came with the Yorktown campaign of 1781, three years after the alliance went into effect. Meantime, Great Britain prepared itself to fend off strikes wherever they came across the globe, all of which increased the likelihood that Americans could win the war—if their soldiers could just endure in the field.

Clinton, who was both contentious and diffident, a man who once described himself as "a shy bitch," did not relish his first assignment as commander—extricating the British army from Philadelphia, the sole prize of the 1777 campaign. Thoroughly disgusted, the new chief loaded a flock of loyalists and some Hessians whom he considered unreliable onto the only available transport vessels, and he prepared to march the rest of his force across New Jersey to New York. Clinton's army of 10,000 set out from Philadelphia on June 18.

Now able to vacate Valley Forge once and for all, Washington immediately took up the pursuit. Still leery of confronting the redcoats in a full-scale general engagement, even though officers like Lafayette, Greene, and Wayne viewed the Continentals as now up to it, the commander chose to peck away at Clinton's flanks. Confusing the whole issue was General Charles Lee, who had recently been exchanged after more than a year as a British prisoner in New York. At first, Lee argued against bringing on a major battle; then, when Washington assigned his advanced units to Lafayette, Lee took the matter as a personal insult, since he outranked the Frenchman and was second in command. Washington yielded. Next, Lee, not coordinating the movements of the regiments under him, bore in early on June 28 on the rear guard of the enemy at Monmouth Court House. He hoped to catch Clinton's troops off guard. The British commander, however, was prepared, wheeled his forward elements about, and stood for the fight with 6,000 men. Lee retreated.

Although Lee had marched into more trouble than anyone could have predicted, Washington was enraged when he discovered the retreat. When he moved forward with the rest of the army on what was an excessively hot and humid day (numbers of soldiers on each side perished of heat prostration), the commander angrily admonished Lee for his behavior. Then Washington took personal charge and rallied the army. As Lafayette described the scene, the Virginian rode "along the lines amid the shouts of the soldiers, cheering them by his voice and example and restoring to our standard the fortunes of the fight." Effectively, the commander in chief built a new line which fought off a grueling series of British thrusts before darkness ended the Monmouth engagement. Clinton, whose army lost 251 killed plus 170 wounded, as well as 600 Hessians who deserted, slipped away toward New York that night, leaving the field of combat to the Continentals, who claimed victory on that basis, despite 267 casualties and 95 missing in action. Once safely ensconced in New York, the British command scoffed at American claims, arguing that they had safely evacuated their army from the middle of enemy territory. Both sides had a case; and Willard Wallace's comment in *Appeal to Arms* (1951) that, if there ever was a draw in battle, "Monmouth was it," certainly summarizes the tactical result.[10]

However inconclusive tactically, Monmouth did pull together a number of threads. Often, the engagement has been depicted as the "coming of age" of the Continental soldier, the point in time when American regulars had traded volley for volley with the best troops Europe had—and held their own. There is no doubt that Steuben's rigorous drill program had begun to take effect. Only manpower handicaps in the months ahead would hold Washington from pressing a general engagement against Clinton's New York base. What is ironic is that Washington could not take advantage of the new circumstances before him, as reflected in Britain's strategy of concentrating on defensible enclaves, even though the army that he now had was up to European standards as a fighting machine. Manpower shortages kept him in his Fabian posture, and that served to lengthen a war that, with France's formal entry, had become almost impossible for the British to win.

On still another dimension, the Battle of Monmouth forced a showdown between Washington and Charles Lee, a man who had once thought of himself as timber to head the army. After the battle, Lee demanded a court martial to clear himself of insinuations that his retreat had cost the rebels a sweeping victory. The panel of officers, heavily influenced by members of Washington's family such as Alexander Hamilton, convicted the former British officer of disobeying orders to attack, of unnecessarily retreating, and of being disrespectful to the commander in chief. Whether the first two charges were just remains a point of heated debate. But as John Shy has reminded us, to have found Lee guilty of disrespect alone would have constituted "a vote of no-confidence in Washington."[11]

Only a few months had intervened since the alleged Conway Cabal. To have treated Lee with leniency might have invited a continuation of needless turmoil in the highest echelon of rebel leadership. The panel of officers thus suspended this brilliant but irascible man from command for a year; and when Congress confirmed the sentence, Lee replied with a string of insults, which resulted in the decision to drop him permanently from the army's rolls. With Lee gone (and Gates neutralized), Washington's firm control was even more complete. The two British professional officers who could have rivaled him for his command had been blocked or eliminated.

Lee's predicament reflected the fact that, while a British prisoner, he had not been able to keep up with fundamental policy decisions on how to conduct the war. When he returned to Valley Forge before his downfall at Monmouth, he still strongly advocated the maintenance of a "republican army." His writings, some of which were made public at the time, clearly contradicted Washington's new modeling course. Lee still advocated a "popular war of mass resistance," as John Shy has described it, "based on military service as an obligation of citizenship."[12] He still argued against any form of a standing army as a fundamental threat to liberty; he certainly did not approve of Steuben's effort to train the Continentals on the "European plan." As Lee warned everyone, "when the soldiers of a community are volunteers [regulars], war becomes a distinct profession. The arms of a Republic get into the hands of its worst members." Yet his pious warnings had a hollow sound in 1778. Washington and his advisors, along with Congress, had followed the path of expediency to maintain an army in the field. Lee's ideas now seemed hopelessly quaint, throwbacks to the *rage militaire* of 1775. He appeared to be completely out of step. Inside the military, he was the last important critic of the Europeanized Continental line. This, too, made him expendable. With Lee's demise, a primary voice of dissent was now gone, which assured that new modeling would virtually have no important critics inside the military establishment as the war continued.

With the British back in New York and beginning to transfer some of their forces to points outside North America, warfare between the two armies in the North became less intense. Clinton continued the well-worn tradition of his predecessor in exhorting the home government to send him more troops (which it could do only with great difficulty but with no net gain in available manpower). Washington dreamed and planned for an all-out assault on New York. Yet the dream remained unfulfilled. All he could do was to nibble at the edges, go into winter camp, and hope for additional manpower the following spring. The Continental army spent a relatively mild winter dispersed around Middlebrook, New Jersey, in 1778–1779, before the one that was so debilitating at Morristown during 1779–1780.

Clinton's forces occasionally fought limited engagements in the southern Hudson Highlands and New Jersey. After the British had taken Stony Point overlooking the Hudson River in 1779, for example, the Americans countered on July 15 with a light infantry raid under Anthony Wayne. The Americans recaptured Stony Point in a well-orchestrated bayonet assault, reminiscent of the Paoli massacre of 1777. The one effect of this turnabout was to deter Clinton from pursuing any campaign in New Jersey against the main Continental army. In June 1780, nearly a year later, the British half-heartedly attempted to carry the war into New Jersey, but American forces turned them back at Connecticut Farms (June 6) and Springfield (June 23). Such sporadic fighting was in complete contrast to the massive British efforts of 1776 and 1777. Yet by 1780 the North ministry and Clinton were attempting to implement a different strategic plan, this time focused on the South.

Washington kept hoping for a concentrated allied campaign effort. The semblance of such an effort took place in Rhode Island during the summer of 1778, directed against royal forces controlling Newport as a land/naval base. However, the joint foray turned into a farce when the French commander, Count d'Estaing, pulled out of the land battle for a potential sea engagement against Admiral Richard Lord Howe. General John Sullivan, who had a history of being caught short in the midst of engagements, had no choice but to retreat from an overextended position, the full impact of which was a healthy round of recriminations among the new allies. The Rhode Island fiasco did not augur well for future joint ventures, even if the French should again offer the extra balance in manpower that Washington so desperately needed.

The British retreat of 1778, followed by the inactive northern campaigns of 1779 and 1780, did not mean that Clinton was more faint-hearted than his predecessors. The British dispersal of manpower, made necessary by so many new threats brought on by global war, effectively changed the primary theater of action in North America. The British ministry, as Russell F. Weigley has pointed out in *The American Way of War* (1973), "decided to exploit their control of the sea to a greater extent than they had previously done and to send expeditions to the South."[13] The idea of the emerging southern strategy was to rally the loyalist population, which the ministry had assumed (somewhat incorrectly) was far more numerous in the South, and to pacify the whole population of that region in piecemeal fashion with a small regular army acting in concert with large bands of partisan loyalists.

While Weigley has called it "a strategy of partisan war," [14] Piers Mackesy has gone further and referred to this new approach as amounting to "a fledgling theory of counterrevolutionary warfare," characterized by two objectives: the desire "to restore civil government in one province and thereby demonstrate that royal institutions were not irrevocably destroyed"; and the hope of "deal [ing] with the militia problem by a methodical plan of counterinsurgency based on the raising of Loyalist militia and special forces." The effect would be to "reverse the institutional revolution which had preceded the war" by crushing rebel militia and reinstituting long-since fallen royal governments. [15] The expectation was that, through attrition, one area after another would once again accept British allegiance. Then the South, in time, could become a vast staging area for yet another campaign devoted to subduing the North.

The southern strategy, with loyalists playing the vital part of manpower substitutes for British regulars, began on a highly successful note in November 1778 when 3,500 troops sailed from New York. Their target was Savannah, Georgia. Joined by loyalist partisans in the vicinity, this expeditionary force quickly subdued the least populous of the American provinces and, indeed, brought a return of royalist rule in one of the 13 rebel states. Suddenly, as 1779 dawned, the war had taken on a dramatic new dimension.

GROWING INTERNAL DIVISION: ARMY AND SOCIETY

While the war turned into a virtual stalemate in the North, the significant pattern of civil-military tensions became increasingly clear. The winter at Valley Forge had convinced both foot soldier and officer alike that they would get little more from republican society than they demanded—and quite often forcibly took for themselves. In the collective mind of the army, the civilian population was simply not doing an adequate job in providing food, clothing, and regular pay. With increasing vehemence, both groups protested in dismay and anger. That officers and soldiers did not work in unison and protest together may have saved the American cause from some form of military autocracy in the end. If they had found the means to express their grievances in concert, possibly representative republicanism would not have characterized the final political settlement of the American Revolution.

Officers and rank-and-file regulars did have one point in common: they resented civilian behavior toward the cause and the army. In particular, the officers objected vociferously to civilians being seduced by wartime prosperity and consequent luxury. In 1780, one irate officer spoke out sharply: "It really gives me pain to think of our public affairs; where is the public spirit of the year 1775? Where are those flaming *patriots* who were ready to sacrifice their lives, their fortunes, their all, for the public?" A New Jersey officer had answered that question in 1779 when he explained that it was "truly mortifying to the virtuous soldier" to see civilians "sauntering in idleness and luxury" while they "despise our poverty and laugh at our distress." The problem was "the cruel and ungrateful disposition of the people" who withheld "from the army even the praise and glory justly due to their merit and services." Self-serving citizens, expostulated Major General Alexander McDougall in 1779, always seemed to "expect Spartan Virtue" from the army while they were "wallowing in all the luxury of Rome in her declining State."

Repeatedly, the officers voiced their disgust in such ominous terms. It particularly rankled them, as gentlemen of means before the war, that some civilians were profiteering at their expense and becoming rich while they were dissipating their personal fortunes. In their kindled anger, they remembered that some congressmen had accused them of "extorting" pensions from the central government. They did not forget the seven-year limitation, which they considered an insult to men of virtue who had demonstrated over and over their willingness to give their all. They would come back to the pension issue time and time again, treating it as a specific measure of the country's appreciation—or lack of it. Before it was all over, their disgust brought the republic to the brink of a military coup d'etat. However, that extreme action developed only when the officers thought themselves desperate, a point that they did not reach in the two years following Valley Forge.

As for rank-and-file soldiers with their modest dreams of postwar prosperity, protest over their sorry plight generally took less extreme, although no less debilitating, forms. Common soldiers practiced the art of defiance through such diverse and common practices as swearing, heavy drinking, looting, deserting, and bounty jumping. At the root of such protest was a sense of civilian disregard for them as human beings. Socially, patriot Americans preferred to keep the regulars at a respectable distance, largely because they were contemptuous of their lower-class origins. Civilians often ridiculed them as troublemakers, drunkards, and mere hirelings. They were the "lesser sort" and, as such, should be happy with next to nothing. After all, that was what they had had before entering the army. James Warren of Massachusetts summarized the perceptions of "respectable" citizens best when he described Washington's troops as "the most undisciplined, profligate Crew that were ever collected" to fight a war. Private Joseph Plumb Martin stated it from a different angle. He noted that when he asked for shelter in patriot homes "wet to the skin and almost dead with cold, hunger, and fatigue," he "experienced" both "scornful looks and hard words."

Too often, scholars have categorized behavior best understood as protest in terms of "time-honored military vices," to use the words of Charles Royster. This type of interpretation has the effect of reducing, if not losing, the impact of what the troops were saying (individually and collectively) about their sense of betrayal in the cause. In fact, it has been common for writers to describe acts of protest as anything but that, since that should impact negatively upon the persistent interpretive illusion of consensus and unity in the patriot war effort. Rather, many historians have thought, as Royster has written, that camp discipline violated "the American soldiers' sense of personal freedom" derived from so much personal liberty in civilian life before enlistment.[16] Whether the down and outers in Washington's ranks ever enjoyed much freedom before direct participation in the war is open to serious question, since it is a well-established point that the poor and indigent groups of late colonial America had little political or economic voice in expressing their public feelings or controlling their personal lives.

Although some acts of defiance may have been in reaction to the travail of camp life or the cruelty of particular officers, much of it boiled down to reactions against the lack of popular support, as manifested in rotted clothing, rancid food, and long arrearages in pay. With their swearing, the soldiery seemed to know that they could upset straight-laced civilians who worried about public morality in the republic, but who did not come out for the fight. Heavy drinking, commonly referred to as "barrel fever" among the soldiers, was a common practice among all Americans and all armies of the eighteenth century. However, in the army it was also a defensive weapon. One general, for example, bitterly complained that many soldiers regularly made it "a practice of getting drunk. . .once a Day and thereby render themselves unfit for duty." By doing so, they were only giving back what they had received—a broken promise. Drinking to excess, when they could get supplied by sutlers on the edges of camps, allowed them to avoid duty that so many civilians had come to assume was the rightful calling of the "poorer sort," despite ideological pronouncements about the obligations of citizenship. It allowed individual soldiers to protest against niggardly levels of support by not being in an effective condition for service, to avoid sacrifice when they alone were expected to carry the burdens of war.

Whether drunkenness, looting, or some other form of defiance, much of it had an individualized character. Only in time did individual protest take on a decidedly group-oriented quality, ultimately involving larger-scale mutinies. Protest rarely resulted in wanton violence against civilians, such as rape or murder. Rather, common soldiers focused on slapping back at the cause or, in some cases, on property seizures and destruction. Their acts of defiance, whether individual or collective, most often varied in number and intensity according to when the army had been supplied and paid. The fewer and more rotten the supplies and the longer the period they remained unpaid, the greater was the likelihood of high levels of individual and group protest.

Beginning with the New York campaign of 1776, when supplies first became a nightmarish problem, common soldier protest started to climb. A Continental sergeant in New York during that campaign described how he and his comrades foraged illegally. Desperate for food, they "liberated" some geese belonging to a local farmer and devoured them "Hearty in the Cause of Liberty of taking what Came to their hand." Next "a sheep and two fat turkeys" approached the men, but "not being able to give the countersign," they were taken prisoner, "tried by fire," and executed for sustenance "by the whole Division of free Booters." When army looting of civilian property continued its unabated course in 1777, Washington threatened severe penalties and emphasized that the army's "business" was "to give protection, and support, to the poor, distressed inhabitants, not to multiply and increase their calamities."

Yet Washington's pleas had little impact. Acts of looting continued unabated as the war dragged on. Incident after incident kept the commander in chief and his staff buried in a daily deluge of civilian complaints. Court martials made almost no dent in such activity. The threat of 100 lashes could not stop hungry and angry soldiers from looting, especially when the victims did not seem to be living up to their republican obligations. In 1780 and 1781, Washington was still issuing pleas and threats but to little avail. Not even an occasional hanging for plundering deterred the defiant soldiery.

The pattern of desertion as a form of protest was somewhat different, complicated by what sociologists and psychologists describe as the phenomenon of "unit cohesion." While it is true that soldiers deserted regularly when food and clothing were short or nonexistent, such as at Valley Forge, primary group identification and cohesion increasingly militated against extraordinarily high desertion rates among Continental regulars. Edward A. Shils, Morris Janowitz, and Samuel A. Stouffer, who studied cohesion among troops in World War II, discovered an important prerequisite for keeping men effectively involved in their duties. It was the "primary group"—the squad, platoon, or company—that nurtured cohesiveness.[17] Specifically, soldiers came to know, trust, and depend on one another. When a web of interrelationships and mutual feelings had been established in a unit, the men were much less likely to desert, despite the adversity of conditions.

So it seems to have been with the Continentals. Thad W. Tate discovered that, in the New York, Maryland, and North Carolina lines, about 50 percent of all desertions occurred within six months of enlistment,[18] and a Delaware company, as another example, experienced a loss of almost a third of its strength within a few days of its formation. Mark E. Lender, in studying desertion rates among Jersey Continentals, found that the rate fell off dramatically through time. In 1777, at least 42 percent deserted; in 1778, 21 percent; in 1779, 10 percent; in 1780, 10 percent.[19] Although it is true that the amount of combat dropped significantly in the North after 1778, the supply situation was as bad if not worse, and pay came ever more infrequently and in increasingly inflated Continental dollars. Unit cohesion thus seems to explain in large part why more soldiers did not strike back through desertion. Another important reason was that by 1779 and 1780 some of these cohesive units were on the verge of resorting to collective protest through mutinies.

The study of these patterns also confirms findings about the makeup of the rank and file. Analysis of the desertion phenomenon does not support the proposition of an embattled farmers' army after 1776. If the Continentals had been freehold farmers, the expectation would be that desertions would have peaked in the fall just before harvest time and that soldiers would not have reappeared or reenlisted until after the spring planting. According to data now available, the bulk of enlistments came in winter (as did desertions) after harvesting but before planting time. Fifty-eight percent of all New Jersey desertions occurred between December 1 and April 30, which were also the prime enlistment months. Stated differently, over 40 percent of all New Jersey desertions took place within three months of enlistment; and over 64 percent within the first six months. Group cohesion, rather than the desire to return to field, hearth, and family (which so many of the post-1776 Continentals could not claim as part of their lives) best explains the varying desertion rates.

Indeed, desertion dropped in importance through time as a form of rank-and-file protest. In 1780, the secretary of the Continental Congress, Charles Thomson, stated with pleasure that desertions were now "comparatively few." What it all amounted to was that the first few months of service were those in which the poor and downtrodden asked themselves whether vague promises of a better life in postwar America were worth the immediate sacrifice and possible death. Many concluded that such an equation was unfairly loaded against them. Since they had little evidence that they could trust the civilian population and the promises of its leaders, they chose defiance through desertion. Group cohesion, in turn, helped to sustain those who made the adjustment to camp life and served to ameliorate the pain of suffering through a long war for the remote chance of greater freedom and prosperity. For those who stayed and became part of Washington's hard core of cohesive regulars, looting, not desertion, was the most widely practiced (and often very necessary) form of protest.

Still another group protested as individuals through bounty jumping. As Washington once mused, it was "a kind of business" among some soldiers. The procedure was simple: enlist, receive a bounty, desert; enlist somewhere else for another bounty, and desert again. Provided the jumper showed some imagination and did not reappear in regiments where he might be recognized, it was a relatively safe activity. John Welch of the Fourth New Jersey regiment, for instance, enlisted in April 1777, deserted in May, and reenlisted in August. He deserted again in September 1778 and joined yet another time in January

1779, never being caught. Others were not always so fortunate. In August 1778, Private Elijah Walker recorded the execution of a remarkably enterprising bounty jumper who had repeatedly enlisted and deserted for seven separate bounties before a firing squad ended his career.

The most extreme form of individual protest was desertion to the enemy. Benjamin Quakenbush of the Third New York regiment, for instance, was caught in the act of going over and "Sentenced to run the Gauntlet through the Brigade twice with fixed Bayonets at his Breast to regulate his pace." That he was not shot perhaps reflected upon the desperate manpower situation. Extreme pain, not death, was the desirable standard of punishment in cases of desertion, looting, and bounty jumping. The hope was that such troops would recover, so that they would be available for future campaigning. As Mark E. Lender has summarized it, "the execution of all recovered deserters would have wiped out a sizable portion of the army," and "excessive severity would have discouraged enlistments."[20]

While officers and the rank and file alike increasingly prided themselves on their competency as soldiers, felt mounting alienation toward civilian society, and protested against lack of patriot support for their army, they almost never expressed defiance in concert. Part of the reason lay in the social gulf separating the two groups. As befit the deferential character of their times as well as concern for military hierarchy, officers, generally drawn from the ranks of the "better sort," expected obedience from the down and outers in the ranks. Their enthusiasm for the Revolution did not extend to social leveling. Indeed, many of them feared that the Revolution might get out of hand and lead to real internal socioeconomic upheaval, especially in the form of widespread property redistribution, if the "common herd" gained too much influence and authority, whether legally or extralegally. In particular, the officers around Washington assumed that it was their duty to administer harsh discipline to deserters, looters, bounty jumpers, and troublemakers in general. They basically supported Washington's desire to set the legal limit for lashes at 500. And many often sanctioned whippings of more than 100 lashes, despite the Articles of War of 1776. As an example, the officers took with relish to Washington's general orders at Morristown in 1780 which allowed them to inflict 100 to 500 lashes instantly on plunderers; and it also became possible to assign up to 50 stripes on the spot, even before court martials occurred. Their concern with the protection of property and societal stability, just as much as the need for good order in the military hierarchy, kept Washington's officers from working with the soldiery when protesting against what they viewed as society's lack of concern and support for the army.

By late 1779, a fundamental question had to do with whether some issue would provoke a sense of commonality of purpose and unity among officers and regulars. If that did happen, the army in its bitterness held the potential to become an awesome threat to the very cause that it was upholding and defending. Equally important, a critical question had to do with whether Washington and Congress, bolstered by the alliance with France, could find some means to win the war and gain acceptable peace terms before some form of internal holocaust, as perpetrated by an army increasingly alienated toward society, occurred. Such perplexing dilemmas would never have existed had the war effort been receiving the united support of what has too often been described as a united and fully committed Revolutionary populace.

NOTES

[1] John B. B. Trussell, *Birthplace of an Army: A Study of Valley Forge* (Harrisburg, Pa., 1976), pp. 33–35.

[2] Charles Royster, *A Revolutionary People at War: The Continental Army and the American Character, 1775–1783* (Chapel Hill, N.C., 1980), p. 88.

[3] Richard H. Kohn, "American Generals of the Revolution: Subordination and Restraint," in Don Higginbotham, ed., *Reconsiderations of the Revolutionary War: Selected Essays* (Westport, Conn., 1978), p. 109.

[4] Mark E. Lender, "The Enlisted Line: The Continental Soldiers of New Jersey," (Ph.D. dissertation, Rutgers University, 1975), pp. 127–34. *See also* Len-

der, "The Social Structure of the New Jersey Brigade: The Continental Line as an American Standing Army," in Peter Karsten, ed., *The Military in America: From the Colonial Era to the Present* (New York, 1980), pp. 29–34.

⁵ Kohn, "American Generals," in Higginbotham, ed., *Reconsiderations,* pp. 119–20. Kohn compared his data with the findings in James Kirby Martin, *Men in Rebellion: Higher Governmental Leaders and the Coming of the American Revolution* (New Brunswick, N.J., 1973), *passim.*

⁶ John Todd White, "Standing Armies in Time of War: Republican Theory and Military Practice during the American Revolution," (Ph.D. dissertation, George Washington University, 1978), p. 279.

⁷ Bernhard Knollenberg, *Washington and the Revolution, A Reappraisal; Gates, Conway, and the Continental Congress* (New York, 1940), *passim.*

⁸ White, "Standing Armies," p. 272.

⁹ Piers Mackesy, *The War for America, 1775-1783* (Cambridge, Mass., 1965), p. 183.

¹⁰ Willard M. Wallace, *Appeal to Arms: A Military History of the American Revolution* (New York, 1951), p. 190.

¹¹ John Shy, "American Strategy: Charles Lee and the Radical Alternative," in *A People Numerous and Armed: Reflections on the Military Struggle for American Independence* (New York, 1976), p. 159.

¹² *Ibid.,* p. 161.

¹³ Russell F. Weigley, *The American Way of War: A History of United States Military Strategy and Policy* (New York, 1973), p. 25.

¹⁴ *Ibid.,* pp. 18–39. This is the title of Weigley's chapter.

¹⁵ Piers Mackesy, "The Redcoat Revived," in W. M. Fowler, Jr. and Wallace Coyle, eds., *The American Revolution: Changing Perspectives* (Boston, 1979), pp. 182–83.

¹⁶ Royster, *Revolutionary People at War,* pp. 70–71.

¹⁷ Edward A. Shils and Morris Janowitz, "Cohesion and Disintegration in the *Wehrmacht* in World War II," *Public Opinion Quarterly,* 12 (1948), pp. 280–315; Samuel A. Stouffer, *et. al., The American Soldier: Adjustment during Army Life,* in Studies in Social Psychology in World War II, 4 vols. (Princeton, N.J., 1949) 1:106–30.

¹⁸ Thad W. Tate, "Desertion from the American Revolutionary Army," (M.A. thesis, University of North Carolina, 1948), *passim.*

¹⁹ Lender, "The Enlisted Line," pp. 203–34. *See also* Robert Middlekauff, "Why Men Fought in the American Revolution," *Huntington Library Quarterly,* 43 (1980), pp. 144–48.

²⁰ Lender, "The Enlisted Line," p. 217.

FIVE

Moral Defeat and Military Turnabout, 1779-1781

DISPERSED WARFARE

While the pace of active campaigning slackened considerably in the North after 1778, it did not let up elsewhere. As already noted, the British launched a major southern offensive before the end of 1778 in retaking Georgia. That effort expanded greatly in 1780 with Sir Henry Clinton's large-scale invasion of

South Carolina. Similarly, combined British/Indian pressures on the frontier resulted in a series of American reactions—most dramatically with George Rogers Clark's invasion of the Illinois country in 1778 and then with General John Sullivan's expedition against the Six Nations of New York during 1779. The war at sea, furthermore, especially with respect to patriot involvement, took on far more significant proportions, largely because of the impact of French involvement. All three of these phases would, in time, affect the final stages of the War for Independence and the level of pressure building in England for a cessation of hostilities and a final peace settlement.

There is no convenient way to summarize warfare west of patriot settlement lines. It represented an endless series of local skirmishes, most often characterized by bloody raids in which acts of human butchery prevailed. Both sides actively contended for Indian support because the most powerful tribes, as Don Higginbotham has observed, "were in a position to influence the balance of power in the hinterland."[1] By and large, the Indian nations, when they did not attempt neutrality, linked arms with the British, who did not represent so direct a threat to tribal lands. British officials, moreover, had an established record of trying to circumscribe white aggression on frontier lands, dating back to the 1760s, and they still had an effective Indian agent network left over from the recent colonial past.

Directly influencing powerful tribes in the Great Lakes region, for example, were Crown officers at the trading post and fortress of Detroit. There Henry Hamilton, a lieutenant governor under the Quebec government, held forth as the Indians' friend. Contemporaries referred to him in disgust as the Hair Buyer. Indeed, Hamilton had been ordered by his superiors to arouse the Indians and to employ them in harassing patriot settlers in Kentucky and Western Virginia. Warriors, seeking scalp bounties, struck with fury and vengeance. Even though historians disagree about how much Hamilton encouraged this butchery, Detroit did an active business in human hair. Hamilton claimed that he admonished his Indian allies against the slaughter of innocent women and children, but his putative pleas dissuaded few warriors. After all, they clearly understood, given the history of white aggression, that they were fighting for their survival as independent peoples. It should also be pointed out that the white record of systematic brutality toward Indians was less than humane.

By 1778, the Virginians had had enough of Hamilton, the Hair Buyer. There was no prospect of relief from the Continental army, which with its constrained manpower could do little to protect settlements on the periphery of the war. Governor Patrick Henry called upon the physically imposing George Rogers Clark, who had been pressing for the assignment. A red-haired 25-year-old of rugged countenance and brash determination, Clark believed that exposed frontier regions like Kentucky could be protected if Virginia irregulars gained control of the Illinois-Indiana country. Thus began his legendary western adventures. With no more than 175 men, Clark headed for French settlements at Kaskaskia, Cahokia, and Vincennes. There his small army convinced the settlers to accept Virginia authority (news of the French alliance was a powerful aid) and threatened local Indians into submission, who also seemed to believe his stories that the British were just waiting for an opportunity to tax them.

Clark's daring venture stirred Hamilton from his lair in Detroit. The Hair Buyer moved south with 235 followers, including 70 Indians and 130 Frenchmen, in October 1778. Hamilton attacked Vincennes, easily overwhelming a small detachment of Virginians there, and reasserted royal authority. He also settled in for the winter season, waiting for the spring thaw before moving against Clark's main force at Kaskaskia. Meanwhile, the Virginian seized the initiative. Hastily assembling a band of 172 men, he moved out in the first week of February 1779. Torrential winter rains flooded the 180-mile path, which included four swollen river crossings. Food became scarce and actually ran out for two days at one critical point. When it was not raining on the irregulars, sharp blasts of cold nearly froze the band in its tracks. Overcoming enormous adversity (in a fashion reminiscent of Arnold's march to Quebec), Clark's party approached Vincennes on February 23. Warning local French inhabitants to stay out of the way, Clark besieged the small fortress controlled by Hamilton. When the Lieutenant Governor refused to surrender, Clark brought forward some Indians who had been recently captured. When taken, they had had white scalps tied to their belts. In full view of the fortress, Clark's men held down four of the Indians, "tomahawked them" to death, as one soldier wrote, and "threw them into the river." Sensing the helplessness of his position, Hamilton surrendered.

Clark sent the Hair Buyer to Virginia where he languished in prison for several months before being exchanged. Furthermore, the red-haired adventurer whom the Indians called Long Knife, persisted in his western campaigning, claiming all lands before him in the name of Virginia. It was beyond the ability of his small irregular force, however, to gain full control of a region of such territorial magnitude. Clark's Rangers did help to hold down the number of damaging Indian raids after 1778, and their exploits did serve to lend credence to American claims to the "Old Northwest" region when peace negotiations began in 1782. But to argue for more on behalf of Clark and his guerilla bands would be stretching the point, especially since the British (with their Indian allies) regained firm *de facto* control of the territory north of the Ohio River after the war and held it well into the 1790s.

Of more immediate effect was John Sullivan's Continental expedition of 1779 against the Iroquois. While some in the powerful Six Nations Confederacy sought neutrality, many warriors did not. For those who allied with the British, Fort Niagara was the staging area for their devastating raids, quite often led by Major John Butler, his son Walter, and their following of loyalist Rangers. Butler's band represented former civilians who had resided west of Albany and had been caught up in the furious partisan clashes that enveloped the New York frontier after 1775. Also aligning with the Rangers were many Iroquois, who quite often operated under the Mohawk chief, Thayendanegea.

He was better known as Joseph Brant, a man of immense sagacity and humanity who had received a formal education in Connecticut before the war.

During 1778, the followers of the Butlers and Brant devastated the Pennsylvania and New York frontiers. In early July they fell on white settlers in the Wyoming Valley of north-central Pennsylvania. Foolishly, the local militia numbering 360 (against 110 loyalists and more than 450 Indians) ventured beyond the protection of the local stockade. In what proved to be one of the worst scenes of frontier carnage, the Rangers and Indians exterminated them. Reputedly, one Indian woman ordered a number of captured militiamen to be arranged in a large circle; while she chanted and danced, she ruthlessly decapitated all twelve. Other whites died by roasting on a spit or by fire at the stake. For the local settlers, it was nothing short of a holocaust.

Other incidents, although not so dramatic in numbers, continued throughout the summer and well into the fall. In early November, the season of atrocities culminated with the Cherry Valley massacre in the Mohawk Valley region. When resisters in that community refused to surrender, Butler ordered the indiscriminate slaughter of 32 men, women, and children—over the vigorous protests of Chief Brant. It had been a gruesome year for frontier warfare, and the patriots had taken the worst of it.

As 1779 dawned, the distresses of so many backcountry inhabitants led Congress to instruct General Washington to put together a punitive expedition. The goal was to secure the Pennsylvania-New York frontier from further Indian/loyalist depradations. John Sullivan, the man of ill-luck at Brandywine Creek and the Rhode Island campaign of 1778, accepted the assignment. Nearly 3,000 Continental soldiers began gathering at Easton, Pennsylvania, during May. Then they marched into the backcountry, hacking out a road as they moved toward the Wyoming Valley. In July they turned north, pointing them straight toward the heart of Iroquois country. At Newtown (Elmira), New York, Indians under Brant, with backup support from Butler's Rangers, chose to make a concentrated stand. Sullivan prepared carefully for the battle that came on August 29. Softening up the Newtown defenders with cannon fire and "a pleasing piece of [regimental] music" which the Indians could not "be prevailed upon to listen to," Sullivan's troops, noted one participant, mowed right through the defenders, who kept "firing and retreating to another tree, loading and firing again, still keeping up the war-whoop." Neither side suffered significant casualties, but the Indian/loyalist party accepted retreat instead of extinction.

The victory at Newtown opened up the Indian settlements to Sullivan's expeditionary force. For the next month, the Continentals burned and destroyed villages and crops wherever they could find them. At least 41 Indian towns were ransacked and leveled. A New Jersey lieutenant, William Barton, wanted some remembrance from so much adventure. Discovering some dead Indians, his men "skinned two of them from their hips down for boot legs, one pair for the major, the other for myself." As for the Indians, one group fell upon a scouting party under Lieutenant Thomas Boyd. They butchered them. Boyd and one of his riflemen were completely mutilated. When the main army found them, their remains had been "stripped naked and their heads cut off, and the flesh of Lieutenant Boyd's head was entirely taken off and his eyes punched out." The commentator also pointed out that the two slain Continentals were "immediately buried with the honor of war."

As these examples suggest, there was no escaping the harsh brutality of frontier war, nor was it just a product of what too often has been described as the "ignoble savagism" of the Indians. Bernard Sheehan, a modern student of the subject, has pointed out that frontier whites were just as savage as the Indians. While "indiscriminate murder, scalping, torture, the taking of prisoners for adoption. . .struck white men as the very antithesis of civilized behavior," frontiersmen, Sheehan has stressed, practiced the same. Sheehan argues correctly that "the irony" of war beyond the established settlements "lay in the apparent determination of the white man to draw the sharpest distinction between civilization and savagery and at the same time to conquer the Indian by becoming more like him."[2]

While the brutality was a shared characteristic of both sides, its overall impact was to weaken further Indian resistance to white aggression on tribal lands. Sullivan's raid, for instance, forced hundreds of Iroquois warriors and their families to become wholly dependent on the British during the winter of 1779-1780. The supplies at Fort Niagara, however, were inadequate, and great numbers of once-proud Iroquois starved to death before spring. After 1779, loyalist Rangers and Indian allies seemed to lack the strength to terrorize the Pennsylvania-New York frontier. Indeed, historians have argued that the Six Nations never really recovered from Sullivan's expedition. Active support of the royal standard became an excuse after the war for clearing the New York frontier of the Indian host. With that, the prospect of enduring in ancient tribal homes was gone.

PATRIOT NAVAL EXPLOITS

The adventures of George Rogers Clark and John Sullivan gave cause for cheer among eastern patriots, even though the war in the main theater did not seem to be getting off dead center. At the same time, the exploits of the fledgling American navy was a source of some rejoicing. With trepidation, the Continental Congress ventured into naval affairs during the fall of 1775. John Adams was among the few enthusiasts who had grand visions for a respectable American fleet, especially in combating British vessels sent out to blockade the coastline and harass commercial carriers and port towns. Other delegates, however, feared the costs associated with a massive naval building program. On October 30, 1775, Congress partially side stepped the issue by establishing its navy committee (later called the marine committee). Within severe constraints, it authorized the committee to seek out and maintain armed vessels for defending the provinces. By January 1776, Congress had purchased eight ships and ordered the construction of 13 new frigates. (Frigates were smaller but normally faster and more maneuverable than ships of the line. The latter could carry as many as 120 guns and crews of up to 1,000; the former rarely contained more than 50 pieces of ordnance and 300 sailors.) Fearful of bankrupting the rebel cause, Congress gave support to what may fairly be described as a very modest naval program throughout the war.

The rapid appearance of various state navies, as well as privateersmen, also militated against the need for a large Continental navy. All told, combined state navies never had more than 40 boats at their disposal. By comparison, over 2,000 American privateering vessels entered the fray before 1783. Anyone with a ship who had secured a letter of marque from one of the states or Congress could join the privateering ranks and prey upon enemy commerce. Any prize coming from a captured and condemned vessel would be turned over to owner, captain, and crew, according to proportions of investment and crew rank on ship. Many privateers were able to make a fortune for owners during the war, so long as they were not run down by British war vessels trying to blockade the American coastline.

Privateering was nothing more than a form of legalized piracy in time of war, and its long and well-developed tradition served the American cause ably. Estimates vary as to how many enemy vessels, quite often carrying vital supplies to the British army, were taken. One figure credits American privateers with 600 prizes, with another 200 going to the American navy. On the other hand, David Syrett, in his revealing study of British transport activities, *Shipping and the American War, 1775–83* (1970), points out that 6,000 British vessels (including American-owned bottoms) were involved in overseas trade as of 1775. Of these, 3,386 fell into enemy hands, with 495 being recaptured and 507 ransomed back to original owners. Permanent seizures, which also would have come to involve French, Spanish, and Dutch maritime activity, amounted to 2,384 vessels.[3] If that number is accurate, total privateering and naval activity had a far more profound impact on Britain's long-distance supply problem than has usually been conceded, even if the British transport service held up well for most of the war.

Whatever the outer limits of vessels seized and condemned, privateering "thus throttled development of a navy" in Revolutionary America, as Howard H. Peckham has phrased it.[4] Also inhibiting the process were the many seamen who preferred privateering duty. For one thing, all prize money went to owners and crew, whereas Continental naval vessels had to turn over at least half the value of each condemned vessel to Congress. For another thing, discipline was generally less rigorous on privateering ships, even though American naval regulations (like the army's Articles of War) were not so harsh as European regulations, befitting a virtuous citizenry-in-arms. Floggings, the standard form of discipline, could run to as high as 1,000 lashes for British mariners; the American code permitted a maximum of 12 stripes, unless the crime was so severe that a formal court martial exacted a higher penalty—and then only with the approval of the naval commander in chief.

The gentlemen-sailors who commanded the American navy, beginning with phlegmatic Commodore Esek Hopkins of Rhode Island, did little to distinguish themselves or the cause of a strong navy, relative to the more aggressive privateersmen. Indeed, what claim to dash and élan the Continental navy earned has focused on boisterous and free-wheeling John Paul Jones, a man whom sailors considered a rigid disciplinarian but extraordinary seaman. Born John Paul in Scotland, the future "father of the American navy" went to sea at an early age and eventually took the surname of Jones to cover his identity after killing a mutinous sailor. Soon thereafter, he joined the Continental navy and, early in the war, took many cargo prizes along the Canadian coastline. Then, in early 1778, Jones showed up in France with the sloop of war *Ranger*. His timing was excellent, since the completion of the Franco-American alliance guaranteed American naval and privateering captains outfitting privileges in French ports. Even before this time, the American commissioners had been urging Congress to send patriot seamen across the Atlantic to harass British commercial carriers in the North Sea and Baltic areas—and even to raid enemy ports. Now guaranteed refitting privileges, Jones was about to earn infamy in his seagoing adventures around Britain.

In April 1778, Jones sailed north through the Irish Sea toward Scotland and raided the border port of Whitehaven, while attacking British merchant vessels along the way. In the heavy shadow of the French alliance, an intrepid patriot seaman thus had carried the war into the vitals of the parent state. Indeed, Jones's raiding expedition served to help unnerve a civilian population heretofore isolated from the war. Such an act spurred a wave of antiwar protest in Britain. It also underscored the important harassing role that the American navy, however limited in vessel strength, could play. With the French accords, the allies could strike the extended British empire at almost any point, inflicting wounds anywhere from the Caribbean Sea to India. After 1778, the maneuverability of allied naval and privateering vessels made the dispersed military assignment of the British ministry a nightmarish task. Britain's critical advantage at sea was now in serious trouble, her dependence on the sea a real liability.

Jones's raid was fundamentally a symbolic warning of the plight confronting the British war machine. In 1779, the commander boldly issued a second manifesto. After his Irish Sea raids, Jones returned to France, dallied with a number of impressionable French belles, and sought a better vessel with which to carry on further seafaring activities. The French government finally turned over to him an old merchant hulk. Jones transformed it into a 42-gun man of war, calling it *Bon Homme Richard* in honor of Benjamin Franklin's almanac character "Poor Richard." On September 23, 1779, while sailing in the North Sea, the American commander engaged the Royal navy's well-armed (50 guns) frigate *Serapis* off Flamborough Head. It was one of the most memorable naval confrontations of the war. Jones's outgunned and outmanned ship eventually went down under withering fire, but not before his mariners had boarded *Serapis,* forced the crew to capitulate, and taken it as a prize.

Furthermore, *Serapis* had been seized within sight of England, some 3,000 miles from the rebel ken. Englishmen had every reason to be more nervous about the increasingly disheveled state of their military effort.

Bon Homme Richard against *Serapis* was a major capstone to American naval warfare, the type of warfare characterized by a numberless list of isolated, small-scale confrontations. These skirmishes on the high seas, especially after the French alliance, exacerbated the problems faced by Great Britain in its attempt to supply its armies and reconquer the North American continent. Moreover, the unremitting harassment provided by Continental, state, and privateering vessels made the Royal navy's blockade of the American coastline more paper thin. The Continental fleet was never large enough to become a threatening force, since Congress did not have the financial means to support a comprehensive naval program. That is just one more reason why the French allies were so important in buttressing the rebel cause. Along with critical manpower on land, the French provided essential naval strength, and it ultimately played a decisive, as opposed to a harassing, role in bringing the war to a successful resolution.

FINANCIAL MORASS ON THE HOME FRONT

Although committed rebels took pride in the exploits of John Paul Jones, George Rogers Clark, and John Sullivan's Continentals, they were also aware that the war effort did not seem to be heading anywhere. The lack of a resolution was one of many reasons why popular enthusiasm and regular army morale had reached rock bottom during 1779 and 1780. Internal divisions were also taking their toll and threatening to drain the last vital signs of life out of the cause. Youthful Alexander Hamilton, serving Washington as an aide-de-camp, suggested many of the debilitating problems when he spoke out in 1779 about "the rapid decay of our currency, . . . the want of harmony in our councils, the declining zeal of the people, [and] the distresses of the officers of the army." These were "symptoms of a most alarming nature," Hamilton fretted. If he had added the military success that the British were then enjoying in the South, his list of critical issues would have been fairly complete.

With each passing day in 1779 and 1780, hardened veterans in the Continental line seemed to become more discouraged. They were not thinking about the nearly impossible global dilemma that British strategists now faced. Rather, their comments focused on mounting alienation toward civilian republicans, especially those taking advantage of the cause. Joseph Plumb Martin may have best captured the sentiments of private soldiers when he reflected on 1780: "We. . .kept upon the parade in groups, venting our spleen at our country and government, then at our officers, and then at ourselves for our imbecility in staying there and starving in detail for an ungrateful people who did not care what became of us, so they could enjoy themselves while we were keeping a cruel enemy from them." Lieutenant Colonel Ebenezer Huntington was even more caustic. "I despise my countrymen," he wrote angrily in 1780. "I wish I could say I was not born in America. . . . The insults and neglects which the army have met with from the country beggars all description." It was Huntington's "cowardly countrymen," holding "their purse-strings as though they would damn the world rather than part with a dollar for their army," who were threatening everything—at the very time that public support for the cause should never have been stronger in the wake of the French alliance.

The dismay and chagrin of dedicated soldiers like Huntington and Martin reflected directly on the growing worthlessness of Continental currency, the primary medium of exchange with which Congress attempted to pay for the war. Beginning in 1775, the delegates, having no source of revenue but facing the hard financial costs of defending liberty, had started to issue paper currency, but without proper financial backing. With enthusiasm and moral commitment running high, the fiat Continental dollars held their face value quite well. Then in 1777, rampant inflation took over. An important source, besides slackened public confidence in the war effort, was that Congress, desperately trying to cover basic expenses, printed its currency at far too rapid a rate, literally glutting the marketplace. The states, which were supposed to be taxing the Continentals out of circulation to stabilize their market value, were not doing so. The states preferred to support the value of their own currencies in taxing their citizens.

From an initial issue of $2,000,000 in the summer of 1775, Congress by early 1779 had put in circulation a total of $191,000,000. It was one matter to ask the army and its suppliers to accept the currency when it was relatively scarce and holding its value. It was quite another to expect republican restraint when the annual salary of a captain would net little more than a pair of shoes. There can be no doubt that the sorry state of Continental finances, given the central government's inability to tax the populace, made it extraordinarily difficult to float a nondepreciating currency, improve the supply situation, or lure in new Continental recruits for that matter. H. James Henderson, in his *Party Politics in the Continental Congress* (1974), stated the matter well: "Congress, in the face of these problems, was not inactive; it was simply increasingly ineffective."[5]

The hyperinflating currency helped to shatter morale where it mattered most—in Washington's army, without which the rebellion would have suffered a fatal blow. Officers of the New Jersey line, for example, began petitioning their state legislature in 1778 asking for solutions to problems ranging from depreciated pay to sorely inadequate stocks of clothing, food, and equipment. In turn, the state insisted that these were Congressional concerns. In April 1779, the officers put more pressure on their legislature by demanding immediate relief. (They understood that Congress, dependent on the states, could not do much of anything.) Their remonstrance pointed out that pay "is now only *minimal,* not real," that "four months' pay of a private will not procure his wretched wife and children a single bushel of wheat. . . . Unless a speedy and ample remedy be provided," they warned the legislature, "the total dissolution of your troops is inevitable." They insisted on pay in specie—"Spanish milled dollars"—so officers and foot soldiers could provide for themselves and their immediate kin. When that occurred, their "complaints shall instantly cease."

It was a strongly worded petition, one that should have been taken seriously. Nothing happened, however, beyond a great deal of legislative windbaggery. Then on May 6, the First New Jersey regiment received orders to march to Easton, Pennsylvania, and bivouac with Sullivan's expeditionary force. The officers responded with a direct threat. In yet another petition to the legislature, they stated that they would resign their commissions *en masse* rather than break camp, unless someone chose to address their pay and supply problems. When Washington learned about these threats, he was "mortified and chagrined beyond expression." The officers had *"reasoned wrong about the means of obtaining a good end."* They had "hazarded a step which has an air of dictating terms to their country, by taking advantage of the necessity of the moment."

In their protest, that is exactly what these officers intended to do. It seemed to be the only way to get someone to pay attention to their grievances, no matter how threatening to the vitals of civil authority. The Jersey lawmakers perceived the implications. Republican purists among them preferred to see "the Brigade Disbanded [rather] than Submit to the appearance of being bullied." But the majority, believing that a fully independent, republican nation was impossible without regulars remaining in the field, rapidly worked toward an acceptable compromise. The solution came out as follows: first, the officers were to withdraw their petition. Second, the state would move to provide relief, "(to all appearance)" by its own volition. Third, the legislature would seek new clothing and immediately pay each officer £200 and each enlistee $40 as a bonus. More or less satisfied, the brigade left winter camp and marched toward Pennsylvania.

Washington summarized the short-term significance of this confrontation most clearly. For "notwithstanding the expedient adopted for a saving [of] appearance," the commander observed, "this cannot fail to operate as a bad precedent." Indeed, that turned out to be the case. With the deteriorating financial situation, individual acts of protest had begun to take on a group character. The hard-core Continentals, separately in the officer corps and in the ranks, had become more cohesive. Groups of officers and soldiers thus began threatening civilian authorities in government out of desperation over their circumstances. If officers and soldiers had learned to cooperate in their protest, they could very well have ripped the republic apart from the inside over the fundamental issue of civilian peculation and indifference. That they did not was more than a testament to their unstinting loyalty to the cause; it was as much a reflection of their well-developed contempt for one another.

When common soldiers employed the tactic of group defiance, civilians called it mutiny. When officers did the same, it earned such epithets as military "extortion" or "blackmail." The officer corps was particularly galled in 1778 that Congressional leaders treated their "request" for pensions as a form of extortion being exacted by so many threats of individual resignations. Damning words from Congress may have helped to spur the officers to raise the issue during 1779. Again they insisted that postwar pensions must be for lifetime rather than only for seven years. The delegates responded by telling them to take their case to their respective states. When Pennsylvania, Maryland, and Virginia responded positively, the corps went back to Congress again, demanding full equality in pensions for officers from states not so generous. Congress, in desperate financial straits, hemmed and hawed while officers refused to back down from their demand. In July 1780, they drew up their most threatening petition to date. Washington's comrades felt that they had needlessly been exposed "to the rapacity of almost every class of the community." If Congress did not promise half-pay pensions for life, they "should be obliged by necessity to quit the service." And if "ill consequences" should befall "their country, they [would] leave to the world to determine who ought to be responsible" for the collapse of the Revolution.

Here was another threat of significant proportions. The officers had made clear that they no longer intended to be whipsawed between a penniless Congress and niggardly state governments. "The officers believed," Charles Royster has written, "that they alone had maintained the *rage militaire* of 1775." They thought "that their virtue could save their country in spite of its people," and half-pay pensions would recognize their sacrifice.[6] Yet it was more than personal honor and public recognition that motivated them. As a group, they were in serious financial trouble, having lost personal income by participation in the war, a condition only worsened by the inflated state of Continental currency. Although Congress had attempted to refinance its currency in March 1780, the program was not going very well. The officers were in dead earnest. The question was whether Congress could respond effectively, given its dearth of resources. It also meant that some members of Congress would have to set aside ideological concerns and accept the pressure for what it was, rather than denigrating it by using slur words like blackmail.

Congress was virtually helpless. By 1780, it was functioning as little more than a front line representative of the states, and it was caught in the middle between the states and the soldiery. Most delegates wanted to act responsibly but lacked the constitutional authority to do so. The obvious weakness was the lack of taxation power and consequent inability to have permanent revenues with which to meet the most pressing needs of the republic. In 1779, for instance, the total amount of fiat Continental money in circulation reached $200,000,000. At this point the delegates stopped the printing press. Then, in March 1780, they endorsed the reevaluation of their paper currency at the ratio of 40 Continental dollars to one specie dollar. The states were to tax the old Continentals out of circulation as quickly as possible. In turn, they were to release the new currency, which was never to exceed a face value figure of $10,000,000. Its relative scarcity was to serve as the major hedge against hyperinflation.

The reevaluation scheme, so precise in theory, hardly functioned at all in reality. The fundamental problem was the states; they did not push to get the old Continental dollars out of circulation. Nor did they show much interest in getting the new money into the marketplace. Congress had to face the fact that it must operate with an all but worthless currency, depending on goodwill and foreign and domestic loans to continue to finance the war and thus appease the anger in the army. Besides the encouragement of mandatory price fixing plans, Congress was doing about all that it could. The states preferred to protect their own interests, leaving the central government almost powerless to deal with a financial morass. This only further fed the retributive wrath of Washington's officers and soldiers and widened the dangerous breach between the military and its civilian master.

Trapped between a restive army and uncooperative state officials, the central government appeared more and more as a long-winded debating society than an agency vigorously supporting the republican cause. Although Washington complained bitterly in late 1779 that "a wagon load of money will scarcely purchase a wagon of provision," he reflected just a few months later that "unless Congress speaks in a more decisive tone" or is "vested with powers by the several states competent to the great purposes of war, . . .our cause is lost." The states, however, were not prepared to hand over greater authority to the central government, when so many republican ideologues kept reminding everyone that the Revolution had resulted, in the first place, because power in the British empire had been too far removed from the people and had been abused by corrupted central government officials. Keeping authority close to the people, specifically in the state legislatures, was necessary for the protection of liberty, they repeatedly claimed. Such reasoning, however, eluded the officer corps during the darkest days of the war. Thus the question remained: Would they resign and leave republican purists and other noncombatants to their own devices in trying to combat the imperial foe?

THE WAR IN THE SOUTHERN STATES

Historians have rather uniformly agreed that the year 1780 represented the nadir of the war effort. The currency finance debacle and a resentful army were only two parts of the problem. Another important source of demoralization was the new British thrust into the South, which appeared to be virtually uncontainable during the summer and early fall of that year. Actually, British interest in retaking the South may be traced back to the fall of 1775. Royal governors in that region had vigorously insisted that the ministry should do everything possible to support a large and supposedly committed loyalist population. In fact, the home government sent out an expedition of regulars to link up with North Carolina loyalists. The royal forces arrived off of Cape Fear in early May 1776, but they had come far too late to be of assistance. At the Battle of Moore's Creek Bridge on February 27, local rebel irregulars had decimated those North Carolina loyalists attempting to rally around the royal standard.

Historian Clyde R. Ferguson has argued that such early rebel success in the South reflected well on "the preexisting colonial militia structure." Scholars such as John Shy, according to Ferguson, who have viewed the pre-Revolutionary militia system there as "degenerate" and "as little more than a social institution whose chief function was the control of slaves," have overstated their case. Indeed, militia activity after 1775 against loyalists and Indian nations such as the Cherokee, which Ferguson has described in terms of "irregular warfare or training for partisan war," resulted in effective rebel control before the southern region became a major theater of war. The work of militiamen as partisan fighters harassing those who were not fully committed to the cause, furthermore, would be an important element in making it extremely difficult for a conventional army to conquer that region when that thrust finally came.[7]

Sustained hit-and-run partisan action was yet to be demonstrated when Henry Clinton, the general in charge of the Cape

Fear expedition, sought to remove his forces and take them north. However, others persuaded him not to waste the opportunity but to seize Charleston, South Carolina, the most significant port city in the South. As it turned out, the Americans were well prepared for the onslaught. Fearing a major British thrust, Congress and Washington had ordered Charles Lee to go to Charleston. There the less-than-diplomatic Lee attempted to badger the local populace into supporting a solid state of preparedness. When Clinton's combined land-naval offensive descended on Charleston in late June 1776, the local patriots, who had not minded much of Lee's advice, put up a brilliant defense and drove off the lion. Clinton's forces then sailed northward to join Howe on Staten Island. That retreat brought an end to major British activity in the South until the end of 1778.

Once the war took on global dimensions and a massive concentration of forces at one strategic point was no longer possible for Britain, the home government reactivated plans for drawing heavily on reputed loyalist numbers as a key to reconquering the southern region. The counterrevolutionary strategy seemed to work well at the outset, yet Clinton was slow to follow up on the initial success in Georgia. Rather, he hung close to New York during 1779, lamenting his declining manpower, worrying about supplies, and fretting that Washington might try at any time to drive him from New York. Clinton became quite testy with his civilian superiors, who kept urging him to push ahead with the southern strategy. "If you wish to do anything," he bluntly told them, "leave me to myself, and let me adapt my efforts to the hourly change of circumstances." Besides clinging to New York, he withdrew the British garrison from Rhode Island to concentrate further his remaining manpower, all preparatory to the planned offensive push that came against South Carolina in 1780.

Meantime, American partisans and Continentals in the Southern Department were active. There was a concerted attempt to drive the British from Georgia. In the late summer of 1779, favorable circumstances brought together the Franco-

American allies outside of Savannah. Admiral d'Estaing commanded the French land-naval contingent, which had been off campaigning in the West Indies. Benjamin Lincoln, who was one of Washington's most trusted generals, had charge of some 1,400 American troops, mostly Continentals. Once again, it was a great opportunity for the allies to demonstrate their ability to work together and to smash the outnumbered enemy. In late September, the forces of d'Estaing and Lincoln put Savannah under siege. Then, with the French commander beginning to worry about the adverse effect of turbulent fall weather on his fleet and with the British defenders demonstrating no signs of capitulation, the unfortunate decision to attempt overrunning the fortifications came. The attack occurred on October 9. It was a slaughter, largely caused by an American flanking party losing its way in the swampy terrain and by the superiority of the British position. The allies sustained 837 casualties before the day was done, compared to 155 for the British. Shortly thereafter, d'Estaing sailed for France; Lincoln had no choice but to retreat to Charleston, leaving the British firmly perched in Georgia.

Satisfied by late December 1779 that an allied offensive against his New York base was not in the immediate offing, Clinton sailed south with an expedition numbering 7,600. Violent weather blew the fleet in all directions, but it reassembled and prepared carefully for the Charleston assault. Knowing that an attack was imminent, Benjamin Lincoln worked feverishly with 3,000 Continentals and 2,500 militia to plan the defense of the city. However, the Americans were now in a relatively weak position, since the defensive works that had proved the key to staving off the British in 1776 had fallen into complete disrepair. Lincoln thought seriously about abandoning Charleston and saving his army. Local leaders pressured him into staying, arguing that the fall of their port city would trigger the collapse of the rebel cause in the South. The British offensive came in early May. When one Clinton sortie cut off an escape route to the North, Lincoln faced two undesirable choices: fight to a sure death or surrender. A furious bombardment convinced fickle

Charlestonians that surrender was the only intelligent course. Lincoln capitulated. For the first time in the war an entire American army, virtually the whole Southern Department of Continental forces, had been captured.

The fall of Charleston, hard on the heels of rebel failures in Georgia, augured well for the British southern strategy. Clinton sailed back to New York in triumph, leaving behind the strong-willed, petulant Charles, Lord Cornwallis. Before embarking, however, Sir Henry had ordered his aggressive subordinate to proceed with caution and to make sure that loyalists had full control of the ground behind the main army. The commander in chief also warned that supply lines be made secure, so that Cornwallis did not find himself cut off from the sea and having to forage off the countryside. Cornwallis, as it turned out, did not listen very carefully.

It was not so much Cornwallis's vigorous campaigning, a quality lacking in so many of the British generals, that eventually got his army into trouble. Rather, it was the renewal of heated partisan war in the region. A sign of the times came at the Waxhaws, near the North Carolina border, on May 29, 1780. The blood bath there involved 400 Virginia Continentals who were marching toward Charleston but who turned back when they learned about Lincoln's capitulation. British Colonel Banastre Tarleton, an odd-looking man with a thirst for human blood, set out in hot pursuit with his green-coated cavalrymen. When they reached the retreating Continentals near the Waxhaws, they overran them. Although the Continentals begged for quarter, Tarleton's men butchered them, with fewer than 100 of the Virginians escaping the tragic confrontation. A new phrase denoting brutality in war, "Tarleton's Quarter," quickly entered the patriots' vocabulary.

The Waxhaws slaughter, in combination with the fall of Charleston, temporarily undercut partisan rebel domination; and Tarleton's bloody ravaging of the countryside certainly encouraged the loyalists. As Russell F. Weigley has noted, "southern Revolutionaries" were "especially cruel in their harassment and repression of Loyalists" before Clinton's 1780 offensive.

With Tarleton setting a "bad example" and the tables turned, "the Loyalists. . .seized the advantage of British occupation to take reprisals in violence against both persons and property."[8] Soon, irregular bands of rebels, which had been so effective in controlling the region since 1775, sprang up again in defense, led by such determined commanders as Thomas Sumter, "Swamp Fox" Francis Marion, and Andrew Pickens. They cowed rampaging loyalist bands in vengeful raids, and they also nibbled away at Cornwallis's army, all of which greatly complicated the Earl's attempts to pacify the region.

Even with the new wave of partisan rebel resistance, the low point of the American effort had not as yet been reached. It came on August 16, 1780, when Cornwallis routed a reorganized Southern Department army under General Horatio Gates near Camden, South Carolina. Gates, so long the darling of New England republicans, had accepted the urgent pleas of Congress that he reassemble some semblance of an army in the wake of Lincoln's capitulation. Washington did not want Gates to have the assignment, feeling that there were others who were more qualified to take on such an extraordinarily difficult military task. Despite Washington's sentiments, the "hero of Saratoga" went south and pulled together a skeleton force consisting of a few Continentals from Maryland and large numbers of untrained militiamen.

With 3,000 soldiers present and apparently fit for duty, Gates incautiously marched right into Cornwallis's arms. Gates's army seemed destined for humiliation and defeat, which is exactly what it got. Once in South Carolina, his columns moved toward Camden, a British outpost, in the middle of night. One American officer reported that "the troops. . .had frequently felt the bad consequences of eating bad provisions; but at this time, a hasty meal of quick baked bread and fresh beef, with a dessert of molasses, mixed with mush or dumplings, operated so cathartically as to disorder many of the men." Unbeknownst to Gates, his temporarily debilitated army was marching straight toward Cornwallis himself, who had hurried out from Charleston with several hundred troops. The two armies bumped into each other in the dead of night. Both pulled back and prepared for a general engagement at daylight.

Gates's inexperienced and incapacitated units never had a chance. The British force completely decimated them, as reflected in the estimated American casualty rate of 750, while the British figure was slightly over 300 killed or wounded. In what many interpreted as an incredible act of cowardice, Gates fled for his life into North Carolina. Much worse, a second Southern Department army had fallen prey to the British in less than one campaign season. The American cause in the South was in deep trouble, despite continued partisan resistance. "Few guerilla campaigns have progressed farther than the phase of terrorist raids without the assistance of at least a semblance of an organized army" to support them, Russell F. Weigley has written.[9] That army was, again, no longer there. Some drastic turnabout was still needed to redeem the cause of the patriots in the South.

TREASON, PENSIONS, AND MUTINIES

In the North, Washington continued to be frustrated in planning for a joint Franco-American land offensive against Clinton. His officers and soldiers were as restive, if not more so, than before. Bounties, which were now normally being paid in specie, did little to lure new recruits. If anything, civilians, regardless of socioeconomic standing, were almost completely unwilling to join the ranks. Washington wondered openly whether he would have enough personnel left to claim to have an army for the next campaign season. The determined commander virtually gave up making plans for the campaign season of 1781. It was both frustrating and ironic not to be able to offer the British a major challenge when he had been able to do so during their concentrated campaign efforts of 1776 and 1777.

With lack of faith and popular commitment in the cause hitting rock bottom in 1779, it perhaps was inevitable that precipitous incidents would take place. None caused greater consternation than the treason of Benedict Arnold. To this day the turncoat behavior of this talented field general has lacked a satisfactory explanation. Too often Arnold has been portrayed as a misfit of unbalanced and egotistical temperament who was little more than a self-interested, vindictive, avaricious person. That Arnold worried incessantly about the declining state of his finances cannot be denied, yet so did many other high-ranking officers. Moreover, he felt strongly that the army had been treated shabbily, as did his comrades. In September 1780, just before going over to the British, he "lamented that our army is permitted to starve in a land of plenty." His words were hardly singular among veteran officers. However, his response to his disillusionment represented the most extreme form of individual protest that any person could have mustered against a cause and a society that was treating its soldiery with indifference, if not outright hostility.

Arnold, as fully committed a republican as there had been in the patriot population of 1775, had become convinced by 1779 that such sentiment had been both a temporary illusion and a sham. With visions of restoring the imperial connection, he hoped through his actions to set the stage for a massive popular return in allegiance to Great Britain. For over a year he flirted with Clinton in secret correspondence, specifically promising to deliver West Point, considered the key to control of the Hudson Highlands, in return for a handsome personal fee and a generalship in the British army. The plan collapsed, however, when dashing Major John André, a personal favorite of Clinton's, fell into American hands in the Highlands region when returning from a secret meeting with Arnold. Thus exposed, Arnold fled West Point on September 25, 1780, and became one of the great villains of United States history. If he had been in better contact with his fellow officers, he would more likely have been pressuring Congress for pensions rather than going over to the British. But he was too much of an individualist, and he has paid for his extremism with a cloud of ignominy ever since.

The popular reaction to Arnold's treason was overwhelmingly negative. In fact, it seemed to bring out guilt in the populace and appeared to help in reviving the flagging popular spirit. Philadelphians were typical in their denunciations. They staged an elaborate parade, centering on a horse-drawn float. Exhibited on the platform was an "effigy of General ARNOLD sitting." The turncoat had "two faces, emblematical of his traitorous conduct," and at his back "was a figure of the Devil, dressed in black robes, shaking a purse of money at the general's left ear." Thousands turned out for the show. Running "through the denunciation of Arnold," Charles Royster has stated, was "the desperate claim that the public virtue of 1775 could survive as the basis for American independence."[10] On the surface, at least, the response to Arnold's treason seemed to bring new determination to a populace apparently guilt ridden by its unsupportive behavior. If it did, the new enthusiasm did not seem to extend very far beyond parades and other forms of denunciation. In October 1780, Washington had 17,586 troops in rank (13,966 effectives). Two months later he had just about half that number (8,742 in rank with 5,982 present and fit for duty)!

A major effect of Arnold's treason, in combination with other problems, was to move Congress off dead center on the pension issue. In October 1780, after another round of debating whether pensions would result in a privileged, unrepublican military caste, the delegates succumbed to reality. The congressmen promised the officer corps half-pay for life, to begin at war's end—predicated on the pious expectation that funds would become available. Despite strong New England antipension sentiment, Congress was not willing to take the chance that other officers, perhaps as disgruntled as Arnold, might retire from the field or, worse yet, follow his turncoat path. One highly visible "renegade from republicanism," as Arnold has been described by James Kirby Martin, was enough.[11] The officer corps seemed to be mollified. The lingering—and vital—question was whether the central government could establish a permanent revenue source to support the pensions.

The seeming resolution of the pension issue came at a critical time, since portentous levels of group defiance among the rank and file had long since become manifest. The most common form of group protest was the line mutiny. Even though there were isolated examples before, beginning in 1779 long-suffering foot soldiers started to "combine" in reaction to their circumstances, as some officers chose to describe the phenomenon. And the step from these secretive and dangerous "combinations" to large-scale mutinies was quite short.

It is plausible to argue that the common soldiers had learned the value of group pressure and defiance by observing the tactics of their officers in the pursuit of pensions. There was also the factor of tightened group cohesion among veteran campaigners. Whatever the specific causes, the year 1779 saw near uprisings among Rhode Island and Connecticut regiments, both of which were barely contained. In 1780, another mutiny involving Connecticut soldiers was aborted only after a dependable Pennsylvania regiment surrounded them and restored order. Tensions among the soldiery led one worried army colonel to conclude in September 1780: "We are in a bad way, and I think a little fighting [with Clinton] would be of great service to our army at present, and put an end to feuds and broils among themselves."

The winter of 1779–1780, spent at Jockey Hollow near Morristown, New Jersey, did little to ease troop dissatisfaction. The winter weather was as severe that year as at any time during the century, much worse than it had been at Valley Forge. Supplies, again, were almost nonexistent, although there was an abundance of food in the surrounding countryside. Local merchants and farmers, however, wanted nothing to do with Continental dollars or other forms of Congressional money, and foraging activity did little to keep stomachs full. About the only things to cheer about at Morristown were the reduced morbidity and mortality rates. While one-third of the soldiery had been on the sick roles at any given time during the Valley Forge winter, the peak at Morristown was never higher than 11.1 percent, based on exceedingly valuable data compiled by Charles H. Lesser.[12] Commensurately, fewer troops succumbed to death in camp. Declining morbidity reflected the presence of hard-core veterans in camp, who no doubt had already suffered through bouts of smallpox, typhus, and other standard camp maladies and had survived and were now immune.

Reduced morbidity and mortality rates during the harshest winter of the war did not serve to uplift soldier morale. The supply situation remained desperate, and pay arrearages became even more pronounced as one winter season gave way to another. To make matters worse, the veterans began grumbling about favors short-term enlistees had received for remaining in service after their terms were up. Such individuals now got bounties in hard money as well as promises of land that exceeded in acreage amounts those that long-term enlistees had been promised. For human beings who had already endured so much pain and hardship, such apparent favoritism, while necessary to keep Washington's declining numbers up, proved to be too much. Surgeon James Thacher understated troop feeling in December 1780 when he drew attention to "repeated disappointments of our hopes and expectations" and pointed out that "the confidence of the army in public justice and public promises is greatly diminished, and we are reduced almost to despair." For many soldiers, the situation had passed beyond despair, now to the awful moment of outright defiance through mutiny.

On January 1, 1781, the Pennsylvania line, suffering through yet another harsh winter in the vicinity of Morristown, revolted. Some 1,000 hardened comrades ostensibly wanted nothing more to do with the army. On a prearranged signal, the Pennsylvanians under the direction of their sergeants, paraded under arms, seized their artillery, and marched south toward Princeton, the ultimate target being Philadelphia. They had had their fill of broken promises. More specifically, they claimed that the period of their enlistments was up. They maintained that they had signed on for three years, not for the duration. So if they were to stay in the ranks, they wanted the same benefits that short-term enlistees and new long-term recruits were obtaining.

Formal military discipline collapsed as the officers who tried to stop the mutineers were brushed aside. The insurgents killed one and mortally wounded two others. Their popular commander, Anthony Wayne, trailed along after them, attempting to appeal to their sense of patriotism. The soldiers, speaking through a committee of sergeants, assured Wayne and others of their essential loyalty—and proved it by delivering up two spies whom Sir Henry Clinton had sent out to monitor the situation. Moreover, the soldiers, despite their anger, behaved themselves well along their route and did not threaten the civilian populace.

While a later check would show that most of the mutineers were duration enlistees, it was a moot point. When the Pennsylvania line reached Trenton, representatives of Congress and the Pennsylvania government negotiated with them. The representatives, caught in an obvious bind, agreed to discharge any soldier claiming to have completed a three-year enlistment. Also, they offered back pay and new clothing along with immunity from prosecution for having summarily left the field. Once discharged, the bulk of mutineers reenlisted for the new bounty. The net loss to the line in terms of manpower turned out to be small. By late January 1781, the Pennsylvanians once more were a functioning part of the Continental army.

The resolution of their most pressing grievances did not come about solely because of the justness of their complaints. Nor was a satisfactory settlement constructed because "the revolt. . .occurred in a country where many of the men were upstanding citizen-soldiers conscious of their rights and liberties," as Don Higginbotham has argued.[13] Few, if any, of the mutineers were upstanding in any economic sense. However, they were quite sure that their fundamental rights had been violated by the long list of broken promises given them. They were also loyal to the cause and certainly as upstanding as any in their commitment to the goal of achieving a republican order in America. They knew that Washington was in desperate need of their manpower, and they used the threat of losing it as leverage for some modicum of financial justice. Unlike the officers, they were not in a position to lobby before Congress. Hence they used the most threatening weapon available to them—and only after less extreme measures had failed to redress legitimate grievances. Committed to the cause, it was not part of the enlistees' thinking to threaten to overthrow popularly based governments, since they had staked their hopes for a better life in the freer republican environment, should the war end successfully. All told, the extreme course of mutiny demonstrated, paradoxically, that they were the most loyal and dedicated of republicans in the new nation, but that they were dangerously close to repudiating a dream that seemed too much like a nightmare.

More worrisome at the time than the issue of appropriate justice for the hardened, enduring veterans was whether the Pennsylvania mutiny, and its aborted predecessors, would trigger additional revolts in the Continental line. Also camped near Morristown during the winter of 1780–1781 were soldiers of the New Jersey line. Officers were aware that the Jersey regulars sympathized with the Pennsylvanians and had been in constant communication with them. One reported that "some men of the 1st regiment have been trying to foment an insurrection yet have been altogether unsuccessful in the 3rd." Other officers naively discounted the possibility. On January 20, the New Jersey line, witnessing the success of the Pennsylvanians, rose in mutiny. Even though each of the regulars had recently received $5 in specie as a token toward back pay, they were upset about bounties and terms of enlistment offered new comrades. The troops first broke loose at Pompton, near Morristown, their leaders shouting: "Let us go to Congress who have money and rum enough but won't give it to us."

Within a few days, the New Jersey line, having been granted liberal concessions, was back under control, except for isolated insults directed at the most overbearing of the officers. Washington, however, had decided that enough was enough. "Unless this dangerous spirit can be suppressed by force," he wrote Congress, "there is an end to all subordination in the Army, and indeed to the Army itself." To back up his words, the commander ordered General Robert Howe and about 500 New England troops near West Point to march to Pompton and to exact an "unconditional submission." Once in control, they were to "instantly execute a few of the most active and most incendiary leaders.'' Howe's contingent reached Pompton on January 27, three days after the New Jersey line had settled its grievances. Surrounding the camp just before dawn, Howe caught the Jersey soldiers off guard and ordered them to fall in without arms. The general singled out three ringleaders and ordered their summary execution, to be shot to death by 9 of their comrades. A Jersey officer intervened in one case, but two were put to death. As Dr. Thacher reported from the scene, ''the wretched victims, overwhelmed by the terrors of death, had neither time nor. . .power to implore the forgiveness of their God, and such was their agonizing condition, that no heart could refrain from emotions of sympathy and compassion.''

Washington's course with respect to the New Jersey line was brutal, but the republican cause, from his perspective, was in sorry shape and depended for survival on a well-disciplined army. He had to maintain control at whatever price, even at the expense of humanity itself. Perhaps because the picture of war brightened so quickly in 1781, there were no major uprisings among Washington's private soldiers after the mutiny of the New Jersey line. Or possibly Washington's harsh actions, directed against men as loyal to the cause as any, had a chilling effect on war-weary and suffering rank-and-file patriots.

SUDDEN TURNABOUT: THE ROAD TO YORKTOWN

Just when the rebel effort in the South appeared to have all but collapsed, the Americans rebounded. There were three fundamental reasons why. First, Cornwallis, flushed with victory at Camden, decided to push into North Carolina. That plan turned out to be poorly calculated, as local partisans rallied and, second, delivered a telling blow at the Battle of King's Mountain. Third, Congress finally deferred to Washington's feelings about who should be the commander of the Southern Department. Washington selected Nathanael Greene, who would soon be running the army of Cornwallis in circles. Greene arrived in Charlotte, North Carolina, on December 2, 1780, where he relieved Gates of duty. Cornwallis's needless aggressiveness, unexpected partisan resistance, and Greene's unorthodoxy as a campaigner were critical elements helping to undermine the British southern strategy.

As Cornwallis pushed northward after the Camden debacle, his left wing under Major Patrick Ferguson found itself being enveloped by rebel partisans. The British goal was to move toward the first line of the Appalachian Mountains. Enraged "over-the-mountain men," coming together in almost leaderless fashion, began to stalk Ferguson's column, which consisted largely of hated loyalists. Beginning to sense real danger, Ferguson ordered a retreat, then found a mountain jutting up from the Piedmont in northern South Carolina. With 1,100 followers, he prepared to defend that promontory. As Ferguson, no doubt apocryphally, announced: "He was on King's Mountain and. . .he was king of that mountain and God Almighty could not drive him from it." He could not have been more wrong. On October 7, 1780, the frontiersmen surrounded him and started moving up from all sides. While brutally cutting the defenders to shreds, the rebels revenged themselves for the maimings and killings of loved ones victimized by the region's partisan war. Major Ferguson died in the midst of battle from several wounds. Before the over-the-mountain men were done, 157 loyalists were dead, another 163 wounded, and 698 were prisoners. The 1,000 frontier rebel irregulars had suffered only 80 casualties.

Not only did the Battle of King's Mountain sever Cornwallis's left wing, it also served to drain much blood from southern loyalist support of the British counterrevolutionary thrust. Colonel William Campbell, nominally leading the King's Mountain victors, permitted summary trials of the most obnoxious Ferguson loyalists. Charges ranged from entering homes and stealing property to raping and mercilessly killing members of patriot families. Nine captured loyalists were hanged; others received gallows reprieves. Again, it seemed, the loyalists were learning that British regiments would not (and/or could not) guarantee them protection. Fewer thus were willing to rush out to defend the King's standard in the critical days ahead.

The effects of King's Mountain did not ease the burdens facing Nathanael Greene. The overall "appearance" of those few troops available to him "was wretched beyond description," complained the Rhode Islander. Notwithstanding, he soon devised a bold strategy for dealing with Cornwallis's superior forces. Greene did the unthinkable, dividing his manpower into three separate columns to make "the most of my inferior force," all of which "compels my adversary to divide his and holds him in doubt as to his own line of conduct." Greene gave 600 regulars and militia to rifleman Daniel Morgan, who was to push south and west toward the British stronghold at Ninety-Six in South Carolina. To the southeast he sent "Light Horse" Harry Lee and his cavalry legion of 280 men to work in concert with Francis Marion's partisan band. With the remaining troops, the numbers of which grew to over 1,000 with hard-sell recruiting and a modest outpouring of militia support, Greene would focus on Cornwallis himself. The effect of his "unorthodoxy" in "violating the principle of concentration," Russell F. Weigley has stressed, was to "make the British army still more vulnerable to partisan harassment and to encounters with his own force, which was not strong enough for a major battle."[14]

Pugnacious Cornwallis, back in South Carolina after the King's Mountain battle, accepted Greene's challenge. His immediate objective became conquering the divided forces by pushing toward Greene and isolating and wiping out Morgan while in transit. To that end, he dispatched Banastre Tarleton with 1,100 soldiers to drive Morgan's force into the trap. Morgan seemed to cooperate, retreating ahead of Tarleton's on-rushing men. The skilled wagon master and rifleman, however, knew that he must avoid being squeezed to bits between two British columns. On January 15, 1781, Morgan reached Hannah's Cowpens, close to the Broad River. There he decided to square off against Tarleton. His numbers now swelled to 1,000 by increments of militia, Morgan set a masterful trap. With the

Broad River at his back, he placed his skittish militiamen in the front lines, ordering them to fire at least two rounds before breaking and running, as experience had taught him that they would. In a second set of lines not visible to the enemy, would be his handful of experienced Continentals, whom he presumed would not falter in the face of concentrated British fire.

Since Morgan did not trust his militia, he wanted the Broad River behind them. "When men are forced to fight," he explained, "they will sell their lives dearly. . . .Had I crossed the river, one half of the militia would immediately have abandoned me." On the morning of January 17, after a forced five-hour march, Tarleton rushed forward into Morgan's hands. The militia line broke, but only after inflicting casualties with some damaging fire. Smelling blood, the British surged forward in disorganized haste, and the second lines, backed up by the militia that had reformed after retreating, ripped them with deadly fire and a bayonet charge; and Morgan also threw in a flanking cavalry assault. Tarleton, who managed to get away, lost all but 140 of his soldiers (339 in casualties and 600 in prisoners). Morgan suffered only 12 killed and 60 wounded. The Battle of Hannah's Cowpens was the second staggering blow against the fortunes of Cornwallis in the South.

Not resting after his success, Morgan regrouped and pushed north to avoid the Earl's slowly advancing main column. After joining Greene, the former Indian fighter turned his portion of the army over to his superior and took a leave of absence, complaining of a severe attack of rheumatism. Shortly, the chase was on between Greene and Cornwallis, the former retreating and the latter desperately trying to catch him. To speed his march, Cornwallis abandoned all his heavy baggage, including his army's supply of rum. Still, he could not entrap the Americans, who retired all of the way into southern Virginia before again turning south. Both armies suffered miserably in the cold, raw weather, but Greene was wearing down his adversary. When the Rhode Islander received reinforcements early in March 1781, he decided to make a stand near Guilford Courthouse in central North Carolina. Even if he lost the engagement, Greene reasoned, he would have inflicted further pain on Cornwallis's harried, exhausted troops.

Russell F. Weigley has accurately characterized Cornwallis when he described him as one who "possessed a quality hitherto rarely displayed by British generals in this war, a thirst for battle."[15] Since Greene had been reinforced, the Earl now had less than half the manpower of Greene (2,000 to 4,300). However, the British general readily accepted the challenge. The Rhode Islander selected a plan of battle similar to that put together by Morgan at Hannah's Cowpens. Early on the afternoon of March 15, Cornwallis moved up to attack. It was a vicious confrontation with neither side gaining a decisive advantage. Finally, Greene, sensing that he had inflicted enough damage on the enemy, withdrew his weary soldiers from the field. Even though the Earl could claim a technical victory, his army had taken the worst of it—506 casualties compared to 264 on the American side. The patriot soldiers had cause for cheering, especially when they learned that the hated Tarleton had been shot in the hand and had lost three fingers. On the other side, Greene was irate that 1,000 North Carolina militia abandoned him during his retreat, which only further fixed him in his strong antimilitia biases.

Cornwallis, finally having had enough and seriously hurt with a 25 percent casualty rate, likewise retreated, his destination being the port town of Wilmington, North Carolina, 175 miles to the southeast. There he could rest his decimated army and get supplies. Although Greene had not defeated his adversary, he had run him all over the landscape and had worn him down while making it impossible for the Earl to support partisan loyalists in South Carolina. Greene had every reason to be satisfied. He and Morgan (along with the over-the-mountain men) had accomplished a phenomenal turnabout in events—and with next to nothing in resources. They had taken advantage of Cornwallis's inherent aggressiveness and had turned it against him. In doing so, they bought vital time and helped to clear the path to Yorktown. Their efforts represented one significant bright spot in an atmosphere of doubt. At last, the elements seemed to be coming together for a critical military victory, despite all the internal turmoil that had made the young nation such an unstable, disunited entity.

NOTES

[1] Don Higginbotham, *The War of American Independence: Military Attitudes, Policies, and Practice, 1763-1789* (New York, 1971), p. 320.

[2] Bernard Sheehan, "Ignoble Savagism and the American Revolution," in L. R. Gerlach, *et al., Legacies of the American Revolution* (Salt Lake City, Utah, 1978), pp. 157, 172.

[3] David Syrett, *Shipping and the American War, 1775-83: A Study of British Transport Organization* (London, 1970), p. 77.

[4] Howard H. Peckham, *The War for Independence: A Military History* (Chicago, 1958), p. 118.

[5] H. James Henderson, *Party Politics in the Continental Congress* (New York, 1974), p. 254.

[6] Charles Royster, *A Revolutionary People at War: The Continental Army and the American Character, 1775-1783* (Chapel Hill, N.C., 1980), pp. 315-16.

[7] Clyde R. Ferguson, "Functions of the Partisan-Militia in the South during the American Revolution: An Interpretation," in W. R. Higgins, ed., *The Revolutionary War in the South: Power, Conflict, and Leadership* (Durham, N.C., 1979), pp. 239-42. For an interpretive overview of the southern phase of the war focusing on Clinton, consult Ira D. Gruber, "Britain's Southern Strategy," *ibid.,* pp. 205-38.

[8] Russell F. Weigley, *The American Way of War: A History of United States Military Strategy and Policy* (New York, 1973), p. 26.

[9] *Ibid.,* p. 27.

[10] Charles Royster, "'The Nature of Treason': Revolutionary Virtue and American Reactions to Benedict Arnold," *William and Mary Quarterly,* 3d Series (1979), p. 191.

[11] James Kirby Martin, "Benedict Arnold: Renegade from Republicanism" (paper delivered at the Columbia University Faculty Seminar in Early American History, 1978); *idem,* "Benedict Arnold and the Sorry State of Civil-Military Relations in Revolutionary America" (paper delivered at the American Historical Association Convention, 1980); *idem,* "Benedict Arnold's Treason as Political Protest," *Parameters: Journal of the US Army War College,* 11 (1981), pp. 63-74.

[12] C. H. Lesser, ed., *The Sinews of Independence: Monthly Strength Reports of the Continental Army* (Chicago, 1976), pp. xxx-xxxi.

[13] Higginbotham, *War of American Independence,* p. 404.

[14] Weigley, *American Way of War,* pp. 29-30.

[15] *Ibid.,* p. 31.

Of War, National Legitimacy, and the Republican Order, 1781-1789

THE YORKTOWN CAMPAIGN

"The Revolution," wrote an aging John Adams in 1818, "was effected before the war commenced. The Revolution was in the minds and hearts of the people. . . .This radical change in the principles, opinions, sentiments, and affections of the people, was the real Revolution." In attempting to give coherency to the era that enveloped so much of his life work, Adams implied that an American identity as separate from Great Britain had manifested itself before the war. This sense of distinctness as a people, in turn, gave unity to the war effort and lent itself readily to the nation-making process that followed, once the patriots had recognized their change of heart and had committed themselves irrevocably to the cause of liberty. Since legitimacy as a separate people was in the American mind well before 1776, the fundamental task in war, Adams seemed to indicate, was to prove the strength of common will and purpose.

Although Adams's observations have a certain romantic appeal, certainly among historians who insist that consensus of purpose rather than conflict over goals and aspirations have been uppermost in shaping the American experience, the "minds and hearts" comment strains historical reality. Specifically, it circumscribes proper appreciation of the war as a source and instrument of national legitimacy and identity. Despite the *rage militaire* of 1775, provincial citizens were not prepared psychologically to display the depth of moral commitment that would be needed to maintain even a facade of unity in the face of concentrated British arms. The extreme volatility of popular enthusiasm that marked the war effort strongly suggests that a sense of national identity had not yet taken much hold, that feelings of separateness undergirding national legitimacy were far from being realized in 1775 and 1776. What the war effort did, above all else, was begin to create a sense of unity and legitimacy of purpose, which was essential to the nation-making process that continued through and beyond the war years. Altered affections did not so much cause as they were vital products of the war.

Nathanael Greene, while running Cornwallis's army in circles, fully appreciated the sensitive task of establishing legitimacy. He rigorously insisted that his small army not plunder the countryside or take advantage of civilians in other ways, no matter how poorly treated or supplied. Cornwallis was not in a position to be so judicious. He let his regular loyalist minions do as they pleased. The British left "the whole country struck with terror," stated one irate North Carolinian. Loyalists with Cornwallis considered it their assigned "business. . .to follow the camps and under the protection of the army to enrich themselves on the plunder they took from. . .distressed inhabitants" unable to defend themselves. As the two armies played at fox and hare, Greene thus made friends for the cause of American identity; ironically, so did Cornwallis. Like Washington, Greene comprehended that restraint toward civilians, regardless of the enormity of army grievances, was essential to having the war effort serve as a mainspring of national legitimacy and resultant nationhood.

Cornwallis blundered in this and many other ways. He did not pacify the ground behind his army, and he did not use the loyalists well as agents of counterrevolutionary activity. Rather, his "misdirected aggressiveness," as Russell F. Weigley phrased it, "carried Cornwallis. . .to his and the British army's final disaster of the war."[1] Had the Earl been a better strategist, he could have done much more to reestablish the allegiance of thousands of citizens who had not yet made an irrevocable commitment to the proposed republican order of the more deeply committed rebels.

In some situations the fate of conflicts hung on the foibles of individual human personalities. Cornwallis was a man who might have undermined the languishing patriot cause but who failed. Personal ambition and the desire for military glory were his weaknesses. The Earl could be blatantly obstreperous when he perceived the world as treating him unjustly. He entered one such moody period at the time of the siege of Charleston. Clinton had just learned that the ministry had rejected his longstanding request to be relieved of the North American command. Cornwallis, positioned to be Clinton's successor, hungered for the job and especially for the potential fame and recognition that came with it. Upon hearing of the ministry's decision, the Earl "withdrew into a shell of self-pity" and "blamed Clinton for his troubles,"[2] Hugh F. Rankin has observed. Not only was he extremely testy with his superior, he studiously ignored Clinton's advice about systematic pacification and maintenance of supply lines. Cornwallis also took out his frustrations by vigorously chasing after rebel armies until Greene's got the best of him. Smashing Greene might have brought glory and renewal of interest at home in the removal of Clinton. Yet having been outduelled, the Earl could not yield. He was going to quench his thirst for glory, and Virginia appeared to be a most attractive oasis.

In December 1780, Sir Henry Clinton had sent a raiding force of 1,500 by sea into the Old Dominion. Commanded by Benedict Arnold, the soldiers were to aid Cornwallis by drawing manpower away from the Southern Department army. Another goal was to establish a site for a naval base to support future British operations in the Chesapeake Bay area. Continental forces under Steuben and Lafayette quickly gathered to check the marauding Arnold, who marched as far inland as Richmond and burned and sacked that thriving town.

Responding to the presence of American regulars, Clinton reinforced Arnold with 2,000 soldiers and named General William Phillips to overall command. The military buildup in Virginia, meant to support Cornwallis, did much more; it drew him there as if by magnetic field. In April 1781, while recuperating with his battered army at Wilmington, the Earl announced by letter to Phillips that he would soon take over operations. Virginia, the forceful Cornwallis had decided, represented a proper theater for the offensive kind of war he so craved. In marching north, he all but abandoned South Carolina, leaving behind only a small army to hold off Greene and local partisan rebels.

Cornwallis's ambition drove him forward into the net that would ensnare him at Yorktown. His defiance of Clinton and virtual repudiation of the southern strategy would bring matters in the land war, at last, to a culmination. And Clinton lacked the strength of character to discipline Cornwallis. Rather, he fussed about the focus of the upcoming summer campaign, waffling among numerous possibilities (much as Howe had done in the spring of 1777). At one moment he thought of retaking Rhode

Island; then Philadelphia struck his fancy. Next he worried about defending his New York stronghold against Washington. Clinton then took to dickering with Cornwallis about relative manpower needs. He wrote and asked for 2,000 of the Earl's troops (Cornwallis now had 7,500 soldiers at his disposal). Cornwallis responded by assuring his commander that he could spare no one. If he could not keep all his soldiers, he would return to Charleston, an offer Clinton should have accepted.

In late July, Clinton ordered Cornwallis to fortify Old Point Comfort at the mouth of the James River as the anchoring point for the British navy. Cornwallis's force of regulars, Hessians, and loyalists now numbered nearly 8,500. After consulting his engineers, he concluded that Yorktown, on the southern shore of the York River near Chesapeake Bay, would make a stronger defensive site than Old Point Comfort. By August 1, the fortifications were going up. All this time, the Earl seethed with rage because his army was to become a garrison force with virtually no opportunity for offensive operations. In fact, Cornwallis retaliated by speaking out sharply about Clinton's ineptness in his correspondence with ministerial leaders in England. Neither he nor Clinton, so busily engaged in picking away at each other, had fathomed that they had put the bulk of the British southern army in an extremely vulnerable position.

While the two generals squabbled, George Washington once again dusted off his plans for an assault on New York. His trump card was a French army of 5,000 under talented, guileless Comte de Rochambeau, which had landed at Newport in July 1780. Both Rochambeau and Washington were eager to mount some major challenge during the 1781 campaign season. Fabian tactics were one thing; yet the American commander realized the debilitating effects of the wave of mutinous turmoil in his army, and he questioned how long his forces could hold together without definitive action. Martial survival, more than ever, depended on operations. Washington and Rochambeau thus met in May at Wethersfield, Connecticut, to set campaign goals. The American commander pushed for full-scale action against New York. Rochambeau countered with news that a large

French fleet might be available to support their combined armies; he favored moving against the British force in Virginia, with the fleet, should it arrive from the West Indies, blocking off any escape route through the Bay. Not knowing that Cornwallis was on his way north, Washington stuck with his New York plan, even though he saw the advantages of a concerted campaign in his native state, should the proper elements blend together.

Most significantly, the Wethersfield meeting signaled the prospect of close allied cooperation, whatever the enemy target. Washington, moreover, needed the 5,000 French troops to put some muscle in his plans, since his own numbers were now so meager. Always persistent, the American commander set July 2 as the day for the New York assault to begin. However, British foraging parties discovered the allied movements, which allowed Clinton to buoy his defenses and throw off the timetable. Then, in early August, the British commander received Hessian reinforcements totaling 2,600, which brought his manpower up to 15,000, somewhat greater than allied strength. Washington began to despair, but bad news quickly turned to the good. On August 14, the commander in chief learned that the rumored French fleet under Comte de Grasse, consisting of 30 ships and 3,000 soldiers, was definitely on its way; its target was Chesapeake Bay. Long since fully aware that Cornwallis was heading for Virginia, Washington embraced the opportunity. Within five days, the first contingents of French and American troops moved out for the long trek south.

During the summer of 1780, Washington had made a telling general observation. "In any operation and all circumstances, a decisive Naval superiority," he wrote, "is to be considered as a fundamental principle, and the basis upon which every hope of success must ultimately depend." If he could get the allied force in front of Cornwallis at Yorktown and the French fleet could seal off the Bay, the Earl would be trapped. The French fleet was an essential factor. It soon would be in place. Admiral de Grasse, as it turned out, was able to move into position and, after three days of maneuvering and heated fighting in late

August, to drive off a British squadron sent out from New York. The French fleet now controlled the Bay. The pincers that would squeeze Cornwallis into unconditional surrender were almost in place.

Leaving behind a small diversionary force to confuse Clinton and to create the impression that the primary allied target was still New York, Washington and Rochambeau moved their armies south with all possible haste. By the end of September, there were 7,800 Frenchmen, 5,700 Continentals, and 3,200 militiamen surrounding Yorktown. Cornwallis, grappling with his likely fate, wrote Clinton on September 23: "If you cannot relieve me very soon you must expect to hear the worst." Still hoping that the Royal navy might break through, the Earl stayed within his well-fortified lines and prepared to hold out against the allied siege. Meanwhile, an exasperated Clinton pushed the navy to get on with another expedition. The relief force ultimately did arrive but with too little and too late. It reached the Bay on October 26, seven days after formal surrender had taken place.

Washington and Rochambeau agreed that formal siege operations should result in capitulation. On the evening of October 6, the allies began digging their first parallel trench, some 600 yards out from the left side of Cornwallis's defensive works. Heavy cannonading began three days later. On October 11, the allies started to construct a second parallel trench, this time 300 yards from the enemy trenches and on a direct line with the Earl's advanced redoubts Nine and Ten. Under cover of night on October 14, separate parties overran the two redoubts, which made it possible to move in with heavy ordnance and proceed with the earth-shattering cannonading.

Cornwallis's forces, besides being devastated by the incessant cannon fire, now faced two other serious problems. Food supplies had become scarce, and smallpox broke out in the ranks. Early on October 16, the British commander began to acknowledge his helpless position by sending out a small column against the second parallel trench. Besides spiking a few cannon, which were back in operation within a few hours, the sortie accomplished nothing. That night the Earl attempted to escape with his troops across the York River to Gloucester Point. A howling storm drove them back. On the morning of October 17, his army facing the prospect of extermination, his artillery all but silent, his parapets crumbling under unrelenting cannon fire, Cornwallis sent forth a lone drummer with a simple message: "Propose a cessation of hostilities. . .to settle terms for surrender."

That the most aggressive warrior among the British generals fell into such a trap is paradoxical. Yet it was just as much Cornwallis's fault as that of anyone else. He had made a mockery of the southern strategy, and he had defied the wishes of his superior officer in the North American theater. His own ambition had got him into a corner at Yorktown. Clinton, too, was more than culpable. He had ordered Cornwallis into a defensive post. Worse yet, he had failed to perceive how vulnerable that army would be if French naval power came to the aid of the rebel commander. That it did stands as one of the major accomplishments of the war, a feat that cost the British an army of over 8,000 at a most unpropitious time.

It took two days to complete the terms of surrender. Washington conceded his adversary almost nothing. He did not promise to protect the loyalists but stated that they would be subject to the dictates of civil authorities. He insisted that British regimental colors be cased in surrender ceremonies, an insult that General Benjamin Lincoln had endured after capitulating at Charleston. Further, the British musicians were not allowed to honor their captors by playing French or American melodies. It was to be an unconditional surrender in every way. With the details worked out, the British army moved out onto a large field on the bright autumn afternoon of October 19. The "indisposed" Cornwallis did not come out. His second in command turned over his superior's sword to Benjamin Lincoln, Washington's second, but only after having tried to offer it to Rochambeau. The Frenchman politely demurred and pointed toward Washington, indicating through his ennobling gesture that the victory belonged to the Americans.

As the defeated British columns began to parade that autumn afternoon, their musicians struck up a melancholy song, "The World Turned Upside Down." No tune could have been more fitting. The mighty and the proud had fallen. A small band of hardened American regulars, dreaming of a better life, had, with inestimable French assistance, endured the dark days of despair following those of sunshine enthusiasm—and now beheld the prospect of triumph. Success at Yorktown would bring the cause of a republican order in America one more vital step closer to legitimacy in the minds of the indifferent and uncommited. On the other side that day, the British had nothing about which to cheer. They had long since fumbled away the initiative in America—and also seemed to be losing it elsewhere across the globe. Whether the people of Britain would allow the war to continue, once they learned about Yorktown, had become the essential question.

The scene on the afternoon of October 19 was emotional, certainly because of everything it signified. The British war effort had suffered another damaging blow. Washington, communicating with Congress, praised "the unremitting Ardor which actuated every Officer and Soldier in the combined Army" which had "principally led to this Important Event." From another part of the field, a distraught British corporal spoke of his musket as he surrendered it in obvious disgust: "May you never get so good a master again!"

FORMULATING A PEACE SETTLEMENT

Contrary to popular lore, the Yorktown triumph was not solely responsible for the first rush in British peace overtures. Matters were far more complex than that. A look at the war map helps to explain why the parent state "had lost its nerve," as incisively stated by Piers Mackesy. "It was the timing of the blow which mattered," argues Mackesy, in making Yorktown so significant.[3] At the end of 1781 and into early 1782, His Majesty's forces would experience setbacks in India and the West Indies.

In February 1782, a sizable Spanish force would begin what would be a successful siege of Pensacola in West Florida. Also, combined Franco-Spanish forces were preparing for a major assault against highly prized Gibraltar, which they had threatened since 1779. The French navy, so crucial in the Yorktown victory, seemed to be able to do as it willed on the high seas. To prove it, French and Spanish vessels had reappeared in the English Channel and were causing havoc. Thus there were threats facing the British everywhere, all of which portended the loss of much more than 13 American provinces. Furthermore, the cost of war had become staggering after seven years of campaigning, yet there was not much to show for the effort. It was in this setting of world war and a towering financial burden that Yorktown loomed so large.

On the other side of the ledger, the British still had 30,000 soldiers deployed in America, controlling vital points from Halifax to St. Augustine. British manpower far outdistanced what was available to Washington, which did not add up to more than 20,000 (with Rochambeau's troops counted in) in all posts. Likewise, the ministry was fully aware of the dissension sapping the patriot war effort from the inside, dissension which did not resolve itself with the elation of Yorktown. For instance, Washington sent the bulk of his army northward to the Hudson Highlands in late 1781. There the veterans settled in and allowed their many grievances to fester—to the point of open revolt by March 1783. As another example, a small number of disgruntled Continentals in South Carolina plotted to seize Nathanael Greene and some lesser-ranking officers during 1782. Their notion was to turn them over to the enemy for ranson payments. Once uncovered, the scheme fizzled; one sergeant was summarily executed, and the other plotters fled to the British. Hence, while a policy of endurance at all costs might have been possible for the ministry, the actual weight of reverses in battle effectively destroyed expectations for an upturn in events. The task now became minimizing imperial losses before the European allies snapped the backbone of the far flung empire.

Yorktown signaled that such a point of unbearable stress

had been reached. Official news of Cornwallis's entrapment reached London on Sunday, November 25, 1781. Germain, the intractable colonial secretary, carried the ominous report to Lord North, who received the news "as he would have taken a ball in the breast." Again and again, the astonished cabinet head exclaimed: "Oh God, it is all over!" North knew that Parliament, increasingly restive about the financial burdens of war and stresses of worldwide military pressure, would not accept the news with equanimity. Even though George III wanted to continue, North's instincts were fundamentally correct. Britain was a war-weary nation that was not to be persuaded with more political rhetoric that the glory of the empire depended upon maintaining all the American appendages. Sentiment for holding on reached its lowest point by March 1782, when Parliament reconvened from its winter recess. The House of Commons on March 4 decreed that any citizen wanting to pursue the war was to be considered an enemy of the realm.

North and Germain, as well as George III, had to accept that verdict. Knowing that he was fully out of step, Germain had already resigned, but not before he recalled Henry Clinton, whom he never liked. Sir Guy Carleton, governor of Quebec, took over as the North American commander through the evacuation process. Much maligned, Lord North surrendered power on March 20, concluding his 12-year tenure with these words as he left the Commons: "Goodnight, gentlemen. You see what it is to be in the secret!" Perhaps to save face, George III mumbled a bit about abdicating. Then he turned to the task of finding a new head minister, one devoted to the construction of peace. Lord Rockingham, who held strong pro-American sentiments and favored the immediate granting of American independence, accepted the office. The moment for serious negotiations thus had arrived with the warmer spring weather of 1782.

At the same time, the challenge facing the designated American peace commissioners in Europe had become more complex by 1782, largely because of French and Spanish diplomatic maneuvering. The Spanish originally had entered the war on the narrowest grounds. Their foreign minister, the brilliant and calculating Count Floridablanca, finally had agreed to do so in 1779 with the permission of his sovereign, Charles III, in return for two basic guarantees: first, that the French would persist in the war until Spain had secured Gibraltar and, second, that any new American nation would be so strictly circumscribed that it would never become a threat to Spain's empire in the Americas. In particular, the Spanish court feared the emergence of a thriving republican nation that could serve as a model for disaffected Spanish subjects in the New World. Absolutists that they were, Charles and Floridablanca did not want to participate in the sanctioning of a political entity that might turn around and become a dangerous threat to Spain's long-term national interests.

Vergennes, no fool, did not question Spanish logic. The French foreign minister certainly comprehended that the creation of a vital New World republic could threaten monarchical and imperial systems everywhere. The real goal, Vergennes believed, was the dismemberment of the hated British foe. Sacrificing American interests, he reasoned, would not hinder this main objective—and might even support it, especially if France and Spain could force the Americans into a state of dependency, primarily commercial, upon the two Bourbon powers. By fusing short- and long-term objectives, France and Spain thus began to imagine that they were going to be major victors in the game of diplomatic intrigue. Great Britain and the 13 states would be the losers. The monarchical-imperial status quo would be preserved indefinitely, yet with a decided shift in the overall balance of power toward the Bourbons.

While the French generously supported the American war effort with men and materiel (which Spain did not do), Vergennes worked diligently, beginning in 1778 and 1779, to see to it that nothing more resulted from the war than a weak political entity, squeezed into constraining territorial boundaries. He also envisioned the formation of an informal commerical empire with French merchants taking up where British commercial interests had left off. That French loans and direct military support were so critical to winning the war when that vital support was being put forth for the creation of a nonnation in the New World is one of the great paradoxes of the times. Only the logic of national self-interest could explain such contradictions.

Over the years the three peace commissioners most in contact with the European courts—John Adams, Benjamin Franklin, and John Jay—had become wary of the intentions of Vergennes and Floridablanca. They clearly had their guard up by 1781, if not before. Vergennes, putting pressure on a Congress fearful of the loss of allied support, a Congress that contained a number of middle state merchants eager for strong commercial ties with Spain and France, got the American central government to agree that, beyond settling the issue of independence, peace commissioners were to claim nothing without France's prior approval. By early 1782, it looked as if Vergennes could dictate a settlement completely favorable to the Bourbon powers, since the nervous Congress had given away more control than the Franco-American alliance specified: The peace settlement was supposed to result from mutual consent, not from the dictates of any one party.

If Vergennes thought that he was in control, he was in for some surprises. The peace commissioners chose to ignore Congressional instructions. Outwardly pleasant, if not obsequious, toward Vergennes, they constructed peace accords without keeping the French minister up to date. Initial meetings began between Franklin and Richard Oswald, an aging Scottish slave trader who was Britain's first emissary to the American delegation, during the spring of 1782. Franklin, vitally concerned about legitimate national interests, promised Vergennes that all proposed terms would have France's approval. Vergennes, perhaps trusting too much in the Philadelphian's republican-looking countenance, encouraged the negotiation of basic points for his review. By the time the French minister saw the details, he had his own reasons for not wanting to scuttle what others had constructed.

Instability in George III's new government after Lord North's resignation did not hurt the American effort. The ministry agreed that the former colonists had to be drawn away from the Bourbon allies. The question was how to facilitate that end. Lord Rockingham preferred to recognize American independence and let the rebels go their own way, so long as the peace treaty did not solidify ties between the former colonists and France and Spain. Lord Shelburne, who had succeeded Germain as the colonial secretary, subscribed to independence in name only. He insisted that proper peace accords would effectively keep American commerce spinning as usual in the old imperial orbit. The difference in approach became a moot point in July 1782, when Rockingham suddenly died. His death cleared the way for Shelburne and the hard-line approach. The new minister would offer only enough to assure that France and Spain did not so weaken the proposed American state that it could be used in some way against Britain. Thus to guarantee firm control over American trade and to give the republic enough strength to stand up to France and Spain, the British made concessions that otherwise might never have materialized.

In the preliminary articles of peace, signed at Paris by Richard Oswald and the American commissioners on November 30, 1782, Great Britain did much more than recognize independence—and set the republicans loose. The articles established the Mississippi River as the western boundary and, in a secret provision, settled 31° of north latitude as the southern boundary. The agreement recognized American fishing rights, although as a "liberty," off the coasts of Nova Scotia and New-foundland; it also stipulated that rebel government confiscations of loyalist property must stop; and it obligated Congress to urge the states to return seized loyalist holdings. The British promised that their army would not carry away slaves upon evacuation, but they refused to concede the vast territorial entity of Canada. On that point, Shelburne was obdurate. Americans did not need such a vast region, he reasoned, to have enough strength to counter future Bourbon New World pretensions.

For years John Adams had feared that the attempt to bring about an enduring republic would not be destroyed in war but in peace negotiations. "America," he wrote, "has been a football between contending nations from the beginning, and it is easy to forsee, that France and England both will endeavor to involve us in their future wars. It is our interest and duty," Adams concluded, "to be completely independent, and to have nothing to do with either of them, but in commerce." Generally, the preliminary peace settlement was satisfactory from that perspective. Certainly, it represented about as much as the former colonists could have expected. It was enough of a base on which to construct a worthy edifice, certainly a broader pedestal than either would have liked. Indeed, it may be assessed as double irony that Great Britain, the enemy in battle, had helped to lay that foundation (admittedly in its own self-interest) when the allies in battle did not really want much of one at all.

It fell to Franklin to explain to Vergennes that the American commissioners had not fulfilled the instructions of Congress. The French minister accepted the news rather passively. In fact, the final construction of preliminary peace accords was well timed. By the fall of 1782, the tide of international war, so decisively against Britain at the end of 1781, had now turned against France and Spain. In April 1782, the French naval force under de Grasse had been shattered in a bloody Caribbean battle with the fleet of Admiral George Rodney. Later in the year the Franco-Spanish expedition against Gibraltar failed to dislodge the British defenders. As with Britain before, the cost of continuing the war with such disasters was putting a terrible burden on Louis XVI's overextended treasury.

Against this backdrop Franklin meekly observed, in communicating the proposed Anglo-American peace accords to Vergennes, *"the English, I just now learn, flatter themselves that they have already divided us."* "I hope this little misunderstanding will therefore be kept a secret," added the disingenuous Philadelphian, "and that they will find themselves totally mistaken." Vergennes must have been amused at Franklin's carefully chosen words. Not to be outmaneuvered, the French minister used the preliminary Anglo-American agreement as an excuse for repudiating Spanish commitments and getting on with the broader peace settlement.

The new American state thus survived the pitfalls of diplomatic intrigue and was about to earn legitimacy among the nations of the world. Still, there was lingering doubt as to whether a republican order could be achieved at home, especially if Washington's army felt too aggrieved by its sense of civilian betrayal to lay down its arms and disband.

THE NEWBURGH CONSPIRACY

The prospect of peace should have made all Americans jubilant, even though no one at the end of 1782 knew exactly how the negotiations were going. The imminence of a peace settlement, however, made the Continental army increasingly restive. The bulk of the Continentals, some 10,000 men and an estimated 1,000 women, had settled into the army's final cantonment at Newburgh, New York, a hilly area slightly north of West Point on the west bank of the Hudson River. Washington's soldiers remained on wartime alert, yet the daily routine in camp was hardly demanding enough to keep the veterans from thinking about opportunity after the war—and obligations still outstanding. Common soldiers worried among themselves about arrearages in pay and whether other enlistment commitments would ever be honored. The officer corps began to fear that the army would be disbanded before Congress addressed the problem of funding pensions. Clearly, the army was more anxious, if not more surly, with each passing week, so much so that Washington, who hoped to spend the upcoming winter of 1782-1783 at Mount Vernon, canceled his plans.

To this day, historians fail to agree on the nature of the drama that was about to unfold at Newburgh. The broad issue was financial justice for an army that thought it had been spat upon and generally abused by an ungrateful civilian populace. According to Richard H. Kohn, the closest student of the Newburgh crisis, the officer corps was sorely divided on the issue of how to guarantee its interests. Washington was in the middle and was the voice of moderation. One group, normally loyal to the commander but very much afraid that a peace settlement would allow Congress to sidestep the pension issue, decided to put strong pressures on the central government. Important leaders in this group were Generals Henry Knox and Alexander McDougall. Another faction, centering on Horatio Gates, second in command at Newburgh, appears to have thought in the strongest of all terms—those of a potential military coup d'etat against the central government.

Richard H. Kohn has described Gates as "an overbearing and sensitive general whose bad blood with Washington was long-standing." He was a man whose "pretensions had suffered for years."[4] Gates, the so-called hero of Saratoga, had been all but sacked from the army for his regrettable performance at Camden. After that debacle, he returned home but repeatedly pestered Congress for a hearing to exonerate his name. To placate him, the delegates restored him to rank as Washington's second in command at Newburgh. Although the commander welcomed Gates back in gentlemenly fashion, he still mistrusted the man whom he believed had been a key principal in the Conway Cabal, a man who, like Charles Lee, had fancied himself as belonging at the head of the Continental army.

Tensions within the disgruntled and divided officer corps, certainly being aggravated by the prospect of peace, intensified dramatically at the end of 1782. The Knox-McDougall group precipitated the flurry when they sent a strongly worded petition to Congress. In it the officers bluntly stated: "We have borne all that men can bear—our property is expended—our private resources are at an end." Then they explained that friends were "wearied out and disgusted with their endless applications for credit." They demanded that half-pay pensions be commuted to five years of full pay; if Congress did not act and guarantee them such severance payments, they pointedly warned, "any further experiments on their patience may have fatal effects."

In 1780, at the nadir of the war effort, the officers had threatened Congress with mass resignations. Now, many of them were hinting rather directly that the force of their arms might be used to exact at least a minimum of financial recompense from civilian authorities. Perhaps, too, they were implying that someone, such as George Washington, might be super-imposed over the government as a dictator, as some had suggested during the most difficult days of the war. The military replacing civil authority would be one means of forcing the population to recognize the accomplishments of the army and to treat it with justice, even if such a precipitous act violated one of the most fundamental and sacred of republican principles about the distribution of power in society. Images of Cromwell—even Caesar—were dancing in many heads at the end of 1782.

To thicken the plot, there was an important bloc in Congress, the nationalists, centering on Robert Morris of Philadelphia. Rotund, florid Morris was reputed to be among the wealthiest citizens in America. That he was a financial genius cannot be denied. That he and other nationalists thought that the central government under the Articles of Confederation was hopelessly weak and in need of a real infusion of authority was also true. Morris and the emerging nationalist group had been appalled by the inability of Congress to deal with basic wartime issues. Their vision of a republic encompassed the need for a central government capable of providing necessary military strength, economic stability, and political endurance. Unlike republican purists, they were not afraid of concentrated power, even when somewhat removed from the people. At the end of 1782, they had already tried to increase the authority of Congress—and had failed. The officers' threatening petition gave them new hope.

Important Morris associates in Congressional dealings were Alexander Hamilton, James Madison, and Gouverneur Morris (no relation to Robert). Robert Morris was serving as Superintendent of Finance, one of three administrative posts along with war and foreign affairs, created by Congress in 1781 to bring greater energy to the war effort. Even before Morris had arrived on the scene, the delegates had approved the Impost Plan of 1781, which was a constitutional amendment to give the central government a permanent source of revenue from duties of 5 percent *ad valorem* on all imports. The Impost represented a modest proposal, one that would assure the central government the ability to pay its war debts, which included outstanding obligations to the army. Moreover, by giving Congress a permanent revenue base, it would have served to finance the officers' pensions or commutation of them into lump-sum payments. Like any amendment to the Articles, the Impost Plan required approval by all the sovereign states. Then in November 1782, Rhode Island dealt the Impost Plan, considered linchpin legislation in the nascent nationalist drive to strengthen the central government, a death blow when the state legislature refused to ratify.

In this context the Morris group grabbed onto the officers' remonstrance. In reinvigorating their plans, as Hamilton was to write, "the necessity and discontents of the army presented themselves as a powerful engine." The idea was simple. It involved using the latent threat of military force as a means of pushing the states into supporting a permanent revenue base for Congress. After all, securing such a base was a fundamental issue in which the army had a vital stake, if it realistically ever wanted to see the payment of back salaries, commuted pensions, or other forms of financial indebtedness.

There was one key to the plan, however, that would have made it truly effective. The nationalists in Congress needed Washington's involvement, perhaps even his willingness to lead the army into the field as a temporary expedient to frighten the states into submission. Yet the nationalists were well aware of Washington's temperament and attitudes. Although the commander openly advocated a stronger Congress, he also realized the dangers of the military intervening in civil affairs. Washington feared the destructive potential of his standing army of embittered veterans. He had scrupulously subordinated his personal desires to civil authority throughout the war. He realized that decision making as a product of martial threats and force was antithetical to rule by civil law and human reason. He understood that the goal of free republican institutions could never be realized if civil officials were overrun, even once, or even seriously threatened by a united, uniformed military force.

Washington wanted the grievances of his army properly redressed, but he refused to countenance the plotters. He saw clearly the imminent danger of the Revolution, begun with a spirit of citizen virtue and moral commitment, succumbing to the tyranny of military dictatorship. Such an ending would have rendered to dust all the human travail and suffering of the past eight years. He was not about to let his army or himself be used as an instrument of coercion and tyranny, the way some standing armies had been in the past.

The Morris nationalists in Congress, despite the odds against involving Washington, were direct in their communications. As Hamilton discreetly explained to the commander in chief, "the great *desideratum* . . . is the establishment of general funds, which alone can do justice to the Creditors of the United States. . . . In this the influence of the army, properly directed, may cooperate." Hamilton sent these calculated suggestions to Washington in February 1783. At that time, informal word about the preliminary peace settlement had begun to reach the government in Philadelphia. If peace came and the Continental army disbanded without incident, the potential leverage of strong military pressure would be forever lost. Washington appreciated those circumstances and prepared himself for the seemingly inevitable confrontation, which he described as the officers throwing "themselves into the gulph of Civil horror."

What Washington suspected was that the Morris group, for lack of alternatives, had struck some sort of a deal with Horatio Gates. Kohn has argued that the initiative itself came from Gates and his "Young Turk" followers, the idea being to supplant Washington at the head of the army and then have Gates lead it into the field.[5] General Gates's most recent biographer, Paul David Nelson, has strongly denied that Gates took any such initiative or had any intentions of trying to undermine Washington.[6] The heavy involvement of Gates's subordinates in the final steps of the crisis, however, does not support Nelson's conclusion. Gates was clearly up to something, and it may have been, as Kohn has argued, that he was working in league with, and was being used by, the Morris nationalists. In fact, Kohn has argued that the Morris nationalists had turned their plotting into "a treacherous double game, fraught with uncertainty." They intended only to have Gates "spark the explosion" of the army, thus serving to break state resistance to revenues for Congress. However, Hamilton warned Washington of the impending upheaval, hoping that he could contain the uprising, once it had occurred, and save the new nation from the likes of Gates.[7] The danger, of course, was that the whole matter could get so out of hand that Washington would be powerless, despite his charisma. In that case, with Gates in the saddle, some form of autocracy could have been the end-product of such machinations.

Whatever the actual extent of Gates's involvement, the crisis came to a head in March 1783. Word from Philadelphia had been received in Gates's camp that it was time to move ahead. On Monday, March 10, John Armstrong, one of Gates's aides, wrote the first Newburgh Address. It was an incendiary document. Once copies had been made, Christopher Richmond, another Gates aide-de-camp, circulated them through camp. The tone was very blunt. Armstrong spoke bitterly of civilian ingratitude for what the army had accomplished; he mocked "the meek language of entreating memorials"; and he warned his fellow officers to "suspect the man who would advise to more moderation and longer forbearance," a clear negative allusion to Washington. If Congress and the states did not guarantee financial justice, the Address declared, decisive action was at last necessary: "If peace, that nothing shall separate them [Congress] from your arms but death: if war, that. . .you will retire to some unsettled country, smile in your turn, and 'mock when their fear cometh on.'" Having argued its case, the Address urged that all officers attend an unauthorized meeting the next day to discuss grievances in full and to prepare for further action.

Washington, outraged by the Address but not surprised that the crisis was at hand, given earlier warnings, prepared himself for the showdown. He had already appealed to the Knox-McDougall group for support. Dislike of Gates helped to bring them around. More secure with this base, on Tuesday morning, March 11, the commander put out general orders that labeled the Address and its proposal for a meeting as "disorderly" and "irregular." Washington advised the officers to meet, but on his authority at noon on Saturday, March 15—the Ides. He would not attend, or so he stated, so that everyone could speak freely. The implication was that Gates, as the ranking officer, would be in charge of the meeting. No doubt fooled by Washington's tactic, which led them to believe that the commander was playing into their hands, the Gates group acceded to Washington's general order through the issuance of a second Newburgh Address. This document, also written by Armstrong, accepted the new meeting date and cautioned the officers that a short delay must not work to "lessen the *independence* of your sentiments."

March 15, 1783, was a day of enormous emotional tension. As the meeting came to order with Gates in the chair, Washington strode into the room and moved forward slowly toward his putative adversary. He firmly asked for permission to speak and then turned to face his angry subordinates. Looking for the right words, he urged patience upon them, while he characterized the first Newburgh Address as a document appealing to "passions" rather than "reason and good sense." How could the army, Washington pleaded, turn against the country "in the extremist hour of her distress." Had it only suffered so much to sow "the seeds of discord and separation" in society? "My God! What can this writer have in view, by recommending such measures? Can he be a friend to the army? Can he be a friend to the country? Rather is he not an insidious foe?"

Sensing that he was still not reaching his comrades, Washington persisted. The commander stated that he wanted to read a letter. He reached into his pocket and pulled out a pair of eyeglasses. The gathering seemed startled; none had seen their leader wear glasses before. Catching their surprise, Washington calmly explained: "Gentlemen, you must pardon me. I have grown gray in your service and now find myself growing blind." His words and their larger meaning caught the assemblage off guard. The commander had verbalized for all of them their sense of personal sacrifice, of thwarted dignity and honor. Suddenly, the officers understood. The army had already established the point that concepts such as citizen virtue and moral commitment, upon which the republic must rest, had meaning in America. Regardless of what so many fair-weather patriots had done, it was the example set by the officers and the regulars that had brought that dream to the verge of reality. Even if the nation never remembered who had really made the sacrifices or gave them proper credit or financial recompense, it did not seem to matter so much now. Each person who had truly sacrificed should be proud of what had been accomplished—and of the legacy that had been left. To ruin it all on the verge of success would have been the most cruel of ironies. The assembled officers thus reflected on the ideals of virtue and moral commitment; and some, the hardiest of dedicated veterans, openly wept. They had been reconciled to their commander in chief and to the cause, despite their lingering bitterness.

The Newburgh Conspiracy thus passed into oblivion, handed down by writers to our own time as basically a minor tempest, until studied more intensively in recent years. Yet to downplay its significance is to support the myth of harmony and unity in the cause, to create the impression that rebels locked closely arm in arm made the republican experiment a functioning ideal. Reality, however, was not such a straight path. The Newburgh crisis would not have occurred had the soldiery not been embittered at the civilian sector. Alienation had been building for at least five years, but it had been diffused and a crisis always averted when civilian government gave in. In late 1782 the war was ending, and the officers knew it. That something more striking did not happen makes the crisis more significant and revealing.

The officers had no way of predicting whether the rank and file would follow them into the field, since the two groups had never identified their interests closely enough to protest effectively in common. Fear of standing alone may have brought some of the officers into line, but recalling their sense of duty cannot be overly stressed. Indeed, what the crisis revealed as a culmination to unstable relations between army and society is that the officers were capable of subordinating self-interest to the public welfare, the essential ingredient of a virtuous citizenry when put to the ultimate test. Because of that restraint, a military coup, with some American Caesar rising out of the ashes, did not eventuate. Washington had controlled his new modeled army, a creature unwanted in 1775 and 1776 but made necessary because of flagging support for the cause. The significance of it all was that the army remained on the side of liberty and republicanism while tempted, even dared by civilians who withheld support and encouragement from 1777 on, to go the other way. When most sorely tried, it reaffirmed subordination of military to civil authority. Paradoxically, this same hardcore group of regulars, so damned by so many patriots (and feared by ideologues as the antithesis of the republican ideal of the militia) set the highest example of selfless behavior in Revolutionary America.

TRANSITION TO A POSTWAR WORLD

Newburgh was one ending in the transition to peace. There would be many others as the new nation extricated itself from war and sought legitimacy with the populace. News of preliminary peace started to spread across the land in early April 1783, and Congress proclaimed a cessation of hostilities on April 11. Final peace terms, involving a settlement among all belligerents, would be ratified in Paris during September. Meanwhile, Great Britain began to evacuate its military forces. Congress, despite the sentiments of nationalists like Robert Morris and Alexander Hamilton, was anxious to demobilize the army before some new threat to civil authority developed. In the aftermath of Newburgh, Congress did commute officers' pensions into lump-sum payments equivalent to five years of full salary. The central body also framed a new impost plan with a 25-year limitation clause, but the states never adopted it, which kept the central government as penniless and powerless as it had been before. Without revenue, Congress was in no position to honor its lump-sum severance payments. By June 1783, the "furlough" of Washington's regulars was well under way. Congress did not want to disband the Continentals officially until British regiments had left New York, Charleston, Savannah, and other east-coast points of concentration.

Most of the army personnel returned to civilian life in relative peace (though with burning resentment on the inside). Each soldier was given three months' pay in "final settlement certificates," hardly what Congress owed them. The idea was to offer the veterans something in the form of fiat money so that they would not go off "enraged, complaining of injustice—and committing enormities on the innocent Inhabitants in every direction," as Washington explained the matter. Not all went off quietly. A large, angry group of Pennsylvania veterans marched on Philadelphia in June. There troops from the southern theater bolstered them. They surrounded the State House, where Congress and the Pennsylvania assembly met, and demanded immediate financial satisfaction. The intimidated delegates, warned ahead of time of the danger, begged the Pennsylvania government for militia protection. State officials offered neither solace nor assistance. While the soldiery shouted insults, the Congressional delegates filed out of the State House and left the scene. So irate were these civil leaders that they ultimately relocated themselves in Princeton, New Jersey, then later at Annapolis, Maryland. There was little else they could do. They had no financial resources and no real authority. With the coming of peace, there were many republican purists who now believed that a central government was a trifle, if not a corrupting luxury.

The confrontation at the State House in Philadelphia was the last major protest from a portion of Washington's army. The commander still hoped that something could be done to reward his veteran troops. In early June, he sent a circular letter to the various states, speaking out in favor of a stronger national edifice and a just financial settlement. With respect to the central government, the issue was whether the nation was to be "respectable and prosperous, or contemptible and miserable." The former condition depended on the establishment of "a Supreme Power to regulate and govern the general concerns of the Confederated republic, without which the Union cannot be of long duration." Washington exhorted the states to support Congress, to give it needed increments of authority, and to convey to it the ability to discharge the wartime national debt (including obligations due the army). He added, poignantly, that he had personally pledged himself "to the Army, that their Country would finally do them complete and ample Justice."

As it turned out, the down and outers who had proved to be Washington's steadiest veterans never received much compensation for loyal services rendered the infant nation. Joseph Plumb Martin, in later life, described the matter rather testily: "The country was rigorous in exacting my compliance to *my* engagements to a punctilio, but equally careless in performing her contracts with me, and why so? One reason was because she had all the power in her own hands and I had none."

Besides settlement certificates, the soldiers retained their muskets, ammunition if they decided to take it, and the clothes on their backs. Furlough papers, which proved honorable discharges, could be used to claim land warrant certificates for promised bounty lands. The land warrants soon became another form of fiat currency, to be traded off quickly for the necessities of life. The result was that few soldiers who dreamed of a freehold stake in the fully legitimized republic realized their goal. It was not long before land speculators moved in on the warrants, started grabbing them up, and enjoyed some easy profits in dealing in the "soldiers' lands" in the Ohio country. Few thus immediately realized their dream of economic well-being. Most reentered civilian life at the same poverty level that they had left behind—and remained there for the rest of their lifetimes. Ultimately, only former slaves and felons clearly benefited from service. The bulk of them had earned their personal freedom.

Joseph Plumb Martin described the readjustment process this way: "When the country had drained the last drop of service it could screw out of the poor soldiers, they were turned adrift like old worn-out horses, and nothing said about land to pasture them upon.'' Martin, who became a humble dirt farmer in Maine, still was not sorry about his personal sacrifices and contributions. He knew that he had measured up to the canons of citizen virtue, and his memoirs demonstrate great pride in an assignment well done, despite the niggardliness of the severance settlement.

Martin also expressed great affection for President James Monroe and others, who in 1818 cleared the way for veterans' pensions in the form of financial relief for dissolute but able-bodied Revolutionary soldiers. (Modest disability pensions had been available before war's end for those unfortunates who had suffered nearly total destruction of life and limb.) Then in 1832 Congress granted all veterans, including militiamen, old age pensions without restrictions. William H. Glasson (*Federal Military Pensions in the United States,* 1918) has estimated that the average living pensioneer was 74-years-old in 1831.[8] Perhaps as many as 60,000 to 65,000 veterans were still alive some 49 years after the final peace settlement and, no doubt, those poor enough to get pensions were grateful for the financial recognition—long since overdue.

What distressed the veterans most of all was the psychological reaction of friends and neighbors to seemingly just financial recompense. Martin's neighbors apparently took to arguing that the pensions were unfair because the Continental army had been ''needless.'' They now asserted that ''the militia were competent for all that the crisis required,'' and that ''it would have been much better for the country to have done it than for us [the Continentals] eating so much provisions and wearing out so much clothing when our services were worse than useless.'' Martin considered ''it cruel to be thus vilified,'' but he had the personal fortitude to slough off such ''hardhearted'' sentiment and to take it for what it was—cracker-barrel commentary. In the end, he took solace in what he and his hardy brethren had done in forging a chain of ''Independence and Liberty'' out of so little in the way of basic war materiel and popular patriot support.

The crushing burdens of poverty and public ingratitude also fell on veterans' wives and families. A few of the hundreds of women who became a part of the rebel army did receive pensions, but the vast majority did not. Many instead shared the hard lot of widows and orphans left by the war. Recognizing at least partial responsibility for their plight, the states had provided some small assistance to these unfortunates. Even this aid, however, came grudgingly. The ordeal of Electa Campfield, for example, the widow of a Continental, typified what happened to other women when they applied for relief. She first wrote to the county court, stating that her husband's death had left her "with one Child and without any kind of support," and that she had suffered "innumerable difficulties during the whole of the war." To receive benefits, she next had to find and then obtain depositions from her husband's former officers, establishing his service record in his New Jersey regiment. The minister of her local congregation also had to supply a deposition testifying to the legality of her marriage, and the local Overseer of the Poor then swore to her legal residency. All this information went to the court, which approved her application and sent it to the state legislature. Widow Campfield then waited seven months for the assembly to approve her request and to authorize payment from the state treasury.

Other orphans and widows never even heard that help was available, and some who had applied became thoroughly disheartened with the arduous application procedures. Worn out by the process, they neglected to follow up on submitted claims, which occasionally meant that approved benefits were never collected. The situation amounted to a tragedy, but it was also indicative of society's misgivings over pensions generally.

Antipension sentiment also hurt deeply because it downgraded the fortitude and ultimate sacrifices of those men and women who had been willing to endure with Washington for the long-term fight. Howard H. Peckham's valuable compilation of American casualties (*The Toll of Independence,* 1974) conservatively estimates a total death figure of 25,674 among Revolutionary soldiers and sailors (7,174 in battle, an estimated 10,000 who succumbed to disease in camp, and an estimated 8,500 prisoners who died while in enemy hands). Another 8,241 were wounded in battle and survived, while 1,426 were missing in action—some of whom may have died with others deserting or returning unnoticed after battle to the ranks.[9] If the basic estimate of 175,000 total participants, including regulars and militia actually in the field, is more or less accurate (Peckham uses the higher base of 200,000), one out of every five soldiers did not come away from the war personally unscathed. Furthermore, since the bulk of the fighting fell to the Continentals, it seems probable that they may have experienced a casualty rate as high as 30 to 40 percent from all causes, dramatically higher than the 13 percent loss figure among Union troops during the far bloodier Civil War.

In his analysis, Peckham points out that the War for Independence, among all wars involving American armies, ranks only behind the Civil War in casualties relative to available total population.[10] Since not that many patriots chose to stay in the ranks for extended periods (over and above short-term service), the debt owed to those few hardened veterans in the Continental ranks should never have been belittled, especially since such a significant proportion did not survive until 1783. Yet memories and arguments have a way of becoming self-serving, as Martin's neighbors so conspicuously demonstrated.

By early 1784, the Continental army had been disbanded for all practical purposes, except for some 600 troops who had responsibility for guarding military stores at West Point and Springfield, Massachusetts, and for assisting with the restoration of civilian government in New York City. It should have been obvious that some form of ongoing military establishment, however circumscribed, should have been necessary. However, the nationalists had begun to despair their prospects for strengthening Congress. Appalled by the inchoate state of public affairs, many had given up and gone home. Typical were Robert Morris, who had left the superintendency of finance, and Alexander Hamilton and James Madison, who had resigned their seats in Congress even before their full terms were up. With localists back in control of the central body, the likelihood that some type of national military establishment would be maintained was quite remote.

There can be no doubt that the leading nationalists believed firmly in a strong military constabulary, even during peacetime. However, the coming of peace meant that their "hopes for a large, centrally controlled standing army evaporated," as Walter Millis described it.[11] All that was left were those 600 troops, not much of a security force to stand up against new external threats or domestic turbulence of any kind.

Washington, now in retirement at Mount Vernon, yet a strongly committed nationalist (as were many of his former officers who had lived with the frustrations of a weak central government for eight years), wanted Congress to keep up a respectable force. Even before his army had been furloughed, he prepared his "Sentiments on a Peace Establishment," derived from the advice of key officers and from wartime experience. The commander knew that a large peacetime constabulary flew in the face of antistanding-army ideology. Thus he recommended a small regular force of 2,631 to protect the new nation's borders and to be ready to deal with domestic turmoil. To back up this core of regulars, Washington recommended a well-trained militia, including all white, male citizens between the ages of 18 and 50. To avoid wartime problems, all militia would train according to uniform guidelines and regulations. Furthermore, some male citizens between the ages of 18 and 25 would be singled out for more rigorous duty in elite units. While the sum total would represent a largely volunteer army, existing because of the obligations of citizenship, it would also be better trained than colonial militia had been, and it would have regulars at the core with vital support from a limited number of elite units. It would also be subject to Congressional as opposed to whimsical and divided state authority.

The "Sentiments" did not go so far as Washington would have liked. He would have preferred to see a larger core of standing regulars, yet the national failure to mobilize such a cadre even during the urgency of war rendered the idea visionary. Moreover, he accepted ideological constraints, just as he had allowed them to govern his behavior as commander in chief. He pointed out to Hamilton, in conveying the plan to Congress, that "a *large* standing Army in time of Peace has ever been considered dangerous to the liberties of a Country." Thus "a few Troops," Washington noted, were all that one could ask for, but they were "indispensably necessary." "Fortunately for us," he concluded, "our relative situation requires but few."

Yet there was also another side to Washington's thinking. The idea behind compulsory training for all male citizens reflected on the obligations of citizenship in the context of wartime manpower shortages and the uneven performance of militia. The commander wrote in the plan: "It may be laid down as a primary position, and the basis of our system, that every Citizen who enjoys the protection of a free Government, owes not only a proportion of his property, but even his personal services to the defense of it." Here was a strong restatement of the fundamental duties of each citizen in a republican polity.

Indeed, Washington was doing much more than simply endorsing the concept of the citizen-soldier and universal military obligation, as essentially argued by the first modern student of the "Sentiments," John McAuley Palmer in *Washington, Lincoln, Wilson* (1930).[12] He was trying to support the legitimacy of the nascent republican order by establishing a mechanism that would result in mandatory virtuous behavior. At the same time, he was being true to his convictions about the necessity of a core standing army as the central unit of defense. Also, as Russell F. Weigley has stressed in *Towards an American Army* (1962), Washington hoped to broaden the hard core base with "a militia in which some men, at least, would be much like regulars." Those in the elite units would become "a special force of carefully trained men, capable of immediate resistance to European regulars, within the general militia."[13]

Despite the efforts of Hamilton and other nationalists, Washington's "Sentiments," as well as similar plans presented by Baron von Steuben and others, would not be fulfilled for 20 years. Congress, reduced to virtual insignificance by the temper of the times and the withdrawal of leading nationalists, declared on June 2, 1784, that the remaining establishment should be discharged, except for fewer than 100 men to guard military stores. Piously, the delegates concluded that "standing armies in time of peace are inconsistent with the principles of republican government." These actions epitomize how weak and helpless the central government had become within a year of the end of hostilities.

MYTH AND TRADITION: A POLITICAL/MILITARY SETTLEMENT

The new nation, somewhat reassured of its republican fervor and moral fiber with independence now a reality, easily retreated into old antistanding-army shibboleths. When Washington officially resigned from service on December 23, 1783, everyone present was on the verge of tears. No Caesar or Cromwell he, the one man who could have become an autocrat offered his "sincere Congratulations to Congress" in "presenting myself before them to surrender into their hands the trust committed to me." Once again, images of Cincinnatus abounded, for it seemed to those present that Washington desired nothing more than the chance to return to his plow.

Yet republican ideologues did not forget that there were those who had urged Washington during the darkest days of the contest to seize power as Caesar once had. When Henry Knox and Baron von Steuben led the officer corps in putting together the Society of Cincinnati in 1783, there were many shrill voices about the unrequited desire for military aristocracy. The officers themselves sought an exclusive fraternal group to which only men of their grade who had been in rank for a minimum of three years or were in uniform at the end of hostilities could belong. Furthermore, they proposed that membership be hereditary with only first sons of succeeding generations to be eligible for membership. Besides exclusiveness, other goals were to continue seeking commutation and to provide a charity fund for former comrades who failed in making the economic transition back to civilian life. Clearly, the officers, through the Cincinnati, were attempting to give each other the recognition that civilian patriots had so long witheld from them. But critics, who were many and vocal, stated that the Society was not only inherently unrepublican but smacked of tyrannical designs. Gossip spread widely—for instance, that the real purpose of the contingency fund was to collect monies for the takeover being planned.

Part of the reaction to the Cincinnati, too, reflected the fact that the officers were largely pro-nationalist in politics, a logical outgrowth of wartime frustrations. That they had insisted on pensions, now wanted more power at the center, and desired a respectable peacetime military establishment made them very suspect to attacks by insecure republican localists (later called Antifederalists). Furthermore, the retired officers seemed to be claiming too much credit for the glory of victory. They were not being fair in neglecting the contributions of noncombatants, who now were demanding a larger share of the limelight with peace at hand.

In this setting, some writers began to explain away why the citizenry had not been more eager to defend liberty. Soon that puzzle was being solved by claiming that they had actually been there all along, all evidence to the contrary notwithstanding. The early evolution of this form of historical imagination may be seen by looking at Mercy Otis Warren's treatment of the war years in her *History of the Rise, Progress and Termination of the American Revolution* (3 vols., 1805).[14] Warren's study typifies how a contemporary's concern with virtue served to modify historical reality and underpin a misleading tradition. Much of her text was written immediately after the war. Even though Warren admitted that participation had fallen off rather sharply after 1776, the real problem, she asserted, had to do with machinating leaders ambitious for personal profit and high political and military offices. What saved the cause from these nascent nationalists was the middle-class citizen-soldier, who behaved with a keen sense of decorum and duty throughout the war. The citizen-soldier was always pure in word and deed and did compose the bulk of the army in the field. To take one example, the "mutinous disposition" of those soldiers who marched on Congress in June 1783 "did not appear to have infested the whole army: many of the soldiers were the substantial yeomanry of the country."[15]

Suddenly, it became the down and outers who were not virtuous, as neatly juxtaposed to morally committed citizens-in-arms. They should have been the great stabilizing influence, so apparently they were there. In turn, those who threatened the cause after 1783 were militarists of the nationalist stripe, individuals who favored the formation of the Society of the Cincinnati, and the lower orders, who could always be duped by designing men grasping after power for its own sake. Warren's characterizations were both highly partisan and inaccurate with respect to the soldiery. But that did not matter in the postwar world. To republican purists, evil, designing men such as Robert Morris, Henry Knox, or Alexander Hamilton, not the virtuous citizenry, were the ones who had to be watched. There was not much ground between the highly partisan reminiscences of Warren and other committed ideologues and the ornate, nationalistic flourishes of George Bancroft, all of which gave a firm base to the myth of true citizen dedication and endurance.

In our own time, however, the hold of the mythology over the War for Independence has been lessening. John Ellis, for instance, in his provocative study of *Armies in Revolution* (1974), has compared levels of popular participation in the American war with those of the English, French, Russian, and Chinese revolutions. Only in the English and Chinese civil wars did he find a harmonious "integration of the civilian and the military" on a mass scale, in the sense that "the act of being a soldier is made inseparable from the desire to be a more fulfilled citizen."[16] In the case of the American war, Ellis argues that "parochial notions of family and district" with no "particular sense of being American," as separate from being an Englishman, held down on high levels of popular involvement and support. He goes on to hypothesize that "though the enemy had been identified," the colonists still lacked a "cohesive sense of solidarity" because they "had little conception of a collectivity beyond that of town or county." With a relatively weak central government, "there was no way in which the more enthusiastic patriots could begin to remedy the deficiencies in national feeling." Thus the most committed rebels "found themselves caught in a vicious circle: regional diversities and divisions fed upon themselves to create an atmosphere of political apathy and helplessness."[17]

To state the proposition somewhat differently, the enemy had been clearly identified by 1776. Yet the sense of being an American (a separate political being) had not as yet become strong enough to ensure unity in the cause, once the *rage militaire* had passed. The problem was to overcome parochial feelings, to create a widespread sense of national legitimacy by giving root to the affections of the people. It meant changing the feelings of the Philadelphian who asserted early on in the war: "Let who would be king, he well knew that he should be a subject." Over time, the actual experience of war did just that, until the point had been reached not too long after the war when many would claim, despite hard evidence, that national duty rather than parochial self-interest had governed their behavior during the war.

Success in war, above all else, completed a vital step in the political conversion process. A more widely held sense of national legitimacy was a critical byproduct of the travail of those few who stood the test of Continental service. In "The Military Conflict Considered as a Revolutionary War" (1973), John Shy has cogently observed that the contest with Britain served as "a political education" by convincing "thousands of more or less unwilling people to associate themselves openly and actively with the cause."[18] This process of forced involvement may easily be brought to mind by recalling operations in the South after 1778. Whether or not local inhabitants in that region liked it, the spread of the war to so many localities helped to break down parochialism and to create new feelings of national identity and legitimacy.

These new feelings were blossoming across the landscape at

war's end. And they were essential to the next step in the process of establishing a fully legitimate national political order. After 1783, the crucial question was what form the republican polity should take. Purists persisted in their faith in public virtue as an organizational concept. The nationalists, by comparison, could not now imagine, after the experience of the war, that citizen virtue could ever serve as a fundamental instrument of enduring political stability. Something had to be done, they kept telling each other. Their chance finally came during 1787 in the wake of Shays's Rebellion in Massachusetts. The national Consititution that they wrote and pushed through to ratification created a structure of government that, from their perspective, would guarantee a national political order that could deal effectively with pressing problems and could endure through time, but would not be dependent on public virtue.

Walter Millis has argued that the Constitution of 1787 "was as much a military as a political and economic charter."[19] Having been denied an effective peacetime establishment in 1783, the nationalists saw to it that such would be possible in the future. Congress now had the stated power to "provide for the common defense" through taxes, import duties, and excises, as well as the authority to declare war, make peace, provide for and maintain a navy, issue letters of marque, and "raise and support Armies." The President, as the highest civil official, was also to serve as commander in chief. There was to be militia, too, which while subject to state authority, could "be employed in the Service of the United States." Equally important, state units were to be trained according to standard procedures of "discipline prescribed by Congress."

The nationalists, in their role as founding fathers, drew heavily upon plans advocating a standing regular force to be supplemented by well-trained militia. As a group, these men were not afraid of military power, with all that it implied, so long as it remained subordinate to civil authority. If they had been blatant militarists, they would not have adopted English precedent and limited military appropriations to a maximum of two years before renewal. There can be no doubt, as Richard H.

Kohn has stated, that the nationalists consciously wanted to give "the new government sharp military teeth," or that they "wanted a government able both to protect the nation from foreign countries and to protect a minority from popular despotism, from the majority, and from the licentiousness of the people."[20] Yet they were not abandoning republican tenets, rather designing them so that regular forces could be there in peace and war to fill the void in public virtue.

There is fundamental irony here. The likelihood of virtue and moral commitment being sustained in the absence of broad-scale consensus about national legitimacy was quite slim. That proved to be the case in 1776. Once that consensus had begun to be achieved, however, there was much greater prospect for the moral fiber of the people to demonstrate itself, both in peace and in war. It is that part of the process of transition and change during the Revolution that the nationalists either did not see or would not concede. As a result, they carried through on sweeping constitutional change in 1787.

Thus it was the experience of war with its concomitant quest for national legitimacy that served as an essential reference point in the definition of enduring republican institutions in America. Those who prevailed in 1787 put the emphasis on order and structure rather than on the abstract concept of public virtue, which from their perspective might forever be wanting. They did also because they viewed military strength as essential to stability and durability as a nation. Opposition whig writings may have served as the framework in their deliberations, but experience cannot be minimized. Thus while carefully providing for the subordination of military to civil authority, the nationalists also sought to emulate Old World models about the need for regular military institutions. The Constitution, so much a product of its times, confirmed that blending of traditions.

Once the new government began to function in 1789, the goal of military effectiveness did not quickly happen. While the nationalists pushed in and out of Congress for a respectable establishment, their political adversaries fought them every step of the way. The opposition party (they soon took to calling themselves Jeffersonian Republicans) branded their political adversaries as militarists eager to ensnare the people in despotic traps. The Jeffersonians retained their faith in militia and the virtuous citizen-soldier well into the nineteenth century. Only time sorted out the two traditions.

In actual historical circumstance, the regular force tradition did find solace and pride in the War for Independence. It owed its viability to the small band of committed individuals who stood with Washington after so many citizen-soldiers went home in 1776. The volunteer force tradition, based on expectation and ideological fervor, in turn, came to dominate in oral and written legend and myth about the War for Independence. In the end, however, Washington's Continental establishment was, of necessity, a standing army, fighting for a populace rather than representing the social composition of that population in war. Even though the army grew to resent and despise the patriot citizenry, it remained faithful in its quest. That army, because of its virtuous fiber, set the stage for a lasting republican order in America. Henry Knox stated the proposition aptly in 1783 when he explained that there was "a favorite toast in the army," that of " 'a hoop to the barrel,' or 'Cement to the Union.' " That may be the way that Joseph Plumb Martin and his comrades would have liked to be remembered, not as the myth has made them, but as the real human beings they were—individuals who secured, militarily, the origins of a stable and enduring New World republic.

NOTES

[1] Russell F. Weigley, *The American Way of War: A History of United States Military Strategy and Policy* (New York, 1973), p. 37.

[2] Hugh F. Rankin, "Charles Lord Cornwallis: Study in Frustration," in G. A. Billias, ed., *George Washington's Opponents: British Generals and Admirals in the American Revolution* (New York, 1969), p. 202.

[3] Piers Mackesy, *The War for America, 1775-1783* (Cambridge, Mass., 1965), pp. 435-36.

⁴ Richard H. Kohn, *Eagle and Sword: The Federalists and the Creation of the Military Establishment in America, 1783-1802* (New York, 1975), pp. 17-28.

⁵ *Ibid.,* p. 25. *See also* Kohn, "The Inside History of the Newburgh Conspiracy: America and the Coup d'Etat," *William and Mary Quarterly,* 3d Series, 27 (1970), pp. 187-220.

⁶ Paul David Nelson, "Horatio Gates at Newburgh, 1783: A Misunderstood Role," *William and Mary Quarterly,* 3d Series, 29 (1972), pp. 143-58, which also includes a reply by Kohn. *See also* Nelson, *General Horatio Gates: A Biography* (Baton Rouge, La., 1976), pp. 266-97.

⁷ Kohn, *Eagle and Sword,* pp. 26-27.

⁸ William H. Glasson, *Federal Military Pensions in the United States* (New York, 1918), pp. 95-96.

⁹ Howard H. Peckham, ed., *The Toll of Independence: Engagements and Battle Casualties of the American Revolution* (Chicago, 1974), p. 130.

¹⁰ *Ibid.,* pp. 131-34.

¹¹ Walter Millis, *Arms and Men: A Study in Military History* (New York, 1956), p. 37.

¹² John McAuley Palmer, *Washington, Lincoln, Wilson: Three War Statesmen* (Garden City, N.Y., 1930), pp. 10-27, 55-71.

¹³ Russell F. Weigley, *Towards an American Army: Military Thought from Washington to Marshall* (New York, 1962), p. 12.

¹⁴ Mercy Otis Warren, *History of the Rise, Progress and Termination of the American Revolution,* 3 vols. (Boston, 1805), 3:268-82. *See also* valuable comments in Lawrence Delbert Cress, "The Standing Army, the Militia, and the New Republic: Changing Attitudes toward the Military in American Society, 1768 to 1820," (Ph.D. dissertation, University of Virginia, 1976), pp. 195-200; *idem,* "Republican Liberty and National Security: American Military Policy as an Ideological Problem," *William and Mary Quarterly,* 3d Series, 38 (1981), pp. 73-96; Lester H. Cohen, "Explaining the Revolution: Ideology and Ethics in Mercy Otis Warren's Historical Theory," *ibid.,* 37 (1980), pp. 200-18.

¹⁵ Warren, *History of the Rise, Progress and Termination of the American Revolution,* p. 277.

¹⁶ John Ellis, *Armies in Revolution* (New York, 1974), pp. 238-39.

¹⁷ *Ibid.,* pp. 46-47.

¹⁸ John Shy, "The Military Conflict Considered as a Revolutionary War," *A People Numerous and Armed: Reflections on the Military Struggle for American Independence* (New York, 1976) p. 222.

¹⁹ Millis, *Arms and Men,* p. 41.

²⁰ Kohn, *Eagle and Sword,* p. 80. *See also* Millis, *Arms and Men,* pp. 40-46.

A Note on Revolutionary War History and Historiography

Until recent decades, military history about the War for American Independence has had a decided "guns and battles" orientation. Many such volumes, dating well back into the nineteenth century, had strong antiquarian interests. Governing questions concerned what personality, battle, or battlefield maneuver contributed most to momentary triumphs or defeats in war. Invariably in the background was the standard patriotic mythology of a determined provincial freeholding populace marching forward arm-in-arm in the struggle to overcome tyranny.

By the standards of our own times, such history was both narrowly conceived and needlessly argumentative. Yet as with any genre of literature, there were exceptions. Readers may still benefit from works such as, for example, Lyman C. Draper, *King's Mountain and Its Heroes* (Cincinnati, Ohio, 1881); Richard Frothingham, *History of the Siege of Boston, and the Battles of Lexington, Concord and Bunker Hill,* 4th ed. (Boston, 1873); Henry P. Johnston, *Campaign of 1776 Around New York and Brooklyn* (Brooklyn, N.Y., 1876); and William S. Stryker, *The Battles of Trenton and Princeton* (Boston, 1898).

There were exceptions of other types, moreover. Some interested students devoted themselves to recovering valuable knowledge and documentation about the wartime period. Peter Force was one such individual. His massive collection, *American Archives,* 4th and 5th Series, 9 vols. (Washington, D.C., 1837–1853), contains a storehouse of information on the early phases of the war through 1776. Then there was Benson J. Lossing, whose *Pictorial Field Book of the Revolution,* 2 vols. (New York, 1851–1852), still remains a seminal guide to Revolutionary battlefield sites. From yet another angle, Emory Upton's *Military Policy of the United States since 1775* (Washington, D.C., 1904), written several years before its publication, denounced the lack of concern about maintaining regular armies and assuring military preparedness in the post-Civil War era. At least part of the blame lay with the Revolutionaries who failed to establish a viable tradition for standing military institutions. As such, claimed Upton, the rebels could not have pulled through had it not been for the intervention of the French and such imponderable factors as luck.

Upton's distaste for militia and his focus on values, policies, and institutions proved to be one basis for a number of newer military studies capable of getting beyond the battlefield.

Claude H. Van Tyne emphasized the ineffectiveness of militia as opposed to regular army units in *The War of Independence: American Phase* (Boston, 1929). In turn, Don Higginbotham has outlined more recent thinking, emphasizing the many contributions made by short-termers, in "The American Militia: A Traditional Institution with Revolutionary Responsibilities," Don Higginbotham, ed., *Reconsiderations of the Revolutionary War: Selected Essays* (Westport, Conn., 1978), pp. 83-103. How leaders in the early republic attempted to balance the two traditions is of paramount concern in the early chapters of John McAuley Palmer, *Washington, Lincoln, Wilson: Three War Statesmen* (Garden City, N.Y., 1930); and Russell F. Weigley, *Towards an American Army: Military Thought from Washington to Marshall* (New York, 1962). Marcus Cunliffe, *Soldiers and Civilians: The Martial Spirit in America, 1775-1865,* 2d ed. (New York, 1973), analyzes the evolution of the "professional," "antiprofessional," and "antimilitarist" traditions in the American experience through the Civil War. The most thorough study of conflicting attitudes, as expressed in postwar policies affecting military institutions in the new nation, is Richard H. Kohn's *Eagle and Sword: the Federalists and the Creation of the Military Establishment in America, 1783-1802* (New York, 1975). Additional light may also be found in valuable doctoral dissertations by Lawrence Delbert Cress, "The Standing Army, the Militia, and the New Republic: Changing Attitudes toward the Military in American Society, 1768 to 1820" (University of Virginia, 1976), and John Todd White, "Standing Armies in Time of War: Republican Theory and Military Practice during the American Revolution" (George Washington University, 1978).

Such literature has demonstrated that much more can be done with war and its related experiences than compiling and arguing about the details of various engagements. Still, a purity of emphasis on martial accomplishments, generally divorced from the concerns of the new republic seeking identity, legitimacy, and stability through rebellion and war, has continued down to our own time. Within this traditional framework, a number of well-received volumes appeared after World War II, perhaps reflecting the new importance being accorded to military matters in the troubled years of the Cold War and beyond. Among the most significant are John R. Alden, *The American Revolution, 1775-1783* (New York, 1954); Robert W. Coakley and Stetson Conn, *The War of the American Revolution: Narrative, Chronology, and Bibliography* (Washington, D.C., 1975); R. Ernest Dupuy, *et al.*, *The American Revolution: A Global War* (New York, 1977); John C. Miller, *Triumph of Freedom, 1775-1783* (Boston, 1948); Howard H. Peckham, *The War for Independence: A Military History* (Chicago, 1958); Marshall Smelser, *The Winning of Independence* (Chicago, 1972); Willard M. Wallace, *Appeal to Arms: A Military History of the American Revolution* (New York, 1951); and Christopher Ward, *The War of the Revolution,* 2 vols., J. R. Alden, ed. (New York, 1952). As companion pieces, two valuable primary source collections are G. F. Scheer and H. F. Rankin, eds., *Rebels and Redcoats* (Cleveland, Ohio, 1957); and R. B. Morris and H. S. Commager, eds., *The Spirit of 'Seventy-Six: The Story of the American Revolution as Told by Participants,* 2 vols. (Indianapolis, Ind., 1958).

There are also a number of specific studies that have appeared since World War II. Representative of this literature on particular battles and regions are Alfred H. Bill, *The Campaign of Princeton, 1776-1777* (Princeton, N.J., 1948); Bruce Bliven, *Battle for Manhattan* (New York, 1956); Burke Davis, *The Cowpens-Guilford Campaign* (Philadelphia, 1962); Richard M. Ketchum, *The Winter Soldiers* (Garden City, N.Y., 1973); Adrian C. Leiby, *The Revolutionary War in the Hackensack Valley: The Jersey Dutch and the Neutral Ground, 1775-1783* (New Brunswick, N.J., 1962); John S. Pancake, *1777: The Year of the Hangman* (University, Ala., 1977); Arthur B. Tourtellot, *William Diamond's Drum* (New York, 1959); and Russell F. Weigley, *The Partisan War: The South Carolina Campaign of 1780-1782* (Columbia, S.C., 1970). Yet there has not been a volume analyzing what common soldiers of the Revolution went through and endured in specific engagements, which is fully comparable with John Keegan's pioneering *The Face of Battle* (New York, 1976), which reconstructs the battles of Agincourt (1415), Waterloo (1815), and the Somme (1916).

The Leiby and Weigley volumes are indicative of the many possibilities inherent in regional history as are two suggestive essays by Clyde R. Ferguson. These include "Carolina and Georgia Patriot and Loyalist Militia in Action, 1778-1783," in J. J. Crow and L. E. Tise, eds., *The Southern Experience in the American Revolution* (Chapel Hill, N.C., 1978), pp. 174-99; and "Functions of the Partisan-Militia in the South during the American Revolution: An Interpretation," in W. R. Higgins, ed., *The Revolutionary War in the South: Power, Conflict, and Leadership* (Durham, N.C., 1979), pp. 239-58.

In comparison with the many general and specific histories of the past three decades, the major thrust of the new military history has been to get beyond tactics and logistics. The new history has sought to grapple not only with war and its conduct but also with its consequences and impact on governments, societies, and peoples. For the period 1760-1790, this approach has meant that "the Revolution was many things, and its military dimension should ever remain an integral part of the whole," as incisively stated by Don Higginbotham in "American Historians and the Military History of the American Revolution," *American Historical Review,* 70 (1964), pp. 18-34. Military historians should not allow their subject to remain something apart from the whole. Rather, it should relate to the broader arena of human action, as demonstrated by those volumes listed above that have probed evolving values, policies, and institutions in the years of the early republic.

A number of recent studies, besides those by Cunliffe, Higginbotham, Kohn, and Weigley, have helped to uncover the rich prospects of the new history. In the first chapter of *Arms and Men: A Study in Military History* (New York, 1956), Walter Millis discussed the impact of the Revolutionary War on social and political developments in the new nation. In "The Military Conflict Considered as a Revolutionary War," *A People Numerous and Armed: Reflections on the Military Struggle for*

American Independence (New York, 1976), pp. 193-224, John Shy looked at the war as an educational experience, particularly in regard to political identity and loyalties. John Ellis's *Armies in Revolution* (New York, 1974), compared rebel armies in the English, American, French, Russian, and Chinese revolutions. He analyzed the role that these armies played in breaking down local attachments and in creating a sense of national purpose and legitimacy among peoples caught up in revolutionary situations. Richard Buel, Jr., in *Dear Liberty: Connecticut's Mobilization for the Revolutionary War* (Middletown, Conn., 1980), produced a valuable case study revealing how the war effort in one state served to wear down the populace and cause a somewhat unbalanced if not unstable economic and political climate in the postwar years. And Don Higginbotham's detailed *The War of American Independence: Military Attitudes, Policies, and Practice, 1763-1789* (New York, 1971), demonstrated the many linkages between the shape of war and the broader Revolution.

Comprehending the relationships between armed forces and the societies creating them has also resulted in important new explorations concerning the composition of armies as reflections of societal values. Many writers, particularly laymen, continue to support the patriotic myth that Revolutionary soldiers were invariably property-holding freeholders and tradesmen. Typical commentary may be found in Charles K. Bolton's otherwise important monograph, *The Private Soldier under Washington* (New York, 1902). A number of quantitative studies, however, have weakened the hold of this long-standing perception. Particularly worthy of notice are Mark Edward Lender, "The Social Structure of the New Jersey Brigade: The Continental Line as an American Standing Army," in Peter Karsten, ed., *The Military in America: From the Colonial Era to the Present* (New York, 1980), pp. 27-44; Lender, "The Enlisted Line: The Continental Soldiers of New Jersey," (Ph.D. dissertation, Rutgers University, 1975); Edward C. Papenfuse and Gregory A. Stiverson, "General Smallwood's Recruits: The Peacetime Career of the Revolutionary War Private," *William and Mary*

Quarterly, 3d Series, 30 (1973), pp. 117–32; John R. Sellers, "The Common Soldier in the American Revolution," in S. J. Underdal, ed., *Military History of the American Revolution: Proceedings of the Sixth Military History Symposium, USAF Academy* (Washington, D.C., 1976), pp. 151–61; and Sellers, "The Origins and Careers of the New England Soldier: Noncommissioned Officers and Privates in the Massachusetts Continental Line" (paper delivered at the American Historical Association Convention, 1972). Together, these investigations indicate that middle- and upper-class Americans were not willing to risk the hardships of long-term campaigning, despite repeated doses of rhetoric about the need for enduring citizen virtue. Given mythology and reality, it is worth comparing the data presented in these studies with those compiled by Sylvia R. Frey in "The Common British Soldier in the Late Eighteenth Century: A Profile," *Societas: A Review of Social History,* 5 (1975), pp. 117–31. See also Frey's *The British Soldier in America: A Social History of Military Life in the Revolutionary Period* (Austin, Tex., 1981), an expansion of her earlier findings.

That the social characteristics of regular soldiers on both sides were so similar suggests that American values concerning what persons should actually bear the burden of extended combat had been heavily influenced by Old World practices. Drawing selectively on poor and politically defenseless people had become an engrained part of the American experience, particularly during the later colonial wars. The implications of this theme as it relates to images of the citizen-in-arms may be traced in John Shy, "A New Look at the Colonial Militia," *A People Numerous and Armed,* pp. 23–33; Gary B. Nash, *The Urban Crucible: Social Change, Political Consciousness, and the Origins of the American Revolution* (Cambridge, 1979); and John E. Ferling, *A Wilderness of Miseries: War and Warriors in Early America* (Westport, Conn., 1980).

In a similar vein, there are other groups, besides long-term Continentals, which are beginning to get long overdue attention. The much neglected role of women in the Revolutionary army has been studied recently in Linda Grant De Pauw, "Women in

Combat: The Revolutionary War Experience," *Armed Forces and Society,* 7 (1981), pp. 209–26; and John Todd White, "The Truth about Molly Pitcher," in J. K. Martin and K. R. Stubaus, eds., *The American Revolution: Whose Revolution?* rev. ed. (New York, 1981), pp. 99–105. These two essays supersede Walter H. Blumenthal's rather straight-laced look at *Women Camp Followers of the American Revolution* (Philadelphia, 1952). As with women, collective information on the men who made up the Continental officer corps still needs further development. Essential on this subject are Richard H. Kohn, "American Generals of the Revolution: Subordination and Restraint," in Higginbotham, ed., *Reconsiderations of the Revolutionary War,* pp. 104–23; and Jonathan Gregory Rossie, *The Politics of Command in the American Revolution* (Syracuse, N.Y., 1975).

Issues about the nature and extent of direct participation in the war by property-holding citizens are critical to discussions of the relative importance of republican ideology as a basis for actual behavior on the part of the Revolutionary populace. Essential background information on the ideology of liberty may be found in Bernard Bailyn, *The Ideological Origins of the American Revolution* (Cambridge, Mass., 1967); and Gordon S. Wood, *The Creation of the American Republic, 1776–1787* (Chapel Hill, N.C., 1969). Concepts about the military obligations of citizens having a clear economic stake in society dated back to at least the period of the Renaissance in Italy. For a discussion of that theme, J. G. A. Pocock's *The Machiavellian Moment: Florentine Political Thought and the Atlantic Republican Tradition* (Princeton, N.J., 1975), is essential. As a related subject, antistanding-army ideology as it affected the coming of the American Revolution has been thoughtfully analyzed in John Shy, *Toward Lexington: The Role of the British Army in the Coming of the American Revolution* (Princeton, N.J., 1965); and John Phillip Reid, *In Defiance of the Law: The Standing-Army Controversy, the Two Constitutions, and the Coming of the American Revolution* (Chapel Hill, N.C., 1981).

In light of the oft-pronounced ideal that the quest for a republican polity depended upon citizen virtue, one would not expect to find persistent manpower shortages and dependency on the poorer classes for long-term military service. On the rapid passing of early enthusiasm for arms, see Allen Bowman, *The Morale of the American Revolutionary Army* (Washington, D.C., 1943); and Charles Royster, *A Revolutionary People at War: The Continental Army and the American Character, 1775–1783* (Chapel Hill, N.C., 1980). Royster argued that the general populace was deeply committed to the cause, even if they eschewed active military service. They thus claimed the war effort as theirs at the end of the contest, despite the fact that they failed to come close to upholding the ideals of republican citizenship.

Royster has also insisted that those unfortunates and ne'er-do-wells who made up Washington's new modeled ranks were by and large motivated to arms by ideological concerns. He has asserted that the quantitative studies of Lender, Sellers, Papenfuse and Stiverson, cited above, overstate the importance of material need as a motivating factor in service. In pitting ideology against material need, Royster has created a false and needless dichotomy. In one of its dimensions, this volume addresses that issue by pointing out that the individual dreams and expectations of the rank-and-file soldier paralleled the broader quest for a new republican order—as represented in the search for greater economic security and personal freedom. Also, it should not be forgotten that the real republicans (those who measured up to ideological standards) were those very men and women whom better-placed Revolutionary citizens encouraged, pushed, or coerced into Continental service. It thus was this small group of determined veterans, rather than the general populace, who deserved the laurels of achievement, laurels that were seized from them on the part of the general populace at war's end. Perhaps more than any other factor, it may have been this postwar displacement phenomenon that helped to establish the myth about widespread popular commitment and involvement in the war.

For more balanced presentations than Royster's on the

motivations of Washington's soldiers, readers should consult the writings of Lender, Sellers, Papenfuse, and Stiverson, as well as Robert Middlekauff, "Why Men Fought in the American Revolution," *Huntington Library Quarterly,* 43 (1980), pp. 135-48; and John Shy, "Hearts and Minds in the American Revolution: The Case of 'Long Bill' Scott and Peterborough, New Hampshire," *A People Numerous and Armed,* pp. 165-79. Also of importance is the general overview by Richard H. Kohn, "The Social History of the American Soldier: A Review and Prospectus for Research," *American Historical Review,* 86 (1981), pp. 553-67, which covers the whole of the American experience.

Over and above these issues, there are other significant dimensions to the new military history. One has to do with civil-military relations and the central concern of keeping military institutions under civilian control. An essential work on this subject is Richard H. Kohn, "The Inside History of the Newburgh Conspiracy: America and the Coup d'Etat," *William and Mary Quarterly,* 3d Series, 27 (1970), pp. 187-220. A second has to do with strategy as it relates to a balanced perspective on the successes and failures of each side. Particularly suggestive inquiries include Ira D. Gruber, "Britain's Southern Strategy," in Higgins, ed., *Revolutionary War in the South,* pp. 205-38; Dave R. Palmer, *The Way of the Fox: American Strategy in the War for America, 1775-1783* (Westport, Conn., 1975); John Shy, "British Strategy for Pacifying the Southern Colonies, 1778-1781," in Crow and Tise, eds., *Southern Experience in the American Revolution,* pp. 155-73; Russell F. Weigley, *The American Way of War: A History of United States Military Strategy and Policy* (New York, 1973); William B. Willcox, "Too Many Cooks: British Planning before Saratoga," *Journal of British Studies,* 2 (1962), pp. 56-90; Willcox, "British Strategy for America, 1778," *Journal of Modern History,* 19 (1947), pp. 97-121; and Willcox, "Rhode Island in British Strategy, 1780-1781," *ibid.,* 17 (1945), pp. 304-31. A third has to do with the war from the perspective of Great Britain. Definitely worth studying are Eric Robson's *The American Revolution in Its Political and Military Aspects, 1763–1783* (New York, 1955), which raises questions about whether British forces could ever have won the war, and Piers Mackesy's *The War for America, 1775–1783* (Cambridge, Mass., 1965), which magisterially reviews the war with particular respect to its international components and the strengths and weaknesses of Britain's leaders. Also of consequence are David Syrett's *Shipping and the American War, 1775–83: A Study of British Transport Organization* (London, 1970); and R. Arthur Bowler's *Logistics and the Failure of the British Army in America, 1775–1783* (Princeton, N.J., 1975).

A number of modern biographies have also influenced the body of new knowledge on the Revolutionary War period. Not all biographies successfully relate their subjects to their times. However, those that follow have transcended the details of particular lives and are well worth reading. Two indispensible collections are G. A. Billias, ed., *George Washington's Generals* (New York, 1964); and Billias, ed., *George Washington's Opponents: British Generals and Admirals in the American Revolution* (New York, 1969). In addition, any sampling of exceptional studies would include John R. Alden, *General Gage in America: Being Principally a History of His Role in the American Revolution* (Baton Rouge, La., 1948); Alden, *General Charles Lee: Traitor or Patriot?* (Baton Rouge, La., 1951); Robert D. Bass, *The Green Dragoon: The Lives of Banastre Tarleton and Mary Robinson* (New York, 1957); George Athan Billias, *General John Glover and His Marblehead Mariners* (New York, 1960); Marcus Cunliffe, *George Washington: Man and Monument* (Boston, 1958); Don R. Gerlach, *Philip Schuyler and the American Revolution in New York, 1733–1777* (Lincoln, Neb., 1964); Louis R. Gottschalk, *Lafayette Joins the American Army* (Chicago, 1937); Gottschalk, *Lafayette and the Close of the American Revolution* (Chicago, 1942); Ira D. Gruber, *The Howe Brothers and the American Revolution* (Chapel Hill, N.C., 1972); Don Higginbotham, *Daniel Morgan: Revolutionary Rifle-*

man (Chapel Hill, N.C., 1961); Bernhard Knollenberg, *Washington and the Revolution, A Reappraisal; Gates, Conway, and the Continental Congress* (New York, 1940); Samuel Eliot Morison, *John Paul Jones: A Sailor's Biography* (Boston, 1959); Paul David Nelson, *General Horatio Gates: A Biography* (Baton Rouge, La., 1976); Hugh F. Rankin, *Francis Marion: The Swamp Fox* (New York, 1973); Charles Royster, *Light-Horse Harry Lee and the Legacy of the American Revolution* (New York, 1981); Willard M. Wallace, *Traitorous Hero: The Life and Fortunes of Benedict Arnold* (New York, 1954); Charles P. Whittemore, *A General of the Revolution: John Sullivan of New Hampshire* (New York, 1961); Franklin B. and Mary Wickwire, *Cornwallis: The American Adventure* (Boston, 1970); and William B. Willcox, *Portrait of a General: Sir Henry Clinton in the War of Independence* (New York, 1964).

The listing of volumes in this bibliographical essay represent but a small portion of the vast body of literature that is available on the War for Independence in the era of the American Revolution. For more detailed bibliographical information, readers should consult John Shy's compilation, *The American Revolution* (Arlington Heights, Ill., 1973); and Frank Friedel, *et al.*, eds., *The Harvard Guide to American History,* rev. ed., 2 vols. (Cambridge, Mass., 1974). On diaries and reminiscences by participants, J. T. White and C. H. Lesser, eds., *Fighters for Independence: A Guide to Sources of Biographical Information on Soldiers and Sailors of the American Revolution* (Chicago, 1977), is a thorough listing. On estimates of wounded and dead, H. H. Peckham, ed., *The Toll of Independence: Engagements and Battle Casualties of the American Revolution* (Chicago, 1974), represents the most trustworthy compilation of statistics to date. And on the numbers of troops in Continental service during various stages of the war, C. H. Lesser, ed., *The Sinews of Independence: Monthly Strength Reports of the Continental Army* (Chicago, 1976), is invaluable.

In the end, all the studies listed herein, as well as many others too numerous to mention specifically, have served to broaden our comprehension of the War for Independence as it came about and as it influenced the texture of American values, institutions, and traditions. Yet there is still much left to be learned. Thus all of us have an obligation to keep raising new questions and working with extant documents, which is the key to comprehending as fully as possible the formative impact that all aspects of the Revolutionary experience have had on the course of United States history.

INDEX

absolutists, 182

Account of Denmark, An (Molesworth), 8

Adams, John, 30, 31, 40, 94, 106, 142, 171, 172, 183, 184, 185

Adams, Samuel, 75

Admiralty, 51

ad valorem duties, 188

Age of Reason, 12

Albany, 84

Alexander, William (Lord Stirling), 106

Allen, Ethan, 37

"American Generals of the Revolution: Subordination and Restraint" (Kohn), 217

"American Hannibal." *See* Arnold, Benedict

"American Historians and the Military History of the American Revolution" (Higginbotham), 214

"American Militia: A Traditional Institution with Revolutionary Responsibilities, The" (Higginbotham), 212

American national identity, 172, 205

American national legitimacy, 207, 212, 215

American Revolution in Its Political and Military Aspects, 1763-1783, The (Robson), 51-52, 220

American Secretary. *See* Secretary for American Affairs

American Way of War: A History of United States Military Strategy and Policy, The (Weigley), 125, 219

André, John (Maj.), 159

Annapolis, Maryland, 195

Antifederalists, 203

antipension sentiment, 198

  See also pensions

antistanding-army ideology, 20-28, 66, 74, 96, 200, 202

antiwar protest, 145

Appalachian Mountains, 166

Appeal to Arms: A Military History of the American Revolution (Wallace), 122, 213

aristocracy, 10

Armies in Revolution (Ellis), 204, 215

Arms and Men: A Study in Military History (Millis), xi, 12, 214
Armstrong, John, 191, 192
army and society, 113, 126–34, 158–65, 186–94
Arnold, Benedict (Gen.), 37, 72, 73, 84, 86, 104, 105, 107, 139, 174, 221
  treason of, 159–60
Articles of Confederation, 42, 188
Articles of War of 1776, 47, 76, 134, 144, 189
Assunpink Creek, 60
Atlantic Ocean, 145
autocracy, 191

Bailyn, Bernard, 6, 10, 11, 31, 217
balance of power, 10, 12, 188
Baltic Sea, 145
Baltimore, 58
Baltimore resolution of 1777, 104
Bancroft, George, 66, 204
"barrel fever," 129
Barton, William, 141
Basking Ridge, 59
Battles. *See* specific places
Bay Colony, 2, 23
"beating up" for enlistees, 88, 89
Bemis Heights, 86
Bennington, 85
Bernard, Francis, 22
billeting of British troops, 21
Bill of Rights of 1689, 11, 24
Birthplace of an Army (Trussell), 103
Birth of the Republic, 1763–89, The (Morgan), 67
blacks, 17, 91, 95
Blue Ridge, 67
Board of War, 42, 111, 112
Bolton, Charles K., 67, 215
Bon Homme Richard, 145, 146
Bordentown, 59
Boston, 1, 2, 22, 23, 24, 25, 27, 32, 34, 37, 40, 41, 47, 48, 53, 55, 88, 211

Boston Massacre, 22, 25, 26
Boston Tea Party, 26
bounty. *See* enlistment bounty
Bourbon family, 16, 182, 184
Bowman, Allen, 53, 218
Boyd, Thomas (Lt.), 141
Braddock, Edward (Gen.), 40
Braintree, 94
Brandywine Creek, 82, 140
Brant, Joseph, 140
Breed's Hill, 37, 38
Britain
  antiwar protest in, 145
  colonial policy of, 21
  empire of, 15
  government structure in, 10
  military obligation in, 17
  military style of, 20
  national debt of, 16, 21, 80
  radical whigs in, 11
  repression of colonies by, 27
  southern strategy of, 174, 219
  standing army in, 11, 12, 13, 14, 21
  and war with France and Spain, 185
  whig perception of, 9
  whigs in, 53
"Britain's Southern Strategy," (Gruber), 219
British Soldier in America: A Social History of Military Life in the Revolutionary Period, The (Frey), 216
Broad River, 167, 168
Brooklyn Heights, 55, 56, 211
brutality, 140, 142
Bunker Hill, 3, 19, 25, 37, 39, 40, 48, 57, 68, 81, 211
Burgoyne, John (Gen.), 37, 80, 81, 83, 84, 85, 86, 87, 88, 116
Bute, Lord, 15
Butler, John (Maj.), 139, 140
"Butler's Rangers," 141
Butler, Walter, 139, 140

Caesarism, 188, 202
Cahokia, 138
Cambridge, 44, 69, 70
Camden, South Carolina, 157, 165, 166, 187
Campbell, M'Donald, 96
Campbell, William (Col.), 166
Campfield, Electa, 198
Canada
  See also specific provinces
  British retention of, 184
  Burgoyne's troops in, 80, 86
  campaign of 1775-1776, 84
  and French and Indian War, 19
  French claims in, 14, 117
  and invasion of, 37, 72-73
Canadians, 84
Cape Fear, 153, 154
Caribbean Sea, 145, 185
Carleton, Guy (Sir), 84, 181
Carlisle Commission, 120
Cato's Letters (Gordon), 8
Chadd's Ford, 82
Charles I (King of England and Scotland), 6, 10
Charles III (King of Spain), 182
Charles, Lord Cornwallis. See Cornwallis
Charleston, South Carolina, 154, 155, 156, 173, 175, 178, 195
Charlestown, Massachusetts, 3, 37, 38, 40
Charlotte, North Carolina, 165-66
Cherry Valley massacre, 140
Chesapeake Bay, 81, 174, 175, 176
Chinese Revolution, 204, 215
Cincinnatus, 36, 65, 73, 202
citizen-soldiers
  British perception of, 37, 38, 39
  Charles Lee's perception of, 41
  and the Continental army, 40
  discipline of, 36, 47, 144
  Gage's perception of, 38
  and Jeffersonian republicans, 208

and Machiavelli, 7
morale of, 63
myth of, 66, 95
and nationalists, 39, 203
and naval discipline, 144
and the Pennsylvania line mutiny, 163
and re-enlistment, 71
and religion, 33
and standing army, 75
and universal military obligation, 201
and Washington, 44, 45, 46
in whig ideology, 5, 6
"citizen virtue." See "virtuous citizenry"
civil authority
  and Arnold, 104
  British, 52, 61
  and Clinton, 154
  in the Declaration of Independence, 54
  and demobilization of the army, 194
  and loyalists, 178
  and military coup, 187-88
  and mutiny of officers, 150, 187
  and nationalists, 206, 207
  and the New Jersey line mutiny, 149
  in New York City, 199
  and republicanism, 188, 189, 194
  and Washington, 42, 44, 106, 189
civil-military relations, 113, 126-34, 158-65, 186-94
Civil War, 199, 212, 213
Clark, George Rogers, 137, 138, 139, 142, 146
"Clark's Rangers," 139
Clinton, Sir Henry (Gen.), 121, 122
  and Arnold, 159
  assumption of command by, 120
  at Breed's Hill, 37, 39
  at Cape Fear, 153
  at Charleston, 154, 155, 156
  and Cornwallis, 173, 174, 175, 178

and the mutiny of the Pennsylvania regiment, 163
at New York, 62, 81, 124, 125, 158, 176, 177
at Saratoga, 84, 87
in South Carolina, 136
Coakley, Robert W., 39, 213
codes of discipline. *See* discipline
Coercive Acts, 26
cohesion among groups, 131, 132, 161
colonial secretary. *See* Secretary for American Affairs
"coming of age" of Continental Army, 122
commerce, 184
"Common British Soldier in the Late Eighteenth Century: A Profile, The" (Frey), 216
"Common Soldier in the American Revolution, The" (Sellers), 216
Commonwealth of Oceana (Harrington), 7, 75
Comte de Vergennes. *See* Vergennes
Concord, 2, 4, 5, 6, 9, 19, 20, 26, 27, 28, 31, 34, 39, 48, 68, 211
Congressional Articles of War. *See* Articles of War
Congressional Board of War. *See* Board of War
Congressional money. *See* inflation of currency
Connecticut, 93, 102, 140, 175
Connecticut Farms, 125
Connecticut infantry, 100
Connecticut regiments, 161
Conn, Stetson, 39, 213
conscription, 13, 90, 91, 93, 94
and republicanism, 94
Constitution of 1787, 5, 206, 207
Continental Congress
and appointment of du Coudray, 106
and Arnold, 105
and Articles of Peace, 184
and Carlisle Commission, 120
and Charles Lee, 123, 124
and Coercive Acts, 26
composition of, 107
and Continental navy, 143, 146
and Conway Cabal, 111, 113
creation of Continental army by, 40
and currency inflation, 148, 151
and demobilization of army, 194
and desertion, 132
and dissatisfaction with officers, 110
early problems of, 69
enlistment standards by, 88
expansion of size of army by, 76
First, 26
and French alliance, 118, 134
and Gates, 157
and invasion of Canada, 72
manpower allocations by, 89
marine committee of, 142
move of to Baltimore, 58
move of to York, Pennsylvania, 82
nationalists in, 188, 190, 199
and naval attack on Britain, 144
navy committee of, 142
and New Jersey line mutiny, 164, 204
officer dissatisfaction with, 104
peace commissioners' instructions from, 183, 185
and Pennsylvania line mutiny, 163
and pension issue, 108, 109, 150, 159, 160, 187, 194
Second, 40
seven-year pension approval by, 109
and South Carolina, 154
and standing army, 75, 200, 201
and surrender of Cornwallis, 179
and taxation powers, 189, 191
veterans dissatisfaction with, 195
Continental dollars. *See* inflation of currency
Continental navy, 143
"convention army," 88, 92

"Conway Cabal," 110, 111, 113, 123, 187

Conway, Thomas (Gen.), 111, 112, 113

Cornwallis, Charles Lord (Gen.)
  at Assunpink Creek, 60
  at Charleston, 156
  defeat of, 177
  at Fort Lee, 57–58
  and Greene, 172
  and loyalists, 173
  in North Carolina, 165, 166
  in the South, 168, 169
  in South Carolina, 157, 167
  surrender of, 178
  in Virginia, 174
  at Yorktown, 175, 176, 181

Coudray, Phillippe du, 105, 106

counterinsurgency, 126

counterrevolutionary thrust, 154, 166, 173

coup d'etat, 75, 110, 128, 187, 194

court martials, 47

Cowpens. *See* Hannah's Cowpens

Creation of the American Republic, 1776-1787, The (Wood), 7, 217

Cress, Lawrence Delbert, 18, 209, 212

Crisis (Paine), 68

Cromwell, Oliver, 6, 7, 9, 75, 78, 188

Cuba, 14

Cunliffe, Marcus, 45, 47, 212, 214

currency. *See* inflation of currency

Customs House, 24

Danbury, 104

Dartmouth, Lord, 26, 27, 50

Deane, Silas, 115

Declaration of Independence, 54, 55

"Declaration of the Causes and Necessity for Taking up Arms," 44

de Grasse. *See* Grasse

de Lafayette. *See* Lafayette

Delaware, 58, 59, 76, 131

Delaware River, 58, 83

democracy, 10, 18

Denmark, 8, 9

desertion, 92, 103, 108, 132, 133
  See also discipline

d'Estaing. *See* Estaing

Detroit, 137, 138

dictatorship, 188, 190

disability pensions, 197

discipline, 11, 14
  and Artemas Ward, 36
  at Brandywine, 82
  in British navy, 144
  in British standing army, 38
  codes of, 11, 14
  Congressional perception of, 78
  in Continental navy, 144
  and Gerry, 32
  and Greene, 46
  and lack of volunteers, 89
  and long-term enlistees, 95
  patriots' perception of, 48
  and Pennsylvania line mutiny, 162
  Ramsay's perception of, 71
  and republicanism, 130
  and short-term enlistees, 73
  in state militia, 206
  Washington's perception of, 45, 47, 62, 69, 74, 165
  Wilson's perception of, 74–75

dispersed warfare, 136–42

distribution of power, 10, 12, 188

Dorchester Heights, 37, 48, 55

draft. *See* conscription

draftees, 94
  See also conscription

drill routines, 17

du Coudray. *See* Coudray

Dutch, 143

Eagle and Sword: the Federalists and the Creation of the Military Establishment in America, 1783-1802 (Kohn), 18, 212

East India Company, 26
Easton, Pennsylvania, 140, 149
East River, 55, 56
*Eighteenth-Century Commonwealth-
    man: Studies in the Transmission,
    Development and Circumstance
    of English Liberal Thought from
    the Restoration of Charles II until
    the War with the Thirteen Colo-
    nies, The* (Robbins), 10
eighteenth-century rationalism, 12
Eliot, Andrew, 23
Ellis, John, 204, 215
"embattled farmers," 66, 67
England. *See* Britain
English Channel, 180
English Revolution, 204, 215
Enlightenment rationalism, 34
"Enlisted Line: The Continental
    Soldiers of New Jersey, The"
    (Lender), 215
enlistees, 158, 162
  see also enlistment
  bonus for, 109
  bounty for, 162
  long-term, 74
  in Pennsylvania line mutiny, 163
  search for, 49, 87–94
  for 1776 season, 70
  short-term, 73
  socioeconomic backgrounds of, 90–
    91
  Taylor's perception of, 78
enlistment, 87–94
  See also enlistees; voluntarism
  and conscription, 93
  and desertion, 132
  long-term, 95
  and New Jersey line mutiny, 164
  and Pennsylvania line mutiny, 162
  and prisoners of war, 92
  and republicanism, 90
  soldiers' perceptions of, 101, 186
  and winter campaign of 1776, 59

enlistment bounty, 78, 88, 89, 128,
    132, 133, 158, 162, 163, 164, 196
enlistment bounty jumpers, 133
Epping, New Hampshire, 94
Estaing, Count d'(Admiral), 125, 155

Fabian tactics, 82, 123, 175
Fabius Cunctator, 79
fair-weather patriots, 193
farmer-soldiers, 73
  See also citizen-soldiers
*Federal Military Pensions in the
    United States* (Glasson), 197
Ferguson, Clyde R., 153
Ferguson, Patrick (Maj.), 166
fiat money, 147, 195, 196
  See also inflation of currency
financial morass, 146
  See also inflation of currency
First Continental Congress. *See* Con-
    tinental Congress
First Newburgh Address, 192
First New Jersey regiment, 149
Fithian, Philip Vickers, 53
Flamborough Head, 145
Florence, 7
Florida, 14, 180
Floridablanca, Count, 182, 183
Fort Lee, 57, 58
Fort Mercer, 83
Fort Mifflin, 83
Fort Niagara, 139, 142
Fort Ninety-Six, 167
Fort Schuyler, 85
Fort Ticonderoga, 37, 39–40, 48, 84,
    85
Fort Washington, 57
France, 50
  aid to Washington from, 175, 176,
    177
  alliance with, 105, 110, 117, 123,
    134, 144, 145, 146, 147, 154–55,
    183
  British naval vessels seized by, 143

commercial ties with, 183, 184
Cornwallis's perception of, 178
diplomatic maneuvering of, 83, 181, 182, 185
Franklin in, 117
and French and Indian War, 14
Gerry's perceptions of, 120
Indians' perceptions of, 16
John Paul Jones in, 144
loans from, 116
and militia, 17
naval power of, 180
North American holdings of, 115
perception of Continental army by, 67
perception of militia by, 33
soldiers' perception of, 118
spy activities of, 32
as threat to colonies, 15
and war with Britain, 12
Franklin, Benjamin, 77, 115, 116, 117, 145, 183, 185
Frederick the Great of Prussia, 62, 113
free blacks, 17
freeholders, 2, 7, 8, 9, 12–13, 18, 19, 20, 32, 36, 67, 71, 90, 91, 93, 95, 131, 196, 211, 215, 217
Freeman's Farm, 86
French Academy of Sciences, 116
French and Indian War, 14, 16, 17, 19, 20, 27, 36, 39, 40, 45, 78, 115
"French menace," 14, 15
French Revolution, 204, 215
Frey, Sylvia R., 13, 216
frigates, 143
"Functions of the Partisan-Militia in the South during the American Revolution: An Interpretation" (Higgins), 214

Gage, Thomas (Gen.), 3, 220
in the Bay Colony, 23, 26, 47
at Boston, 34, 37
at Breed's Hill, 38
at Concord, 2
Dartmouth's perception of, 27
firing of, 39
Lexington, 9
perception of militia by, 19
Gates, Horatio (Gen.), 157, 190, 221
appointment of as adjutant general, 41
and Arnold, 86
Burgoyne's surrender to, 87
and "convention army," 88
and Conway Cabal, 111
and Newburgh Conspiracy, 187, 191, 192
and New England militia, 85
in North Carolina, 166
Northern Department command of, 84
in South Carolina, 157, 158
Southern Department command of, 157
and Washington, 112, 113, 123
"General Smallwood's Recruits: The Peacetime Career of the Revolutionary War Private" (Papenfuse and Stiverson), 215
George III (King of Great Britain), 15, 26, 50, 54, 181, 183
Georgia, 51, 76, 91, 126, 136, 154, 155, 156, 195
Germain, George (Lord), 50, 52, 53, 80, 81, 87, 181, 184
German mercenaries, 13, 50, 93
Germantown, 82, 83
Gerry, Elbridge, 32, 118
Gibraltar, 180, 182, 185
Glasson, William H., 197
Glorious Revolution, 10, 11
Gloucester Point, 178
Glover, John (Gen.), 56, 60, 220
See also Marblehead mariners
Gordon, Thomas, 8, 10
Grasse, Comte de (Admiral), 176, 185
Gravesend, Long Island, 56

Great Lakes, 137
Greene, Nathanael (Gen.)
  army commission to, 41
  and British deserters, 92
  and Cornwallis, 174
  and du Coudray, 105
  at Fort Lee, 58
  and national legitimacy, 172, 173
  perception of militia by, 46, 169
  perception of soldiers by, 121
  quartermaster general, 102
  in South Carolina, 166, 167, 168
  and South Carolina conspiracy, 180
  Southern Department command of,
    165
Green Mountain Boys, 37
Grey, Charles (Sir), 82
group cohesion, 131, 132, 161
Gruber, Ira D., 57, 62, 219, 220
guerillas, 16, 139, 158
Guilford Courthouse, 168

"Hair Buyer." *See* Hamilton, Henry
Halifax, Nova Scotia, 48, 51, 180
Hamilton, Alexander
  and Charles Lee, 123
  as a nationalist, 194, 201
  and Newburgh Conspiracy, 188,
    189, 190, 191
  perception of inflation by, 146, 147
  republican purists' perception of,
    204
  resignation from Congress by, 199
  and Robert Morris, 188
Hamilton, Henry, 137, 138, 139
Hannah's Cowpens, 167, 168, 169
"hard money," 162
Harrington, James, 7, 8, 10, 75
Head of Elk, 81
Henderson, H. James, 148
Henry, Patrick, 138
Herkimer, Nicholas (Gen.), 85
"hero of Saratoga." *See* Gates, Horatio

Hesse-Cassel, 50
Hessians
  at Bennington, 85
  at Bordentown, 58–59
  British perception of, 61, 62
  enlistment of in Continental army,
    88, 90, 91, 92, 95
  influence of on Congress, 76
  at Monmouth, 122
  in New Jersey, 121
  in New York, 56, 57
  origin of, 50
  at Trenton, 58–59, 60
  at Yorktown, 175, 176
Higginbotham, Don, 16, 46, 49, 96,
    137, 163, 212, 214, 215
Hillsborough, Earl of, 22, 23, 26
History of the American Revolution
    (Ramsay), 71
*History of the Rise, Progress and
    Termination of the American
    Revolution* (Warren), 203
*History of the United States from the
    Discovery of the American Conti-
    nent, The* (Bancroft), 66
Hopkins, Esek (Commodore), 144
House of Commons, 10, 181
House of Lords, 10
*Howe Brothers and the American
    Revolution, The* (Gruber), 57,
    220
Howe, Lord Richard (Admiral), 51,
    55, 56, 125
Howe, Robert (Gen.), 164, 165
Howe, William (Gen.), 53, 81, 111
  at Boston, 37, 47, 48
  at Breed's Hill, 38, 39
  and campaign of 1776, 78–83
  recall of, 120
  indecisiveness of, 174
  and loyalists, 61
  in New Jersey, 58, 59
  in New York, 51, 55, 56, 57,
    154

in Pennsylvania, 99
perception of colonists by, 62
replacement of Gage at Boston by, 47
and strategy of 1776, 53
Washington's perception of, 100
Hubbardston, Vermont, 85
Hudson Highlands, 52, 58, 80, 124, 159, 180
Hudson River, 57, 58, 72, 81, 124, 186
Hugh, Lord Percy, 3
Huntington, Ebenezer (Lt. Col.), 147
Huntington, Jedidiah (Gen.), 107

Ideological Origins of the American Revolution, The (Bailyn), 6, 10, 217
ideological transmission, 9–15
"ignoble savagism," 141
  See also white aggression against Indians
Illinois, 137
Illinois-Indiana country, 138
import duties, 188
Impost Plan of 1781, 188, 189, 194
impressment, 22, 90
  See also conscription
indentured servants, 17, 90, 91, 92
India, 145, 179
Indiana, 138
Indians
  atrocities by, 140, 142
  and British army, 16
  Cherokee, 153
  at Cherry Valley, 140
  at Fort Schuyler, 85
  and Hair Buyer, 137
  Iroquois, 139, 140, 142
  and militia service, 17
  Mohawk, 139
  at Newtown, 141
  in New York, 84
  and St. Leger, 86

Six Nations of New York, 137, 139, 142
  at Vincennes, 138, 139
  and white aggression, 15, 137, 142
  in Wyoming Valley, 140
indigents, 17
indirect taxation, 21
inflation of currency, 101, 107, 131, 146, 147, 148, 151, 152, 161, 195, 196
  Hamilton's perception of, 146, 147
  and republicanism, 148
"Inside History of the Newburgh Conspiracy: America and the Coup d'Etat, The" (Kohn), 219
Irish Sea, 145

James II (King of England and Scotland), 10, 11
James River, 175
Janowitz, Morris, 131
Jay, John, 183
Jeffersonian republicans, 208
Jockey Hollow, 161
Jones, John Paul, 144, 145, 146, 221
"Journal of the Times," 23

Kaskaskia, 138
Kentucky, 137, 138
King-in-Parliament, 24, 26
King's Mountain, 165, 166, 167
King Street, 24
Knollenberg, Bernhard, 111, 221
Knox, Henry (Gen.), 48, 105, 107, 187, 191, 202, 204, 208
Knox-McDougall group, 187, 191
Kohn, Richard H., 18, 106, 186, 187, 190, 206–7, 212, 214, 217, 219

laborers, 24
Lafayette, Marquis de, 100, 113, 121, 122, 174
Lake Champlain, 37, 72, 84
land redistribution, 133

land owners. *See* freeholders

land speculators, 196

Laurens, John, 114

Lee, Arthur, 115

Lee, Charles (Gen.), 32, 36, 41, 58, 59, 121, 122, 123, 124, 154, 187, 220

Lee, ("Light Horse") Harry, 167

Lender, Mark Edward, 64, 90, 106, 131, 133, 215, 218, 219

Lesser, Charles H., 89, 161

Lexington, 1, 2, 3, 4, 5, 6, 9, 19, 20, 26, 27, 28, 31, 34, 36, 39, 48, 211

liberty, 6–9

Lincoln, Benjamin (Gen.), 155, 156, 157, 178

Livingston family, 73

London, 15, 181

Long Island, 55, 56, 57, 63, 82

looting, 129–30, 133

Loring, Joshua (Mrs.), 61

Louis XVI (King of France), 115, 116, 117, 185

Lovell, James, 108

loyalists

abandonment of by Howe, 61

and British occupation of Charleston, 157

and British southern strategy, 125, 126, 154

and British strategy of 1776, 52

and Continental justice, 93

and Cornwallis, 156, 172, 173, 175, 178

and escape from Boston, 48

at Fort Schuyler, 85

at King's Mountain, 166

and Knox, 107

militia, 126

in Mohawk Valley, 86

in New Jersey, 121

at Newton, 141

in North Carolina, 153

number of, 76

in Pennsylvania, 83

and the Pennsylvania-New York frontier, 142

and Treaty of Paris, 184

in Wyoming Valley, 140

Loyalists and Redcoats (Smith), 61

loyalty oaths, 53, 58, 61

McCrea, Jane, 85

McDougall, Alexander (Maj. Gen.), 107, 127, 187, 191

Machiavelli, Niccolò, 7

Mackesy, Piers, 50, 120, 126, 179, 220

Madison, James, 188, 199

Maine, 51, 72, 197

Manhattan, 55, 57

manpower

quotas, 93

shortages, 69, 70, 87, 89

search. *See* enlistment

Marblehead mariners, 56, 60, 220

marine committee of Congress, 142

Marion, Francis ("Swamp Fox"), 157, 167, 221

Martin, James Kirby, 160

Martin, Joseph Plumb (Pvt.), 54, 93, 100, 128, 147, 196, 197, 208

Maryland, 40, 90, 91, 131, 150, 157, 195

Maryland Provincial Convention, 32

Massachusetts, 5, 9, 19, 22, 26, 31, 37, 40, 41, 56, 76, 91, 108, 128, 199, 206

Massachusetts Provincial Congress, 34

Mease, James, 102

mercenaries, 13, 34, 49–50, 54, 78, 93, 95, 107, 113

See also Hessians

merchants, 183

Middlebrook, New Jersey, 80, 81, 124

Middle Department, 111

Mifflin, Thomas (Gen.), 101
military aristocracy, 202
military-civil relations. *See* civil-military relations
military code of 1775, 76
"Military Conflict Considered as a Revolutionary War, The" (Shy), 205, 214
military dictatorship, 190
military establishment, 199, 200, 203
  See also standing army
military obligations, 18, 19, 201, 217
militia
  and Arnold, 104
  British plans to deal with, 126
  at Charleston, 155
  citizens' perception of, 197
  at Concord, 2, 3, 6
  Connecticut, 37
  conscription of, 94
  and Constitution of 1787, 206
  exemption from, 90
  financing of, 116
  at Hannah's Cowpens, 167, 168
  Howe's perception of, 81
  ideological basis of, 6-9
  Jeffersonian republicans' perception of, 208
  at Lexington, 2, 3, 6
  loyalist, 126
  in Massachusetts, 9
  New England, 111
  New Jersey, 53-54, 58, 96
  New Hampshire, 85
  patriots' perception of, 31, 32, 55
  Pennsylvania, 59, 87
  and republicanism, 194
  in 1776 campaign, 88
  in the South, 153
  in South Carolina, 157
  vs. standing army, 74
  structure of, 18
  unreliability of, 87
  Washington's perception of, 45, 46

Washington's recommendation for, 200, 201
  in Wyoming Valley, 140
  at Yorktown, 177
Millis, Walter, xi, 12, 13, 200, 206, 214
Minden, 50
Minutemen. *See* militia
Mississippi River, 184
Mohawk Valley, 85, 140
Molesworth, Robert, 8, 10
monarchy, 10
money. *See* inflation of currency
Monmouth, 122, 123
Monmouth Court House, 121
Monroe, James, 197
Montgomery, Richard (Gen.), 72, 73, 84
Montreal, 84
Moore's Creek Bridge, 153
Morale of the American Revolutionary Army, The (Bowman), 53, 218
Morgan, Daniel, 72, 86, 167, 168, 169, 220
Morgan, Edmund S., 67, 68
Morris County, 107
Morris, Gouverneur, 188
Morris group, 189
Morris, John Ford (Ensign), 107
Morris, Robert, 188, 190, 194, 199, 204
Morristown, New Jersey, 60, 79, 80, 89, 93, 102, 124, 134, 161, 162, 164
Mount Vernon, 186, 200
muster days, 17
mutiny, 129, 150, 158-65, 175, 204
  See also discipline
Mutiny Act, 11

national debt
  in America, 196
  in England, 16, 21, 80

national identity, 171–72, 205
nationalists, 188, 190, 199, 200, 201, 202, 203, 204, 206, 207
national legitimacy, 171–73, 202–9, 212, 215
" 'Nature of Treason': Revolutionary Virtue and American Reactions to Benedict Arnold" (Royster), 63
naval activities, 142–46
navy committee of Congress, 142
Negro in the American Revolution, The (Quarles), 95
Nelson, Paul David, 190
Netherlands, 117
neutrals, 61
Neville, Henry, 10
New Brunswick, New Jersey, 58, 60, 78, 79, 81
Newburgh Addresses, 191, 192
Newburgh Conspiracy, 113, 186–94, 219
Newburgh, New York, 186, 187
New England, 17, 19, 23, 36, 37, 38, 40, 41, 43, 45, 51, 52, 67, 80, 83–84, 87, 108, 116, 118, 157, 160, 164
Newfoundland, 184
New Hampshire, 59, 94
New Jersey, 33, 52, 58, 59, 60, 61, 63, 68, 78, 90, 93, 94, 107, 124, 125, 127, 132, 141, 148, 149, 161, 164, 165, 195
New Jersey line mutiny, 164–65
New Jersey regiment, 198
"New Jersey Soldier, The" (Lender), 64
"New Look at the Colonial Militia, A" (Shy), 216
"New Model army," 6, 7, 69–78, 186–194, 202–8
Newport, Rhode Island, 62, 125, 175
Newtown, New York, 140, 141
New York, 21, 41, 72, 76, 86, 116, 130, 131, 140, 142, 186, 220

New York campaign, 53–60, 68, 79, 130
New York City, 23, 52, 53, 61, 62, 63, 73, 80, 81, 84, 121, 122, 124, 126, 154, 155, 156, 175, 176, 177, 195, 199, 211
New York regiment, 133
North Africa, 50
North Bridge, 2
North Carolina, 131, 153, 156, 158, 165–66, 168, 169, 173
northern colonies, 125, 126, 131, 158
Northern Department, 111, 116
North, Lord, 48, 50, 120, 181, 183
North Sea, 145
Nova Scotia, 48, 184

officers
  anger of, 103–10
  pay of, 103, 186, 187
  and pensions, 118, 127, 150, 151, 186–94, 196–98
Ohio, 67, 196
Ohio River, 139
Old Dominion. *See* Virginia
"Old Northwest," 139
Old Point Comfort, 175
"Origins and Careers of the New England Soldier: Noncommissioned Officers and Privates in the Massachusetts Continental Line, The" (Sellers), 216
Oriskany, 85
Oswald, Richard, 183, 184
"over-the-mountain" men, 166, 169

pacification, 173, 174
Paine, Thomas, 68
Palmer, John McAuley, 201, 212
Paoli Massacre, 82, 125
Papenfuse, Edward C., 90, 215, 218, 219
paper currency. *See* inflation of currency
Paris, 115, 117, 184, 194

Parker, John (Capt.), 2
Parliament, 10, 11, 21, 22, 26, 181
partisan activity, 153, 154, 156, 157, 158, 165, 166, 167, 174
Party Politics in the Continental Congress (Henderson), 148
pay
  of officers, 103, 186, 187
  severance, 195
  of soldiers, 108, 109, 129, 148, 149, 162, 163, 164, 189
peace settlement, 179-86, 190
Peckham, Howard H., 67, 144, 198, 199, 213, 221
Pennsylvania, 40, 54, 58, 60, 63, 81, 82, 83, 85, 140, 142, 149, 150, 162, 163, 195
Pennsylvania campaign of 1777, 99
Pennsylvania line mutiny, 162-64
Pennsylvania regiment, 161
Pennsylvania State House, 195
Pensacola, Florida, 180
pensions
  and Continental Congress, 108, 109, 150, 159, 160, 187, 194
  and Impost Plan of 1781, 189
  and mutiny, 158-65
  and the Newburgh Conspiracy, 186, 187
  officers' demand for, 150, 151
  officers' expectation of, 118
  officers' perception of, 127
  officers' proposal for, 108
  opposition to, 198
  and republicanism, 108, 109
  United States Congress's settlement of, 197
  and women, 198
People Numerous and Armed: Reflections on the Military Struggle for American Independence, A (Shy), 214-15, 216
Perth Amboy, 79
Philadelphia, 31, 40, 51, 80, 81, 82, 83, 99, 100, 111, 117, 118, 121,
160, 162, 175, 183, 185, 188, 190, 191, 195, 205
Phillips, William (Gen.), 174
Pickens, Andrew, 157
Piedmont, 166
piracy, 143
  See also privateering
Pitcairn, John (Maj.), 2
Pocock, J. G. A., 7
Politics of Command in the American Revolution, The (Rossie), 43, 217
Pompton, 164, 165
Pontiac's Rebellion, 15
postwar transition, 194-202
power, 6-9
  balance and distribution of, 10, 12, 188
  centralization of, 152, 195, 196
Prescott, William, 38
Preston, Thomas (Capt.), 24, 25
price fixing, 152
Prince, The (Machiavelli), 7
Princeton, New Jersey, 58, 60, 62, 63, 78, 79, 80, 162, 195, 211, 213
privateering, 116, 143, 144
Private Soldier under Washington, The (Bolton), 67, 215
property holders. *See* freeholders
property redistribution, 133
Provincial Congress, 41
provincial militia tradition, 15-20
Prussia, 110, 113, 114
"public virtue." *See* "virtuous citizenry"
Puritans, 7, 75
Putnam, Israel, 36, 38, 41

Quakenbush, Benjamin, 133
Quakers, 41, 87
Quarles, Benjamin, 95
Quartering Act of 1765, 21
Quebec, 19, 72, 74, 84, 104, 137, 139, 181
Quebec campaign, 74
Queen's College (Rutgers), 78

radical whigs, 5, 6, 8, 10, 11, 14
rage militaire, 31, 45, 68, 69, 75, 78, 124, 151, 172, 205
Rall, Johann (Col.), 58, 60
Ramsay, David, 71
Ranger, 144
Rankin, Hugh F., 173
rationalism, 12, 34
reconciliation, 43, 44, 57, 117, 159
recruitment. *See* enlistment
recruits. *See* enlistees
redistribution of property, 133
regular army. *See* standing army
republicanism, 217, 218
  and Arnold, 159
  and centralization of power, 152, 195
  and civil authority, 188, 189, 194
  and conscription, 94
  and Conway Cabal, 113
  and discipline, 130
  and enlistment requirements, 90
  and Franklin, 117, 183
  and the French alliance, 118
  and Gates, 157
  as goal of the war, 20, 30-34, 78, 97, 102, 179, 186, 208
  and inflation, 148
  influence of the war on, 5, 194-208
  Jeffersonian, 208
  lack of commitment for, 173
  and militia, 194
  myth of, 4
  and nationalists, 204, 206, 207
  in New Jersey legislature, 149
  and officer dissatisfaction, 188
  and Pennsylvania line mutiny, 163, 164
  and pensions, 108, 109
  and postwar policy, 206
  soldiers' perceptions of, 103, 147
  and standing army, 34-40, 94, 95, 96, 202
  and universal military obligaton, 201

"Republican Liberty and National Security: American Military Policy as an Ideological Problem" (Cress), 209
"respectable army," 76
Revolutionary People at War: The Continental Army and the American Character, 1775-1783, A (Royster), 31, 68, 218
Rhode Island, 41, 62, 91, 125, 140, 144, 154, 161, 167, 168, 169, 174–75, 189
Richmond, Christopher, 191
Richmond, Virginia, 174
Riot Bill, 24
Robbins, Caroline, 10,11
Robson, Eric, 51, 220
Rochambeau, Comte de, 175, 177, 178, 180
  Wethersfield meeting, 176
Rockingham, Lord, 181, 184
Roderigue Hortalez & Cie, 115, 116
Rodney, George (Admiral), 185
"Roman Delayer." *See* Fabius Cunctator
Rossie, Jonathan Gregory, 43, 217
Royal navy, 21, 49, 55–57, 143, 145–46
Royster, Charles, 31, 33, 63, 68, 103, 128, 129, 151, 160, 218
rule by civil law, 189
  See also civil authority; republicanism
Russian Revolution, 204, 215

St. Augustine, Florida, 180
St. Johns, New Brunswick, 84, 85
St. Leger, Barry (Col.), 85, 86
Saratoga, 86, 105, 111, 116, 219
Saratoga campaign, 83-87
Saunders, John, 93, 96
Savannah, Georgia, 126, 155, 195
scalp bounties, 137
  See also Hamilton, Henry

Schuyler, Philip (Gen.), 41, 84, 85, 91, 220

Schuylkill River, 99–100, 102, 106

"scortched-earth" policy, 52

Scotland, 144, 145, 183

Second Continental Congress. *See* Continental Congress

Second Newburgh Address, 192

Secretary for American Affairs, 22, 26, 50, 51, 81, 181

Sellers, John R., 91, 216, 218, 219

"Sentiments" (Washington), 201

Serapis, 145, 146

settlement certificates, 195, 196

See also pensions

Seven Years' War. *See* French and Indian War

severance payments, 195

See also pensions

Shalhope, Robert E., 28

Shays's Rebellion, 206

Sheehan, Bernard, 141

Shelburne, Lord, 184

Shils, Edward A., 131

Shipping and the American War, 1775-83: A Study of British Transport Organization (Syrett), 143, 220

Shy, John, 19, 39, 123, 153, 205, 215, 216, 217

Sidney, Algernon, 10

Sinews of Independence: Monthly Strength Reports of the Continental Army, The (Lesser), 89, 221

Skenesborough, 85

slaves, 17, 90, 91, 92, 95, 196

smallpox, 73, 84, 101, 162, 177

Smith, Francis (Lt. Col.), 1, 2, 3

Smith, Paul H., 61

smugglers, 21

"Social Structure of the New Jersey Brigade: The Continental Line as an American Standing Army, The" (Lender), 215

society and the military, 126–34

See also civil-military relations

Soldiers and Civilians: The Martial Spirit in America, 1775-1865 (Cunliffe), 45, 212

Society of Cincinnati, 202, 203, 204

South Carolina, 137, 154, 155, 156, 157, 166, 167, 169, 173, 174, 175, 178, 180, 195

southern colonies, 17, 91, 125, 126, 136, 147, 153–58, 165, 168, 205

Southern Department, 92, 154, 156, 157, 158, 165, 174

southern strategy of Britain, 125–26, 153–58, 174, 219

Spain, 12, 14, 17, 50, 117, 143, 180, 181, 182, 183, 184

specie, 149, 151, 158, 164

See also inflation of currency

Springfield, Massachusetts, 125, 199

Stamp Act of 1765, 21, 22

"Standing Armies in Time of War: Republican Theory and Military Practice during the American Revolution" (White), 212

standing army, 6–9, 211, 217

in Britain, 12, 13, 14

British regulars as, 5, 26

Charles Lee's perception of, 124

Congress's disbanding of, 202

and Declaration of Independence, 54

nationalists' support of, 27, 206

opposition to, 20–28, 66, 74, 96, 200, 202

Parliament support of English, 11

in peace time, 108, 110

vs. republicanism, 34–40

Samuel Adam's perception of, 75

tyranny of, 20–28

Washington's perception of, 45, 63, 74, 189, 201

whig perception of, 15, 109

"Standing Army, the Militia, and the New Republic: Changing Attitudes toward the Military in American Society, 1768-1820, The" (Cress), 212

Stark, John (Gen.), 85

Staten Island, 51, 76, 154

Steuben, Baron Friedrich von (Gen.), 110, 113, 114, 115, 124, 174 201, 202

Stillwater, New York, 86

Stirling, Lord. *See* Alexander, William

Stiverson, Gregory A., 90, 215, 218, 219

Stony Point, 124

Stouffer, Samuel A., 131

"strategic defensive," 79

Stuart kings, 10, 11

Sullivan, John (Gen.), 59, 82, 84, 105, 125, 137, 139, 140, 141, 142, 146, 149, 221

"summer soldiers and sunshine patriots," 63, 68

Sumter, Thomas, 157

Suprintendent of Finance, 188
See also Morris, Robert

surrender of British, 178
See also Cornwallis; Yorktown

"Swamp Fox." *See* Marion, Francis

Syrett, David, 143, 220

Tarleton, Banastre (Col.), 156, 157, 167, 168, 169, 220

"Tarleton's Quarter," 156

Tate, Thad W., 131

taxation, 9, 21, 138, 148, 151, 206
See also inflation of currency
indirect, 21

Taylor, John, 78, 79

terrorist raids, 158

Thacher, James (Dr.), 34, 162, 165

Thayendanegea, 139

Third New York regiment, 133

Thomson, Charles, 132

Thoughts on Government (John Adams), 30

Toll of Independence: Engagements and Battle Casualties of the American Revolution, The (Peckham), 198, 221

Tourtellot, 213

"Toward a Republican Synthesis: The Emergence of an Understanding of Republicanism in American Historiography" (Shalhope), 28

Toward Lexington: The Role of the British Army in the Coming of the American Revolution (Shy), 39, 217

Towards an American Army: Military Thought from Washington to Marshall (Weigley), 201, 212

Townshend duties of 1767, 21

treason, 105, 158-65
of Arnold, 159-60

Treaty of Paris of 1763, 14, 15, 115

Treaty of Paris of 1783, 184

Trenchard, John, 10

Trenton, 59, 60, 62, 63, 76, 80, 163, 211

Trussell, John B. B., 103

typhus, 101, 162

unit cohesion. *See* group cohesion

United States Congress, 197

universal military obligation, 18, 19, 201, 217
See also conscription; republicanism

Valcour Island, 84

Valley Forge, 99-103, 106, 108, 110, 112, 113, 114, 118, 121, 123, 126, 128, 131, 161

Van Tyne, Claude H., 46, 212

Vergennes, Comte de, 115, 116, 117, 182, 183, 185

Vermont, 37, 85
Versailles, 32, 116, 117
Vincennes, 138, 139
Virginia, 17, 32, 40, 41, 42, 45, 91, 115, 137, 139, 150, 168, 174, 176
Virginia Continentals, 156
Virginia irregulars, 138
Virginia riflemen, 72
"virtuous citizenry," 31, 32, 34, 94, 95, 109, 160, 193, 194, 207, 218
    defined, 7-8
voluntarism, 55, 66, 89, 93, 94, 114, 124, 200, 208
von Steuben, Friedrich. *See* Steuben

Wadsworth, Jeremiah, 102
Waldo, Albigence (Dr.), 100
Walker, Elijah (Pvt.), 133
Wallace, Willard M., 122, 213
Walpole, Robert (Sir), 11
Ward, Artemas, 36, 41
war debts, 189
War for America, 1775-1783, The (Mackesy), 50, 220
War for Independence: A Military History, The (Peckham), 67, 213
War of American Independence: Military Attitudes, Policies, and Practice, 1763-1789, The (Higginbotham), 16, 215
War of 1812, 114
War office, 51
War of Independence: American Phase, The (Van Tyne), 46, 212
War of the American Revolution: Narrative, Chronology, and Bibliography, The (Coakley and Conn), 39, 213
Warren, James, 128
Warren, Joseph (Dr.), 25, 26
Warren, Mercy Otis, 203, 204
Washington and the Revolution, A Reappraisal; Gates, Conway, and the Continental Congress (Knollenberg), 111, 221
Washington, George, 44, 114, 155, 218, 219, 220
    and Arnold, 104
    and British surrender terms, 178
    and centralization of power, 196
    and Charles Lee, 32, 121, 122, 123, 154
    and civil authority, 42, 106
    Congress's expectations of, 41
    and conscription, 93
    and Conway Cabal, 111, 112, 113
    and discipline, 45, 47, 133, 134
    and enlistment campaigns, 88
    Fabian tactics, 79
    and Gates, 157
    and inflation, 152
    and looting, 130
    and manpower shortages, 69, 70, 87, 89
    at Monmouth, 121, 122, 123
    naming of as commander in chief, 40
    and national legitimacy, 173
    and Newburgh Conspiracy, 186, 187, 188, 189, 190, 191, 192, 194
    in New Jersey, 58, 59, 60, 62, 63, 80, 81
    and "New Model" army, 74
    in New York, 55, 56, 57
    and officer dissatisfaction, 43, 103, 158
    and Pennsylvania line mutiny, 163, 164, 165
    and pensions, 108, 195
    and republicanism, 94
    resignation of from army, 202
    in Rhode Island, 125
    "Sentiments," 201
    1781 campaign strategy of, 175, 176
    and soldier dissatisfaction, 158
    and standing army, 124, 200, 201

and universal military obligation, 201
at Valley Forge, 100
Wethersfield meeting, 176
and women in camp, 92
at Yorktown, 177
Washington, Lincoln, Wilson: Three War Statesmen (Palmer), 201, 212
Watchung Mountains, 60, 79
Waxhaws, South Carolina, 156
Wayne, Anthony (Gen.), 82, 102, 121, 124, 163
Weigley, Russell F., 79, 125, 126, 156, 158, 167, 169, 173, 201, 212, 214, 219
Welch, John, 132
Westchester County, New York, 57
West Florida, 180
West Indies, 117, 120, 121, 176, 179
West Point, 159, 164, 186, 199
Wethersfield, Connecticut, 175, 176
whigs, 109, 120, 207
  in Britain, 53
  and the British army, 23
  and the Howe brothers, 57
  at Lexington, 2
  perception of British army by, 38
  perception of British colonial rule by, 54

perception of militia by, 20
perception of Montgomery by, 73
perception of standing army by, 9
radical, 5, 6, 8, 10, 11, 14
and the "virtuous citizen," 31
white aggression against Indians, 137, 138, 142
Whitehaven, 145
White, John Todd, 42, 74, 75, 110, 113, 212, 217
White Plains, New York, 57, 58
William Diamond's Drum (Tourtellot), 213
Wilmington, North Carolina, 169, 174
Wilson, James, 74, 75
Wolfe, James (Gen.), 19
women in the army, 92, 186, 198
Wood, Gordon S., 7, 217
Wright, Aaron (Pvt.), 54
Wyoming Valley, 140

York, Pennsylvania, 82
York River, 175, 178
Yorktown, 169, 180
Yorktown campaign, 121, 171–79
Young recruits, 90
"Young Turks," 190
Young, William, 54